Grappling
BEST OF CFW
2001
Jose Fraguas

Grappling
BEST OF CFW
2001

By Jose Fraguas Copyright © 2025 I&I SPORTS SUPPLY. All rights reserved. Published by I&I SPORTS SUPPLY ISBN 978-0-934489-82-9

Dedication

To all of you—those who deserve the most of the credit, the writers who supply us with an enormous amount of material every year to fill the pages of our magazines.

Acknowledgements
Our special thanks go out to the usual suspects, our staff editors, for taking time and effort to make every article better and comprehensive for the reader.

Contents

Foreword 10
  Jose M. Fraguas

Wallid Ismail's Killer Weight-Training Program 13
  Loren Franck, story and photos

Stefanos Miltsakakis: Terminate the Takedown 21
  Todd Hester

Stefanos Miltsakakis' Takedowns Clinch 27
  Todd Hester

The Legacy of Shuai-Chiao's King, Grandmaster Chang Teng Sheng 33
  Matt Furey

Double Trouble: The Fighting McCully Brothers 39
  Todd Hester, story and photos

The 2000 Brazilian Jiu-Jitsu World Championships 47
  Kid Peligro, photos by Gustavo Aragao

Frank Shamrock's Ultimate Training and Fighting System 59
  John Steven Soet

Notes written from under the bleachers at the Abu Dhabi 2000 Submission Wrestling World Championships 65
  John G. Keating, MD, photos by Bill Curry

Shonie Carter—Semper Fi 75
  Todd Hester, story and photos

6 Attacks That Really Work from the Guard 85
  Edward Lee Vincent, photos by Clenice Vincent

Erik Paulson: Training for a Fight 91
  Todd Hester, story and photos

Get a Grip! Four Can't-Miss Defenses Against the Standing Grab 97
  Todd Hester, story and photos

Shark Attack! 103
  Todd Hester

Tito Ortiz: Still Climbing III
  Thomas Gerbasi

'Twas the Tournament Before Christmas: The 2000 International Pro-Am of Grappling 117
  Kid Peligro, photos by Koichi Kawasaki

Antonio McKee: The Great Mandingo 127
  Todd Hester, story and photos

Heath Herring: From Amarillo to Amsterdam— The Odyssey of a Small-Town Superstar
... 133
  Todd Hester, story and photos

How to Beat a Black Belt... 147
  Todd Medina

Franco Columbu and Francisco Bueno: A Rock and a Hard Place.................................. 153
  Todd Hester

Fabiano Iha: The Brazilian King Midas 159
  Loren Franck

Jermaine Andre: Some Bash, Some Splash, and a Whole Lotta' Class 167
  Todd Hester

Cage Fighting Strategies 175
  John Lewis, photos by Todd Hester

Royler Gracie: The Heart of a Champion.. 181
  Kid Peligro

Rodrigo "Comprido" Medeiros: The Tao of Hard Work 189
  Kid Peligro, photos by Todd Hester

Fabiano Iha's Winning Fight Strategies... 197
  Loren Franck, story and photos

Joe Hurley: They Call Him The Rapper... 205
  Loren Franck

John Lewis: Warlord of the New Millennium 211
  Todd Hester

5 Spinning Killer Knee-Bar Attacks.. 219
  Erik Paulson

Foreword

To say we get a lot of mail at CFW Enterprises would be quite an understatement. Every year we receive literally hundreds and hundreds of story submissions for all of our various magazines. These manila envelopes contain works ranging from fascinating to—well, to put it diplomatically, "fanciful." Yet we open nearly each and every piece of mail to separate contents from the envelope while doing our best not to commit an eco-crime.

Kidding aside, what we look for in the mail is the best martial arts writing in existence. To be considered "the best" there are some basic criteria which must be met. The editors at CFW Enterprises carefully evaluate the articles they receive to finally decide those which will be published. It is not an easy task since many variables are involved in the process.

Needless to say, while we receive a lot of good submissions we also, as an occupational hazard, have to read a lot of "really bad stuff." Fortunately, after years of working as an editor you develop an instinct and can quickly identify an unusable submission.

That's what this series is all about: bringing you the "Best of Grappling" for each year, without prejudice in terms of the writer, the source, or the subject. Our aim is to provide the readers with a wide selection of styles and systems. The collection includes many different authors who offer their own perspectives of the arts and the influences of their respective arts in the field. All of them have expressed their ideas in a very different way. But whether expressed in the language of the teachers, the language of the students, or the language of the thinker, there is truth in concepts, philosophies and techniques that so many martial artists have believed and lived by for decades.

Here at CFW, we have made every effort to present each article and work as accurately as possible within the limitations of the book format. In addition to being a resource for researches, writers, students and teachers, we hope this collection of works will provide comfort and inspiration for all those who love the martial arts. There are many excellent books about the martial arts with more on the way. My hope is that this book of collective works and articles will prove a worthy companion to them in two main ways: first, in its size and scope; second in its practicality and ease of use.

There have been many changes in the martial arts but some things are still the same. A well-written article is one of them. Our job and responsibility at CFW as the world leaders in the publication of martial arts magazines, videos, and books is to inform and educate the reader, promoting all the styles and approaches without being limited by any of them.

As early as I can remember. My house was filled with martial arts magazines from around the world. For many years, I gathered publications and became curious about many of the authors who wrote for them. The more I researched, the more I realized that those "great people" were a lot more like you and me than they were different. Today I have written hundreds of articles in magazines around the world, more than a dozen of books under my own name and a couple under some else's. At CFW, our editors have read, written, edited and re-written more articles and books than one could possibly imagine. Although it is unlikely any of us will ever be awarded the Nobel Prize, the writing that we like is the writing that we like. Nothing can change that.

I bring all this up because I believe all the writers who have submitted material to be published in the different magazines owned by CFW Enterprises have followed similar paths.

Walk on!

—Jose M. Fraguas General Manager CFW Enterprises

Wallid Ismail's Killer Weight-Training Program

*Brutal, Grueling, and Super-Intense—
It's The Secret of His Success!*

Loren Franck, story and photos

Standing outside of Gold's Gym in Venice, California, Wallid Ismail looked scary, ready for the biggest brawl of his life. But fighting was the last thing on the mind of the grappling icon, still praised for choking out the seemingly invincible Royce Gracie in their infamous December 1998 bout.

The IVC (International Vale Tudo Championships) top middleweight and one of the world's most respected grapplers, Ismail was waiting for his personal trainer and strength coach, Gilbert Coppage, to arrive. It was leg-training day, and Ismail, always eager to hit the weights, couldn't wait to begin.

Both men are a familiar sight at the sprawling muscle factory, long hailed as the Mecca of muscledom. It houses every piece of workout equipment imaginable. After nodding hello to Lou Ferrigno, a former Mr. Universe and star of *The Incredible Hulk* TV series, Ismail and his trainer headed straight for the squat racks.

"This is going to be a *great* workout," Ismail quipped. "I can feel it." And he was right. In fact, all of Ismail's workouts have been excellent since he teamed with Coppage two years ago.

Nothing But The Best

Ismail has always craved success, and he's willing to pay any price for it. While living in his hometown of Rio de Janeiro, Brazil, he was an eight-time Brazilian jiu-jitsu champion. Still not satisfied, however, he wanted to become the most successful—and the most feared—grappler in the world. To do that, he needed cutting-edge techniques in the ring and to be in his best physical condition.

The fighting skills weren't a problem. To a large extent, he already had them. But he needed to train his body to perfection. So, uprooting his life in Brazil, he moved to Marina del Rey, California, a posh Los Angeles suburb. It's the perfect venue for getting in top shape.

"One of the first things I did after moving to L.A was contact Pro Camp Athletics, which is based next to Gold's Gym in Venice," Ismail recalls. "It trains some great athletes, including Chris Chelios of the Detroit Red Wings, the New England Patriots' Willie McGinnis, Glen Murray of the Los Angeles Kings, and the Chicago Bears' Cade McNown. I figured if I was going to become the best in my sport, I needed a good trainer."

Shortly after signing on with Pro Camp, Ismail met Coppage, one of the organization's most savvy instructors, and the two hit it off immediately. Their relationship now extends beyond the sets and repetitions found in the gym. "We're good friends, a lot like family," Coppage confides. "I take a real personal interest in Wallid, and he knows I'm here for him."

Such commitment is vital to Ismail's weight-training program.

Why Weights?

Early in Ismail's grappling career, few of his opponents knew Brazilian jiu-jitsu. He remembers those days well. Weighing 190 pounds, Ismail easily defeated big, beefy guys who weighed 250. The reason? He knew jiu-jitsu and they didn't. But now, most professional grapplers are skilled in the art, so Ismail needs an extra advantage. And that advantage is weight training.

Unlike those who lift weights only to make their physiques look good, Ismail pumps iron strictly to help him fight. As a whole, professional grapplers are incredibly strong and agile, making an effective weight-training program a required tool of the trade. It can never replace Brazilian jiu-jitsu, though, which Ismail maintains is a grapplers most lethal weapon. Nevertheless, if done correctly, weight training can bring out the best in any grappler.

An Inclusive Philosophy

Training philosophies are in rich supply, especially at Gold's Gym. Yet, many athletes have a hard time discerning which philosophy works best for them. Fortunately, this has been fairly easy for Ismail, who approaches his training eclectically. Incorporating the best of all available workout philosophies, his program is dynamic and complex, multiphasic and multidimensional.

"Grappling is the toughest sport in the world, so I have to train in jiu-jitsu, boxing and wrestling every day to stay ahead of the competition."

Wallid Ismail's Death-Defying Diet

Pulling no punches, Wallid Ismail decided to reap grappling gold when he moved to Los Angeles recently from Rio de Janeiro, Brazil. After quickly becoming a regular at Gold's Gym in Venice, he hired Pro Camp Athletics to whip him into shape. All Ismail lacked was a rock-solid food plan.

And just when Ismail needed dietary help the most, he met Pro Camp nutritionist Alfred Krautgartner, who expertly matched the champion grappler with a customized food plan.

"My goal was to determine what nutrients Wallid lacked, what mistakes he made in his diet, and what his underlying nutritional problems were," Krautgartner explains. "Afterward, I put him on an eating program that met his needs and preferences."

Careful investigation, including blood tests, urinalysis and a food-intake history, revealed how Ismail's diet affected not only his muscle recuperation, but his injury pattern and performance in the ring as well. Armed with that knowledge, Krautgartner put Ismail on a sensible, effective eating plan.

Protein: Before embarking on his new food plan, Ismail ate too much starch and not enough complete protein. The body needs complete protein, which is rich in essential amino acids, to build and maintain muscle. Ismail ingests plenty of egg whites and protein supplements (egg, soy and whey) to obtain the amount of complete protein he needs. A strict vegetarian, he gets no protein from meat.

Carbohydrates: Unlike some athletes who don't eat simple sugar, Ismail consumes a fine-tuned mixture of simple and complex carbohydrates. "I drink several types of high-nutrition shakes," he explains. "Each type provides different kinds of carbs." His preworkout shakes, for example, have more grams of complex carbs than his postworkout shakes do.

A correct blend of carbohydrates at the right time is crucial to Ismail's nutrition program and, in turn, to his results at the gym and in the ring. "In the preworkout shakes," Krautgartner explains, "I'm more picky about the carbs Wallid consumes because I don't want him to have an insulin spike. Some athletes eat too much simple glucose before going to the gym, then burn out halfway through their workouts because their insulin starts to rise."

That's why Ismail eats fruit and complex carbs before lifting weights. "Fruit is good," he explains, "because my body assimilates it quickly, but not too quickly."

There's little chance of postworkout insulin spikes because the body is usually sugar depleted at that time.

Consistency: One of Ismail's biggest challenges while getting in top shape has been a consistent schedule. "Most people go without eating for as long as six hours," he observes. "That's a big mistake, and I changed that in my diet when I learned it wasn't a good idea. Now I eat every three hours."

Preworkout Meals: Ismail eats these meals an hour and a half to two hours before a weight-training session. This gives him the energy he needs for his workouts. Preworkout meals contain a carefully calculated balance of protein, simple and complex carbs, fat and other essential nutrients. They're usually about 65 percent carbs and 10-15 percent protein.

Postworkout Meals: Like preworkout meals, these are rich in muscle-building nutrients and are usually 50 percent protein and 50 percent carbs. Very important meals, they restore the glycogen in Ismail's body after hard workouts and help it repair broken-down tissue.

Fluid Intake: Healthy fluids are a key to Ismail's food plan. "I drink 100-120 ounces of water a day," he admits. And though he sips limited amounts of green tea, he shuns coffee and other stimulants. "They provide energy but can overstress your internals," Krautgartner warns. "This stress can run your body down very quickly."

Supplements: Ismail takes vitamins and minerals every day in addition to his daily protein shakes. Some of the most vital are antioxidants, which help detoxify the body and help Ismail recuperate quickly from his grueling workouts. Besides a multiple vitamin supplement, he takes a joint-support formula that helps repair tendons, ligaments and other connective tissue.

"Wallid's weight-training program isn't limited to one workout philosophy," Coppage emphasizes. "We take the best training theories and techniques and apply them to Wallid's needs in the ring. There are all kinds of beliefs about training, and they all have their good points. I just put them in order for Wallid."

Essentially, the program seeks to maximize the muscular endurance Ismail needs for fighting. "I continually work my muscles past fatigue," he explains. A secondary goal is to increase muscular strength. It doesn't matter whether he uses free weights or machines, low repetitions or high, few sets or many, as long as he gets the results he wants.

As Easy As One, Two, Three

Ismail's three-phase approach achieves two objectives. First, it helps him implement the best workout strategies available. Second, it offers flexibility so he can structure his weight-training workouts to optimize his preparation for fights.

Phase One: The first phase increases muscle endurance, which helps prevent Ismail from tiring during a fight. Light weights and high repetitions are the rule here.

In phase-one workouts, Ismail may begin by performing 12 repetitions per set for each exercise. He'll later increase the number to 15-20, depending on the muscle he's training. He also focuses on range-of-motion issues in this phase.

Phase Two: "In this phase," Ismail points out, "I start to lift heavier weights and, as a result, do fewer repetitions per set than I do in phase one."

He doesn't mind if he adds a little muscle mass here, but it's not his main goal. Instead, he strives to maximize the strength needed for grappling. Unlike the other two phases, the second phase resembles a bodybuilding workout.

"I perform basic exercises in phase two such as flat and incline dumbbell presses," Ismail elaborates. "I also do movements to help me in the ring such as good-mornings [while standing, bending forward and then straightening at the waist with a barbell behind his neck] and cable rows with a rope."

In another sport-specific movement, Ismail shoots toward an imaginary opponent's leg and picks him up, just as he would while executing a takedown in the ring. Special lunges, during which Ismail wears a weight belt, also strengthen his legs for fighting.

Phase Three: This final phase combines the first two. The goal? To build endurance and agility. The most unique part of phase-three training is its brutal one-hour weight-training circuit. Designed exclusively to condition Ismail right before a match, it's perhaps his most effective pre-fight workout tool.

He begins with a group of exercises such as rope jumps, push-ups, lunges, then returns to rope jumps. The circuit consists of 12-14 exercises. Ismail does them all, one immediately after the other, until he completes the circuit.

Between circuits, he rests for a minute, sips water, then repeats the excruciating regimen for an hour, often stronger and more energetic at the end of the workout than at the beginning.

"The circuit shows how Wallid's body would react under the pressure of being worn down in the ring," says Coppage, who painstakingly sought the circuit-training exercises that would best benefit his client. "What's even more valuable is it let's both of us monitor his mental state after he reaches high levels of fatigue."

Workout Anatomy

Ismail's weight-training program may well be one of the most aggressive conditioning regimens ever devised. It takes full advantage of the latest training techniques commonplace at Gold's Gym, which is ground zero for new muscle-building strategies.

When a new training technique surfaces, Ismail and Coppage analyze it thoroughly and determine if it fits into the program. "Something may be good for phase three, so we stick it there," Coppage says. Likewise, a new exercise (or simply a new way to do an old one) will become popular, and it will be perfect for Ismail's abdominals, hips, rotators or other core-training areas. Accordingly, the exercise might find a home in phase one.

Most of Ismail's workouts have five stages. When first entering the gym, Ismail warms up. That's stage one. After a thorough warm-up, he passes through stage two, which is rotator work to maintain deltoid flexibility.

Stage three is resistance training, while stage four increases his agility. Abdominal training, always performed at the end of resistance workouts, is stage five. "All workouts end with a cool-down stretch," Coppage adds.

Muscle Isolation

Cheating is a proven weight-training tool that helps build strength and muscle mass. For example, while performing standing barbell curls, using a little upper-body momentum to swing the bar up helps you lift more weight and therefore build bigger, stronger biceps. But Ismail refuses to cheat. Instead, he isolates each muscle by maintaining strict form throughout every exercise.

Hardcore Sets and Reps

All of Ismail's weight-training workouts differ a little from each other. Some are longer, more intense and more complex than previous sessions. Exercises vary too. But whenever he lifts weights, thoroughness and intensity prevail. Ismail believes biceps are primarily a cosmetic muscle for grapplers, so he limits his biceps training to one exercise.

The Foundation: A scientifically sound advanced weight-training program designed for Ismail after he received blood tests, a soft-tissue scan, nutritional assessment and other evaluations. **The Philosophy:** An exhaustive, eclectic approach that optimizes the use of all available weight-training philosophies.

The Program: A multiphasic, multidimensional workout system tailored to maximize Ismail's skills as a professional grappler.

PHASE ONE
3 Sets of 10-20 repetitions

Day One
Chest: Smith machine bench presses, Smith machine incline presses, flat cable flies, push-ups.
Upper Back: Lat pull-downs, seated cable rows, Hammer Strength reverse pull-downs, Smith machine stiff-leg dead-lifts.

Day Two
Thighs: Leg extensions, seated leg curls, leg presses (single leg), barbell squats, single-leg squats, singleleg lunges, balance-board work.

Day Three
Shoulders: Rotator-cuff exercises, shoulder-alignment rotations, shoulder presses, cable rear laterals, cable side laterals, cable front raises.
Biceps: Cambered-bar curls or dumbbell curls.
Triceps: Triceps push-downs, lying triceps extensions.

PHASE TWO
3 sets of 6-10 repetitions (increased resistance)

Day One
Chest: Dumbbell bench presses, dumbbell incline presses, dumbbell flies.

Day Two
Upper Back: Lat pull-downs, single-arm lat pull-downs, good mornings, standing cable rows with rope, single-arm multidirectional cable pulls, dead lifts.

Day Three
Thighs: Seated leg curls, leg extensions, leg presses, squats, weighted single-leg lunges, weighted cable lunges with a weight pick-up at the end, balance-board work.

Day Four
Shoulders: Shoulder presses, hang cleans and presses, dumbbell side laterals, dumbbell bent-over rear laterals, front raises (dumbbells or straight bar).
Biceps: Cambered-bar curls or dumbbell curls.
Triceps: Triceps push-downs, cambered-bar triceps extensions, close-grip bench presses.

PHASE THREE
Circuit training is the essence of this phase. Ismail begins by performing circuits two days on and one off. As he gets used to the demands they place on his body and shortens his recovery time, he circuit trains more days consecutively before resting a day, such as three on and one off.

"I isolate each muscle while working it," he confides. "When training abdominals, for instance, I contract them while keeping my other muscles stationary. In the same way, when working triceps, I use only my triceps to move the weight, isolating every muscle I train whenever possible."

The weight machines Ismail uses also aid muscle isolation, which can be difficult when he trains with barbells and dumbbells. Free-weight compound exercises such as bench presses, rows and shoulder presses often work multiple muscle groups simultaneously. To minimize this effect, Ismail maintains strict form during free-weight movements.

Timing Is Everything

Haphazard workouts, whether for building muscle or perfecting fighting skills, are a shortcut to haphazard results. And Ismail probably knows this better than anyone. Much of his success in the gym results from frequent, consistent training.

Because grappling requires tremendous skill and speed, Ismail works on his fighting techniques daily. "I have to," he admits. "Grappling is the toughest sport in the world, so I have to train in jiu-jitsu, boxing and wrestling every day to stay ahead of the competition."

But weight training is different. Ismail lifts only three or four days a week, his fighting schedule largely determining the details of his meticulously planned workouts. His days off, so crucial in maintaining strength and muscle tone, let his body recuperate and return stronger the following workout.

"We know where we're going with each of Wallid's workouts," Coppage says, "especially when he has a fight coming up soon because, ultimately, that's where the training leads."

Turning Up The Heat

When observing one of Ismail's arduous muscle-blasting sessions, it becomes clear that he doesn't just go through the motions at the gym. He loves to train. It's his life. And he loves the results his can-do attitude and all-out efforts achieve.

"I remember doing circuits recently," Ismail recalls, "and I could tell when I had a good workout by how tired I felt afterward. It sometimes takes me a half-hour to fully recuperate from circuit training."

You can also see in Ismail's face when he's had a great workout—and when he hasn't. And he can tell how his workouts are going by how precisely he performs his exercises. Sloppy form or lagging energy suggests he's missing the mark. But when he picks up the pace—his movements crisp and intense from first rep to last—he's firing on all cylinders, and he knows it.

What's most incredible, however, is when Ismail is so fatigued that he's ready to pass out. Yet he digs in, turns the key to his inner power, and increases his efforts another notch. "Without thinking," Ismail reflects, "I'll take a minute or two off each pass through the circuit or cut the time spent on other exercises."

That's when he knows his efforts are leading to another victory, another title, and when he's taken another step closer to winning it all.

Loren Franck, a Los Angeles-based, freelance writer and martial artist, is a frequent contributor to Grappling.

Stefanos Miltsakakis
Terminate the Takedown

For a striker to defeat a grappler they must first neutralize the takedown with punches, keep their legs and body free to keep from being clinched, and then push the grappler away and continue to strike.

Todd Hester

Greek-born All-America wrestler Stefanos Miltsakakis is a complete fighter who possesses a range of useful and practical skills developed from his background of streetfighting in his native land, and then in America after his family immigrated. Turning his natural strength and aggression to the wrestling mat on the advice of a high school coach, Stefanos immediately excelled in the grappling arts, becoming a high school champion and then a North Carolina State All-American before being named to the Greek Olympic Team.

Moving to California to pursue an acting career, Stefanos trained grappling with Rickson Gracie and then won the WVC Superfight Championship, a title which he still holds. Unable to fight as often as he would like due to his successful acting career, Stefanos nevertheless trains almost daily with world muay Thai champion Maurice Travis, perfecting his stand-up and striking skills. This combination of world class skills allows Stefanos to see a fight from the perspective of both a grappler and a striker, and has given Stefanos a unique perspective on how to both take down a striker and defeat a grappler.

While inside control for a grappler is the basis for near all wrestling styles and is almost second nature, keeping inside control for a striker is not nearly as natural and requires training and discipline. Trained to throw punches and kicks from a distance, most strikers lose their composure when a grappler pressure them and comes into their neutral zone, often responding by either throwing wild punches or trying to clinch the grappler, which plays right into their hands. The key, says Stefanos, is for the striker to keep inside control of the grappler.

Q: As a stand-up fighter, how do you keep someone off you who is trying to take you down and get you off your feet?

A: No matter what, a striker has to keep striking. As the grappler comes into range, the striker has to be active with jabs and kicks and force the action. The worse thing a striker can do is be passive and wait for a grappler to come at them. Strikers have to be aggressive and force the action as much as possible. Keep moving forward—moving backwards against a grappler is certain death. Also, don't surrender to a standing clinch and make it easy for the grappler to get into takedown range. Stay busy with the hands. Remember that you're a striker and that strikers strike!

Q: But isn't it almost impossible to keep a good grappler away for an entire fight?
A: Of course, no matter what you do as a striker, the grappler will eventually come in by looking for either a poorly thrown punch to duck under or a weak kick to follow in. Once they get inside, they will try to gain inside control with the arms around the body. So as a striker I have to make sure to keep fighting for inside control myself, or at least fight to keep the grappler from establishing inside control. I have to make sure that I don't throw any stupid punches—by this I mean wild, uncontrolled swings that a grappler can duck under, get to my body and clinch. Telegraphed kicks are also very dangerous. You can throw a high kick, but you have to set it up with low kicks first. Most clinches that are given up by stand-up fighters are the result of wild swings or sloppy kicks. The punches have to be directed, controlled, go towards a specific target and then snap back quickly, ready to fire- out again. The same holds true for kicks. As a grappler myself, I know what the grappler is trying to do. He's going to try to establish inside control of my body by underhooking my arms, or he is going to go downstairs by shooting in, take control of my legs, and then get to my back. So when he comes in I have to strike, clinch, gain inside control, push away, and then get ready to strike again.

Q: What is most common way a grappler will enter?
A: Very often a striker will try to time a grappler's entry and catch him with a punch or a kick while he is coming in. This takes amazing timing and will mostly be dependant upon luck. If you catch it, good for you, but the odds are against it. More often than not the striker is going to either not connect, or at best catch the grappler with a glancing blow. This might slow him a little but will not keep him off you. Gilbert Yvel from Holland is famous for catching grapplers coming in with a flying knee and knocking them out. This has worked for him against some fighters such as Dennis Reed, Carlos

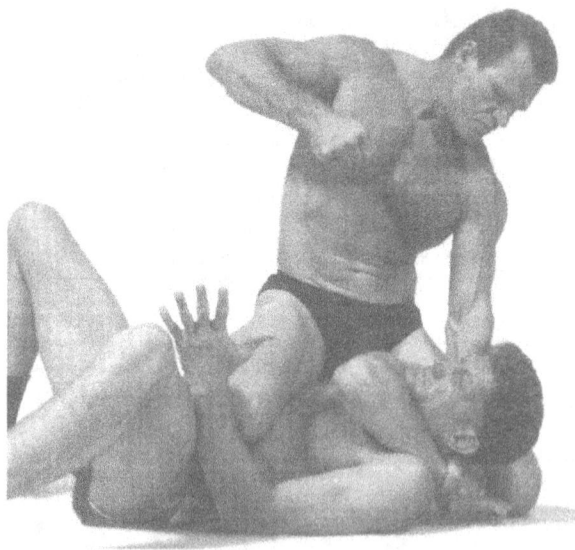

Takedown Defensive Keys for Strikers

1. Keep striking as the grappler comes in.
2. Neutralize the takedown by not moving back and staying low.
3. Keep your body and legs from being clinched by maintaining inside control.
4. Push the grappler's shoulders away to create distance.
5. Attack the grappler with strikes and kicks as he moves away.
6. Keep your feet and don't be tempted to follow the grappler to the ground.

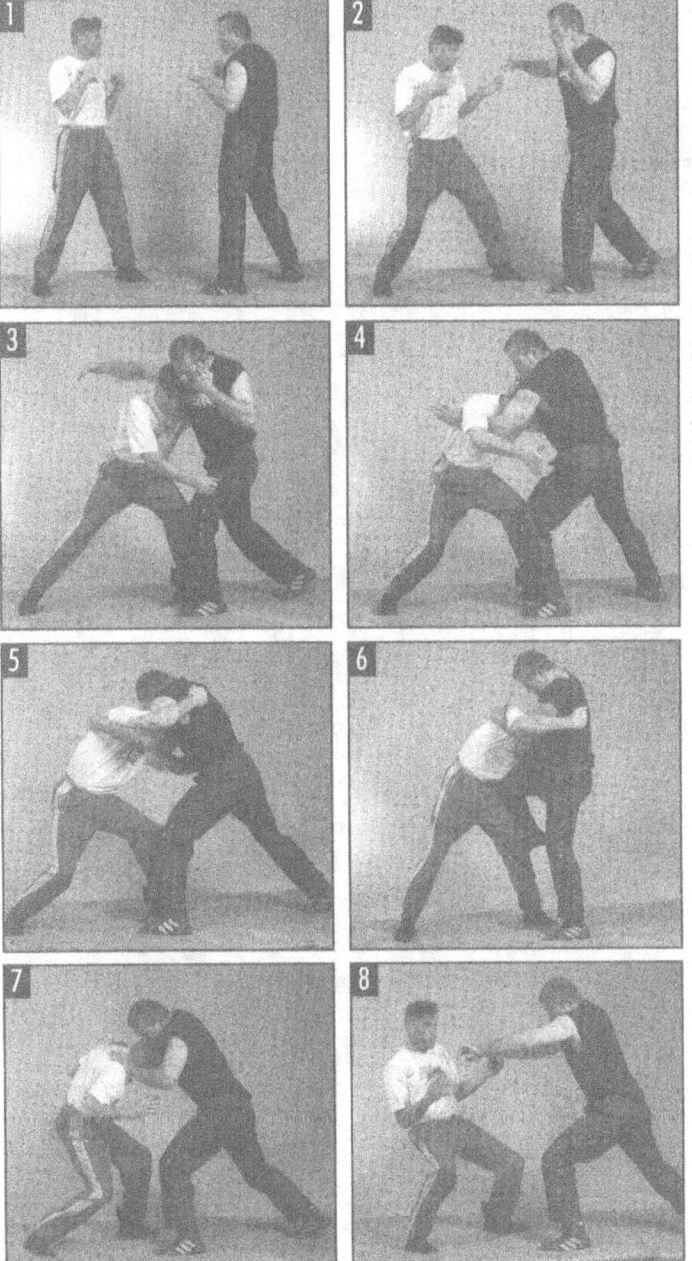

Upper-Body Clinch Counter

Facing a grappling opponent (1), Stefanos Miltsakakis throws a cross (2), which the grappler slips under and tries to clinch (3). Underhooking the grappier's arm to maintain inside control (4), Stefanos traps the head and steps back (5), and then knees to the ribs (6). He then places his hands on the grap- pier's shoulders (7), and pushes him away, defeating the takedown attempt (8).

Baretto, and several others. But this strategy has backfired on him more often than it has worked, and he has been taken down in Pride and

Q: Summarize the basic steps a striker must do against a grappler.
A: It is best to strike as the grappler comes in, move your feet

Q: Do you think that strikers really have a chance against a good grappler?
A: Of course they do. The old myth that a grappler would always defeat a striker was broken years ago when Maurice Smith knocked out Conan with a kick to the head. When you look at the recent Pride and UFC events you'll see that more often than not, the striker with grappling experience will take out the pure grappler. Anymore, I don't think that any top no-holds-barred fighter will be purely considered a grappler or a striker. Nowadays, all the top

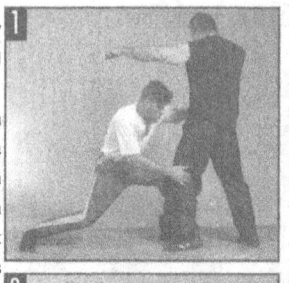 

Single-Leg Takedown Counter
Stefanos Miltsakakis faces a grappler who shoots under his left jab and goes for a singleleg takedown (1). Stefanos pushes down on the attackers shoulders to break his momentum (2), then sprawls low and underhooks the grappler's arm to establish inside control (3). Pushing the grappler's head down to control the body (4), Stefanos then cocks his leg into the air (5), and hammers a knee to the grappler's head (6). Not wanting to risk staying on the ground with a grappler he then pushes away (7), and comes back to a standing position, ready to strike (8).

fighters are truly mixed fighters who have studied jiu-jitsu, submission wrestling, boxing, muay Thai, or whatever. Even within the grappling community you see cross-training going on, with jiu-jitsu guys learning takedowns from wrestlers, and wrestlers learning submissions from jiu-jitsu fighters. It's a whole new world out there and you have to adapt or you'll get left behind.

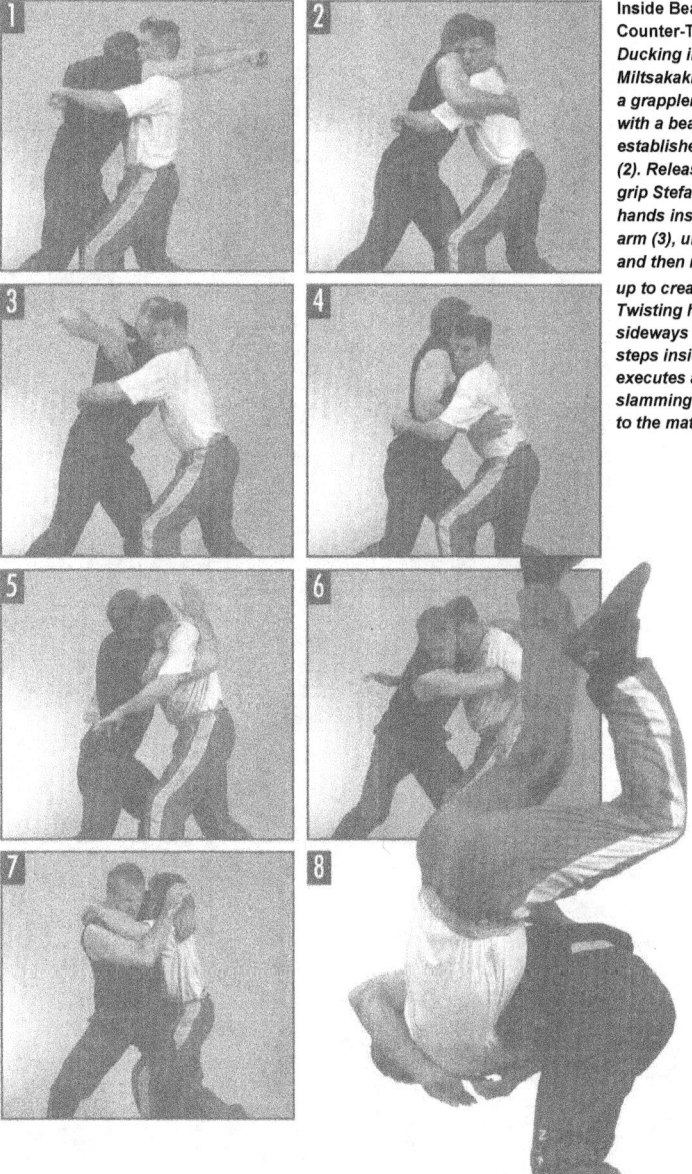

Inside Bear-Hug Counter-Throw
Ducking inside Stefanos Miltsakakis' right cross (1), a grappler clinches inside with a bear hug and establishes inside control (2). Releasing his outside grip Stefanos shoots his hands inside the grap pier's arm (3), underhooks (4), and then raises both arms up to create space (5). Twisting his opponent sideways (6), Stefanos steps inside (7), and executes a hip throw (8), slamming his opponent to the mat.

Stefanos Miltsakakis' Takedowns Clinch

Grapplers who hope to take down skilled and dangerous strikers have to be patient, have to be smart, and have be ready to commit immediately when an opening arises.

Todd Hester

Stefanos Miltsakakis is one of no-holds-barred most well-rounded fighters. A Greek immigrant who learned to fight out of necessity during his early teens growing up in rough East Coast neighborhoods, Stefanos found in wrestling an outlet for his frustration at being teased for being an "outsider with an accent." He eventually won a scholarship to North Carolina State where he became an All-American wrestler and eventually won a berth on the Greek Olympic team. Bitten by the acting bug after getting a part as an extra in the Van Damme movie, *Cyborg,* Stefanos moved to Los Angeles in the early '90s where he began pursuing his acting career. It wasn't long before he made the acquaintance of Rickson Gracie and also Rob Kaman, two fighters who added greatly to his wrestling skills by introducing him, respectively, to the arts of Brazilian jiu-jitsu and muay Thai, which Stefanos considers the world's two most efficient combat arts.

Eventually landing larger and larger rolls in action films and television shows, and currently appearing as a semi-regular on the hit series *Nash Bridges,* Stefanos never forgot about his fighting roots. With a desire to test himself, he eventually agreed to a fight in Aruba for the WVC World Superfight Championship, a fight he won against Joe Charles, and a title he still holds to this day. Even though his fighting career has been put on hold due to his success on the screen—he has a large role in the upcoming television series *Big Apple*—Stefanos still plans to return to the ring within the next year to defend his WVC title.

"Personally, I think I do my best work when I'm most afraid, because that's the time my instincts are most alive," Stefanos says. "I refuse to let fear intimidate me. Instead, I focus and use that energy to my advantage. Fear can be your best friend. Some people get addicted to the adrenaline. Controlling it requires some form of meditation. It is considerably easier to meditate on a beautiful sunset than in the heat of battle fighting on the front line with a sword or a spear or with your bare hands. I'll always look for situations that will scare the hell out of me, that will make me shake with fear. That is why I want to continue to fight. It keeps me in touch with fear."

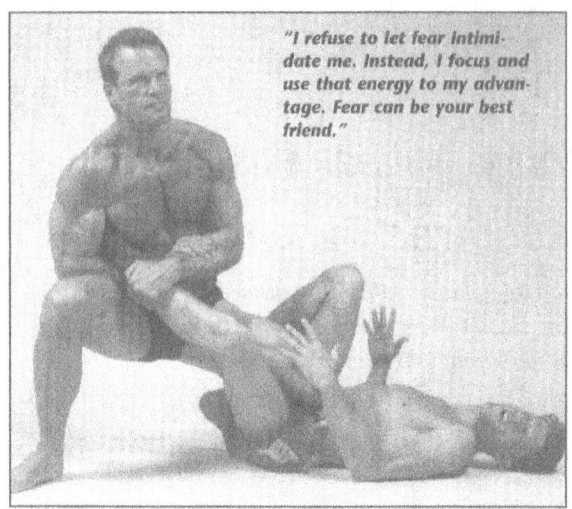

"I refuse to let fear intimidate me. Instead, I focus and use that energy to my advantage. Fear can be your best friend."

The Three Keys to the Clinch

"I believe that one of the most basic positions that applies to both grappling and striking is the clinch," Stefanos says. "Too many people either concentrate on the takedown, or they concentrate on the strikes, but they do not take the time to explore the possibilities of the one position that has elements of both—the clinch. Whether you are a grappler attacking a striker, or a striker defending against a grappler you can use the same principles of clinching in order to best defeat your opponent."

While trained a both a grappler and a striker, Stefanos maintains that the clinch can be approached by breaking it down into a series of basic maneuvers. "There are basically three parts to getting into, and then controlling, the clinch," he says. "The first is to either wait for your opponent to make a mistake, or to force him into a mistake. The key here is patience. If you try to rush in when your opponent is set, then even if a double-leg takedown is executed correctly, there is a chance that you will be caught on the entry by a knee, elbow, or punch. However, if you wait for a punch or kick and then it in, or you wait until his weight is on his back foot, or you kick his leg to make him move backwards, then even if you get hit it will be a glancing blow and you won't get hurt.

The second part when you make the entry is to stay very close to your opponent. Clinch him tightly around the neck or the body, and then tuck your head against his chest in order to take away his striking angle. Also, keep you face down so any blows that do come in bounce off your head. Always remember that your skull is a lot harder than anyone's fist. They will break their fist if the strike against the head. Make sure you move your feet in the clinch while he moves, and most importantly, maintain inside position. The person who maintains inside position in a clinch will be the one who controls the clinch. This means keeping your arms inside of his arms, and not letting him into your body. Fight him constantly. Always be moving to keep inside control. More than anything else, this is the key to controlling the clinch.

The next part is the takedown and, like the entry, should come off your opponent's mistake. When I'm in a clinch, and have my head tucked and am maintaining inside control, I hope that he throws a knee or a punch at me because this will give me the opening I need in order to take him down. He is unbalanced when he attacks as long as I have maintained inside control. So there is no need for me to expose myself—I just need to wait for the attack, feed off his energy, and then take him to the ground."

Common Mistakes

Most mistakes made from the clinch come from a lack of patience and from trying to much to force the action, Stefanos maintains. An avid reader of historical battles and somewhat of a scholar when

Clinch and Takedown Against a Front Kick Stefanos Miltsakakis faces opponent Maurice Travis (1). Blocking Travis' kick to the inside (2), Stefanos throws down the leg (3), and gains the inside clinch against Travis' back (4). Travis' attempted elbow strike is ineffective because of Stefanos' tight spacing (5), and gives Stefanos an opening to lift Travis into the air (6), and slam him to the ground where Stefanos gains top control (7).

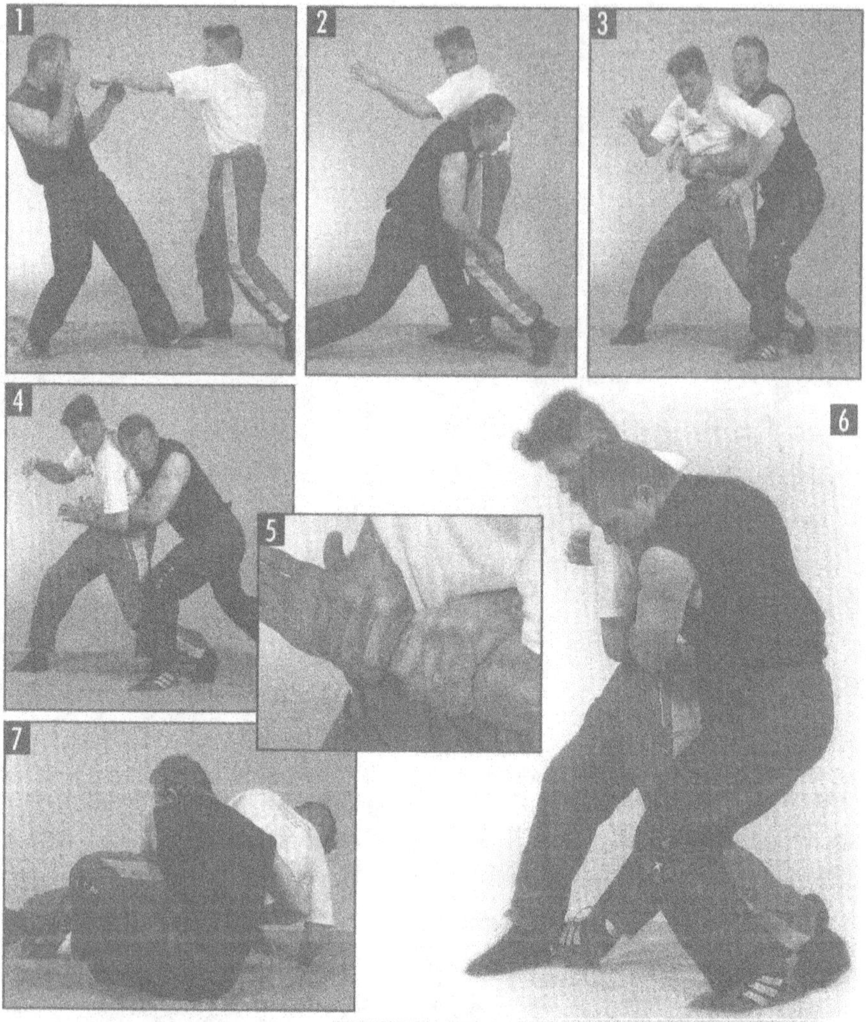

Clinch and Takedown Against a Left Punch

Stefanos Miltsakakis leans back to avoid the blow from opponent Maurice Travis (1). Stepping inside he clinches tightly (2), spins to the back (3), and places his face tightly against Travis' back to avoid potential backfists or elbows (4). Controlling his opponent by a double-handed grip (S), Stefanos then puts his leg out (6), trips his opponent down (7), and gains back control (8).

it comes to the classic battle strategies of such generals as Alexander the Great, Stefanos says that the lessons learned from history can be applied inside the ring as well.

"You have to be patient," Stefanos insists. "But when the time comes to act, you must act decisively and without hesitation. Personal combat is all about strategy, especially when you are a grappler taking down a striker. You have to be especially careful to not get caught and that means biding your time and waiting for a mistake. But when you see an opening, act quickly. More than anything else you're playing a game of chess, and to successfully come in on a striker, clinch with him, and then take him to the ground, you have to be smart, wait for an opening, and then strike like a bolt of lightning."

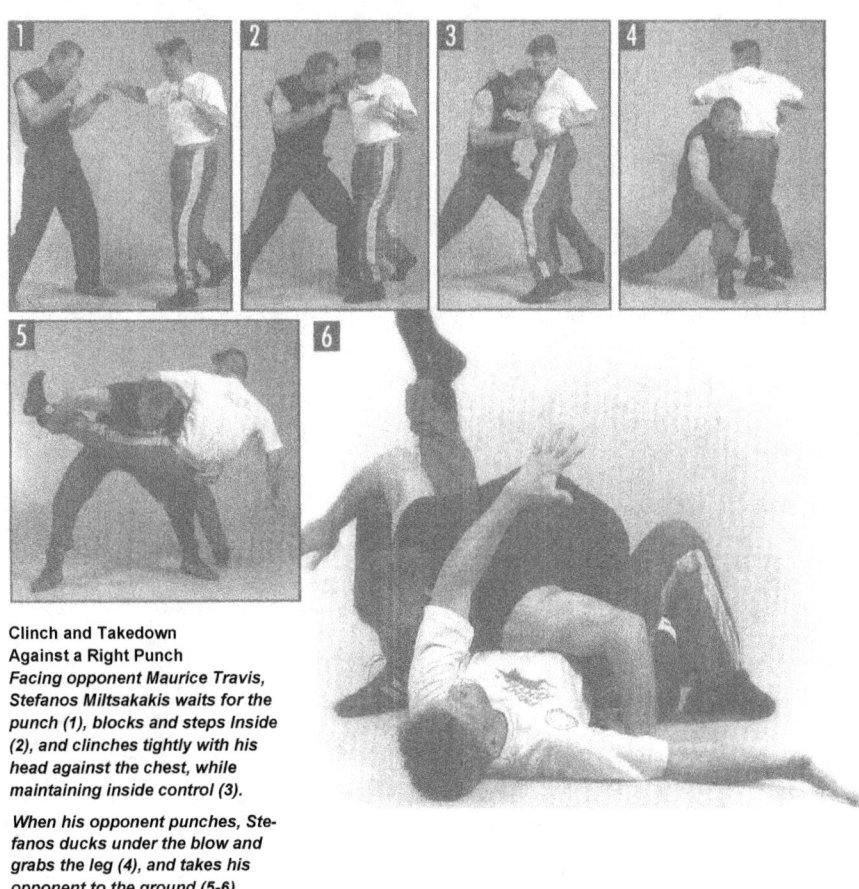

Clinch and Takedown Against a Right Punch
Facing opponent Maurice Travis, Stefanos Miltsakakis waits for the punch (1), blocks and steps inside (2), and clinches tightly with his head against the chest, while maintaining inside control (3).

When his opponent punches, Stefanos ducks under the blow and grabs the leg (4), and takes his opponent to the ground (5-6).

The Legacy of Shuai-Chiao's King, Grandmaster Chang Teng Sheng

Called "The Butterfly That Can Kill," Chang Teng Sheng will go down in history as the greatest fighter that Chinese shuai-chaio wrestling has ever produced.

Matt Furey

Every style of combat has its heroes; people we draw inspiration from. As a young boy I had many heroes, but Muhammad Ali was one of my biggest. I loved the way he flung his jab in the ring, and how he verbally jabbed his opponents non-stop outside it. His elusive, backpedaling style of fighting frustrated many foes, and the lightning speed of his punches was unmatched.

Ali wasn't much of a student, but that didn't keep him from reciting poetry. His own, that is. Many of his poems predicted the outcome of his fight, others belittled his opponents—but none were more famous than the swaggering, "Float like a butterfly, Sting like a bee."

A butterfly who stings like a bee. In the world of combat, it's hard to find a fighter described as a butterfly. A monkey, a snake, a crane, a tiger, a dragon? Yes. A butterfly? No. But hold on to your seats folks. In the world of Chinese martial arts, there was a man, known as Chang Teng Sheng, who practiced the ancient kung fu grappling art known as *shuai-chiao*. He was not the butterfly who stung like a bee. He was "the flying butterfly—the butterfly that can kill."

Unlike Ali, who gave himself the name, Grandmaster Chang was given the butterfly label by those who saw him fight, and Chang will undoubtedly go down in history as "the greatest" in his style of combat. This kung fu style is different from what many think of as "grappling." When I first began learning it, I had to put on the beginner's hat again. That's not easy for someone who has more than 25 years of wrestling experience. Most wrestling movements require you to apply force in one direction. All shuai-chiao movements are unique in that you are taught to apply simultaneous force in at least two different directions. This makes learning each move a chess game, but once you have a move down, it feels effortless.

Those who practice shuai-chiao know that no one has ever demonstrated the effectiveness of its throwing techniques better than Grandmaster Chang Teng Sheng. He began studying at the age of eight. In 1933, he won his first national title. In 1948, at the age of 39, he won his last national title, then retired unbeaten. When he died at the age of 80, he could rest in peace knowing that he was the best his art ever produced.

Any experience I have of Grandmaster Chang has been limited to the teachings of his top student, Dr. Chi Hsu Daniel Weng, who teaches the art to students in Cupertino and San Francisco, California.

Single Leg Counter
To counter a single leg Furey grabs his opponent's belt and executes a leg blocking throw.

Grandmaster Chang's 3 Keys to Fighting Success

1. Opportunity—an assessment of your opponent's strong and weak points, and a determination as to which techniques will work on him. Plan a number of moves, the create a strategy of how to use them, just as if playing chess.

2. Timing—knowing when to execute your techniques. If the movement is flawless, but the timing is off, the movement won't work and your opponent can counter.

3. Angle—be in a proper position so that you have maximum leverage to complete the technique. If the opportunity is present, and the timing is right, but the technique doesn't work, the problem lies with the angle.

He tosses his opponents through the air like he's flipping pancakes. As they land on the ground, he is still standing. This is the trademark of a perfectly executed throw in shuai-chiao.

The footage I have seen of Chang on videotape is mind-boggling. He tosses his opponents through the air like he's flipping pancakes. As they land on the ground, he is still standing. This is the trademark of a perfectly executed throw in shuai-chiao. Instead of going to the ground with an opponent, your goal is to throw him hard enough that he won't be able to get up.

An example of this is evident in the following story. When Chang was nearly 70 years old, King Hussein of Morocco invited him to give a demonstration of his martial art. During the demonstration he was unexpectedly attacked by a fourth-degree black belt in another martial art. Chang quickly back-stepped, pivoted to his opponent's rear, then nailed him with a strike and throw that catapulted him through the air, knocking him unconscious.

Of greatest importance to those who are striving to become wrestling champions, is Grandmaster Chang's unyielding dedication. From an early age, young Chang's desire to succeed was so great that he sought the counsel of any shuai-chiao master who possessed a technique he didn't know. On one occasion he worked in the bellows of a blacksmith shop for more than a year, silently doing his job, hoping that the proprietor, who was a shuai-chiao master, would teach him his techniques. Chang's hard work eventually paid off and the master taught him.

World-renowned kung fu master, Adam Hsu, who rarely has anything positive to say about any martial artist, had nothing but respect for Grandmaster Chang. In an article entitled *King of Shuai-*

Adam's Hsu's 4 Levels of Skill Required for Mastery
1. **Tan, or courage—a brave, frearless spirit.**
2. **Li, or power—strength in muscles, tendons, and sinews.**
3. **Kung fu, or hard work—the dedication and perseverance necessary to learn.**
4. **Yi, or art—using all techniques effectively and effortlessly.**

Snap Down
Furey grabs the top of his opponent's jacket. When he gets his opponent leaning too far forward, he pulls his right leg back to make room, then snaps him to the ground.

Chiao, Hsu told about the four different levels a martial artist must go through to become an expert. No matter what form of combat we are talking about, you can see that the levels are the same.

According to Hsu, "The first level is *tan* (courage) a brave, fearless, spirit; second, *li* (power), which refers to the development of strength in muscles, tendons and sinews. The third is *kung fa* (hard work) which means the dedication and perseverance necessary to learn. And finally there is *yi* (art), the highest expression of the very highest level, in which all techniques can be used effectively and effortlessly, demonstrating complete mastery of a style." Hsu further stated that Grandmaster Chang's mastery of shuai-chiao was so complete that his opponents were unable to find a weakness in his style. And because he could use any technique he wanted, and readily adapted to any fighting situation, his opponents literally lost the bout before it began. After more than 70 years of training in shuai-chiao as well as other kung fu styles, Grandmaster Chang was asked to distill the secrets of his success. He narrowed his answer down to three basic principles. Take a close look at these principles, then ask yourself if they apply to your situation. I'll bet they do.

The first principle is opportunity, which involves an assessment of your opponent's strong and weak points, and a determination as to what techniques will work on him. Chang believed in planning a number of moves, then creating a strategy on how to use them, just as if he was playing chess. The second principle, timing, involves knowing when to execute your techniques. If the movement is flawless, but the timing is off, the move won't work and your opponent can effectively counter. The third principle, angle, involves being in proper position so that you have maximum leverage to complete the technique. If the opportunity is present and the timing is right, but the technique still doesn't work, the problem lies with your angle. Correct the angle and the move will work much better.

Grandmaster Chang left a great legacy behind, in deeds as well as words. Shuai-chiao is a great art in and of itself, and using its tactics will prove useful for any grappler who trains with or without a gi or jacket.

Matt Furey is a national collegiate wrestling champion, world kung fu champion and student of Karl Gotch. He is the author of Combat *Conditioning: Functional Exercises for Fitness and Combat Sports. To order this book for $29.95 plus $5 S&H, call 813-994-8267 or visit Matt on the Web at* www.combatwrestling.com.

Cracking
To counter a lapel grab, Furey crosses his arm beneath his opponent's arm, locking the elbow. From this position he steps in with his left leg and throws.

Counter to Hip Throw
To counter a hip throw Furey pivots his hips and steps inside, executing the same throw his opponent tried.

Double Trouble
The Fighting McCully Brothers

Brothers Sean and Justin McCully are martial artists and gym owners who are known in Europe and Japan for their all-around fighting and wrestling ability—all they ask for in their home country of America is a little R-E-S-P-E-C-T.

Todd Hester, story and photos

With a father involved in law enforcement his whole life, who was always working out in boxing and wrestling, it seemed natural that sons Justin and Sean would follow in his footsteps as fighters—and that's just what happened.

"Our dad was always cross-training in everything," Justin says. "You name it, he did it—lifting weight, swimming boxing, judo, kickboxing, or whatever—he was a Secret Service agent, police officer, and worked for the Strike Force in Los Angeles. So he always felt that being in shape and training in martial arts was a way to protect himself."

"We always had a heavy bag or a speed bag up," older brother Sean recalls. "And as young as the ages of 4 and 7, he'd throw the gloves on us and let us duke it out whenever we had an argument."

"So we took it a step further," Justin adds. "I even remember us putting on having impromptu boxing matches and boxing with the neighborhood kids. For us, it was just natural because it was something that we'd always seen our father do."

Justin, the younger and yet bigger of the two siblings agrees. "Yeah, where most kids get stressed out by having to fight it was no big deal to us. We never had a hang up or anything because there was never a time we weren't doing it."

As the two grew older, Sean gravitated to boxing and then eventually kickboxing, preferring the striking arts to the grappling arts. "I'm a banger," he admits. "I always have been. I actually got interested in martial arts from Kung Fu Theater," Sean laughs. "I watched it all the time and then hit my dad up for lessons when I was just 8 years old. From there I just naturally gravitated toward competition, going from point fighting, to boxing, to full contact kickboxing, and finally to no rules fighting—almost by accident—when I got into the World Combat Championship. Somebody just approached me and asked what I'd think about doing something like the UFC. I asked how much did it pay? When they said $120,000 for first prize I said, 'Where do I sign up?' After that I just kept going."

As the younger brother, Justin recalls having to put up with getting experimented on growing up, by Sean as he learned different fighting techniques. "I was his whipping post for about 10 years," he says. "And then I got a little bigger and started training myself in some different things, more as a way to survive at home," he laughs. "Then when I was about 14 I got serious and started taking taekwondo and some kickboxing for a few years. Then for a good 3 or 4 years I got out of martial arts and concentrated on team sports in high school and didn't get back into it until after I finished playing football at Orange Coast College. I was just kicking around and saw that a guy named Alan Goes had opened a school down the street and started teaching Brazilian jiu-jitsu. This was around the time of the second Ultimate, and the first World Combat show that Renzo Gracie won. I thought that BJJ was overrated so I wanted to check it out for myself. I went to Alan's school with an attitude and he gave me a whipping that I'll never forget. This was when Alan was with Franco de Camargo. I was there with both of them, and then when Alan left to start his own school, I went with him. This was actually really good for me, because he used me as a practice dummy for his private students to try out moves on. So I was with him for 4 or 5 hours a day just training with guys and listening to Alan give them pointers—more than anything else, all that mat time is what helped me to improve."

With both brothers now involved in the fighting arts, Sean decided that it was time to open his own school, Extreme University, which soon became a place for some of the nation's top wrestler and no-holds-barred fighters to train. "EU was my idea and I hooked up with a couple of friends of mine, who were my students, and we pooled our money and made a very big investment in this place and hoped that it would take off. It was a great idea but there were three different guys who had three different ideas about how to run the school—which is not uncommon in partnerships—so that turned out to be a negative factor in making it work. I wanted to make money from the beginning, but we

Facing brother Sean (1), Justin grabs the lapel (2), puts the knee on the hip (3), falls to the side (4), and puts him into an arm bar (5).

Demonstrating a kickboxer facing a grappler (1), Sean defends the attempted takedown from Justin(2), steps to the side (3), and shin kicks to the face (4).

put too much money into it up front and the debt load was just too much for us to sustain paying— a beginner's business mistake. But we did have some top guys there: Mark Kerr, Mark Coleman, Maurice Smith, Randy Couture—you name it, there were there."

"Yeah," Justin agrees. "All the EU partners had good ideas, looking at it as an outside observer, but they had the ideas at different times and they just ended up inadvertently pulling EU apart."

"I'd like to think that we were a little ahead of our time," Sean agrees, "but the truth of the matter was that we were probably just inexperienced in business. The next gym I opened, L.A. Boxing in Costa Mesa, is the one I have right now and have had for 8 years. It's very successful and I think a lot of that is from the lesson I learned at EU."

After WCC, Sean was given an in to fight in Japan by friend Todd Medina, who had earlier made a connection to the Japan fighting circuit. So Todd hooked me up with some of the bookers, and had me work out in from of them, and then they asked me to go over and start working in Rings, whom I worked for at least three or four times. From there I just expanded my contacts and brought Justin in and we worked for New Japan, All Japan Kickboxing, and UWF A lot of the wrestling shows, which are huge in Japan, will have shoots that they'll do inside the wrestling shows. So once you get in with them you work across a lot of organizations."

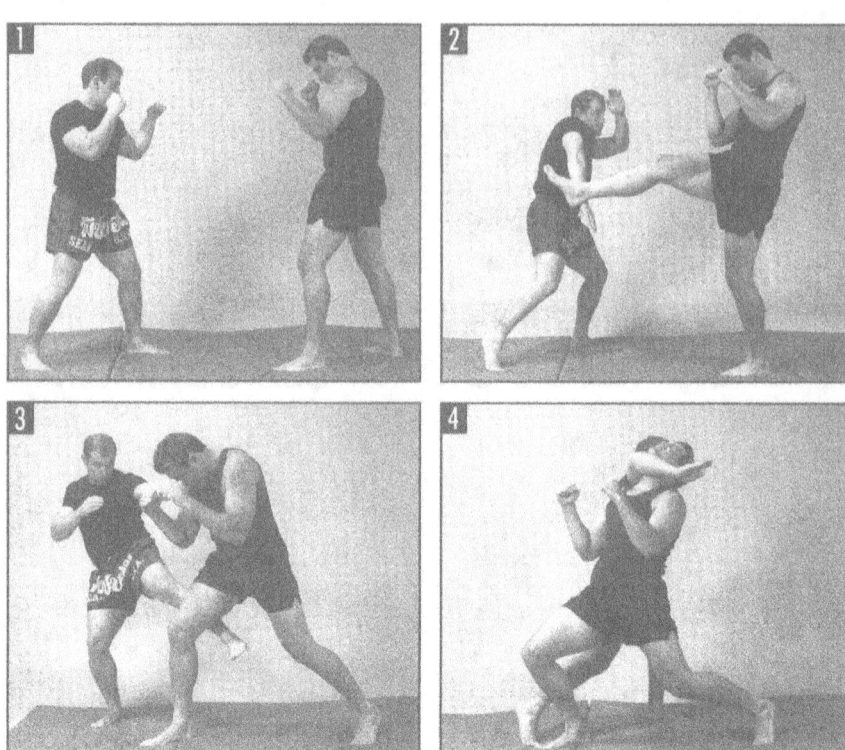

Sean faces Iustin (1), blocks his kick (2), lands a lead-leg kick of his own the thigh (3), and ends with a devastating clothesline strike (4).

Once I got in," Justin agrees. "I worked for Pancrase, Daido Juko, Rings, and also World Vale Tudo. So we've both had our share of fighting out of the country."

The brother have sometimes worked together on shows. One of their most memorable experiences came in Frederico Lapenda's World Vale Tudo IX, where Justin, given no chance against Brazilian black belt Mario Sucata, actually tapped him with a knee as just a purple belt, and Sean punched-out highly rated lute livre fight Joao Bosco in the first round, after taking the fight on 12 hours notice. But for all their international experience, the two are not really known in the United States outside of the hardcore fighting community—where they have are well-known and well-respected as teachers, trainers, and fighters.

"I think part of the lack of respect or notoriety," Justin says, "Is the fact that the only real event people know here is the Ultimate. The public thinks the guys who fight in that are the toughest guys in the world and that anyone else isn't really top notch. But when you look at it there are a lot of top guys who don't fight in it, and fight a lot out of the country, who don't get the credit they deserve. It's not for me to say that we fall into that category, but I will say that we've both paid our dues."

"We do make money," Sean says, "but we're in the martial arts because we love it. So when you so something out of love it is nice to get a little recognition in your own country, just not overseas."

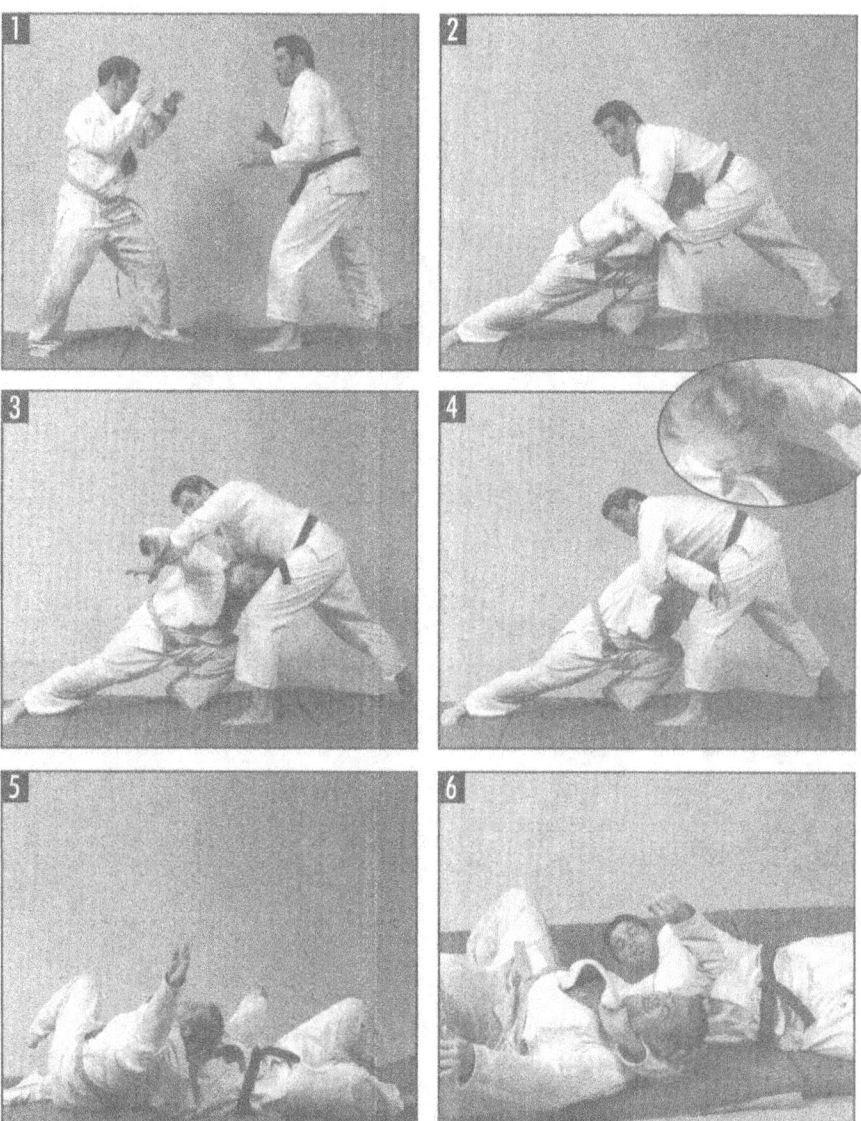

Facing off in gis (1), Sean shoots in (2), which Justin counters (3), then secures an under-grip on the lapel (4) barrel-rolls Sean to the ground (5), and applies the side-choke (6).

Starting from inside the guard (1), Iustin pressures the knee and breaks the leg scissors (2). Trapping the legs (3), he pressures the neck (4), and then goes to the side (5), and slides to the back (6), where he puts the hooks in (7), and apply a finishing leg lock (8).

The fact that the two are extremely well thought of is evidenced by the fact that several of the biggest Japanese fighting organizations routinely bring some of their top fighters over to stay for weeks at a time and have the McCullys train them for their biggest fights.

Justin and Sean McCully, though, seem determined to keep going in the martial arts regardless of the course they need to follow to stay on the fighting path. Accidentally related by birth, but brothers in spirit, the McCully brothers are leading figures of the dedicated grass root no-holds-barred network that is growing the sport in the United States and making a real difference to those who will follow in their footsteps.

But martial arts are their blood, and even if no-holds-barred were to get banned, and even if there was no money to be made in kickboxing, you'd undoubtedly find the McCullys setting up a ring in their backyard, throwing a barbecue, and inviting their friends and neighbors to stop by on a sleepy Sunday afternoon "to duke it out," just for kicks.

Justin and Sean McCully are available for group and private lessons in boxing, kickboxing, grappling, no- holds-barred fighting, and general

recreational fighting fitness programs for men, women, and children by calling LA Boxing at 949-722-3533, 2380 Newport Blvd, Costa Mesa, California 92627.

Comprido controlling the action.

The 2000 Brazilian Jiu-Jitsu World Championships

The greatest jiu-jitsu players in the world assembled to find who was the best in the world with the gi. But there were some surprises in store—most notably in the form of American BJ. Penn—who became the first non-Brazilian to ever win a black belt world championship.

Kid Peligro, photos by Gustavo Aragao

The fifth edition of the Brazilian Jiu-Jitsu World Championships, held at the Tijuca Tennis Club in Rio de Janeiro, on July 27th-30th, and had a lot of history to live up to, both negative and positive. Was this going to make a lasting mark in the history of the sport, or was this going to be merely another ho-hum event in which most of the stars stay away from the hard match-ups? There are so many black belts now, due to jiu-jitsu's popularity, both in Brazil and around the world, that a bottleneck is beginning to form in each weight division as so many claim to be the best.

Mondial 1996

The first Mondial was held in 1996 at this same venue and was the first time that any black belt could truly declare themselves to be a world champion. The attraction of the title brought out most of the stars to compete. All the big guns at the time—names like Royler Gracie, Fabio Gurgel, Murilo Bustamante, Leo Castello Branco, Ricardo Liborio, Amaury Bitteti and Wallid Ismael—were there ready to play. There were also new names in the black belt scene about to earn a reputation for themselves, most notable were newly promoted black belts Ze Mario Sperry, Saulo Ribeiro, and Roberto "Roleta" Magalhaes. Even though there was much excitement surrounding the first event, the championhips were hardly dramatic—sure winners like Royler Gracie, Fabio Gurgel and Amoury Bitteti asserted themselves one more time with Murrillo Bustamante falling in the finals to archrival Gurgel. And even though Sperry and some others won, the field at the top in the weight divisions was relatively thin. This first year greatest surprise was by "Roleta" Magalhaes. During the semifinal against favorite and feared Wallid Ismael, "Roleta" using all of his called *" esquijitsu"* (weird jitsu) somehow survived the pressure applied by Wallid. Wallid had the match in the bag when, with about 35 seconds to go, Roleta pulled one of his weirdest and newest moves, "The Helicopter Sweep" and managed to get Wallid in a bad position for a split second, where he proceeded to take Wallid's back with 10 seconds to go for the surprise win. Roleta then defeated Wallid's teammate "Bebeo" Duarte and won the title.

Mondial 1997

The next year, still at the same venue, marked the real appearance on the jiu-jitsu scene of Robson Moura and Saulo Ribeiro. Robinho, who had won the Superfeather title in the purple belt division the year before, came back to the same arena to claim the same division now, however, as a black belt. Ribeiro, on the other hand, was starting to make his fantastic run of world titles, each year in a different weight division. Ribeiro, who had won the year before as a lightweight, was coming back as middleweight and defeated all that stood in the way to get the title. Royler Gracie, Gurgel, Roleta, Sperry, and Bitteti also repeated their success. Royler, on this day, fought eight matches, five as a featherweight and three more in the Absolute, as the 150lb. technician managed to beat two giants, 330 lb. Aguinaga, and 220 lb. Leo Dalia, before losing to a fresh 220 lb. Bitteti by a slim margin. Royler was elected the most technical athlete of the tournament that year.

Mondial 1998

The third edition highlighted some rising stars such as new black belts Leo Vieira and Vitor "Shaolin" Ribeiro, who had been sensational in the lower belt divisions. These young lions were now pushing the established champions for a little bit of sunlight and some success of their own. Saulo Ribeiro, who was going up in weight once again to compete as a medium-heavyweight, would have his work cut out for him as he would have to face superstars Gurgel and Bustamante on the same night. Ribeiro successfully defeated Gurgel by a takedown, and then Murillo with the same move, to win his third consecutive title. If that wasn't enough drama, there was Royler going into the finals against "Shaolin" and getting swept early in the match only to come back and use the momentum from his opponent's sweep to pay him right back and apply pressure to become the first person to win three consecutive jiu-jitsu world titles.

In the Heavyweight division, two previously undefeated two-time world champions were there—Sperry and Roleta. It was obvious that someone was going to have to lose as the congestion of top competitors was beginning to show. Roleta drew first blood and took out Sperry in the heavyweight finals. This gave Sperry, for the first time since he was a brown belt many years ago, the taste of defeat in a major competition. Sperry didn't like the taste and promptly signed up for the Absolute division. Roleta, still reeling from the win and the new title, and looking for more, also signed up, thus raising the stakes. If Roleta beat Sperry for the second time in one evening, he would undoubtedly be declared the best jiu-jitsu fighter of the year. On the other hand, another Sperry loss would do serious damage to his reputation. In a gutsy performance, Sperry defeated Roleta in the emotional final and conquered the Absolute division.

B.J. Penn became the first American to win a black belt world title

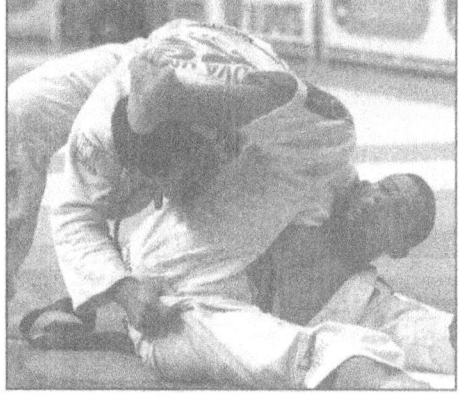

Mondial 1999

The fourth world championship saw the bar raised even higher, as fresh faces were starting to show-up in the Brown Belt division. Archrivals Fernando "Margarida" Pontes, and Flavio "Cachorrinho" Almeida made the finals of their weight division and had one of the most fantastic matches ever seen. At one point in the match, while behind on points, Margarida had Cachorrinho in such a tight arm bar that in order to escape and eventually win, Cachorrinho had to suffer a hyperextension of the elbow joint. Royler Gracie once again had some memorable fights. Having been sick with fever for several days going into the tournament, he faced newcomer Leo Santos in the semifinals, who he managed to defeat with last minute heroics. He then had to go against Leozinho Vieira, who had dropped in weight in order to face the most dangerous Gracie. Royler was once again successful and took his unprecedented fourth consecutive world title, a result that was almost considered just a given. Saulo Ribeiro, now fighting as a heavyweight, faced Roleta, the last man to beat him (by arm bar submission) a few years back. Saulo took the opportunity to pay back Roleta and maintain his incredible string of victories for that year, having just won the State title a month prior to the event. Sperry, however, ran out of silver bullets. He fought many matches in the Super Heavyweight and the Absolute divisons only to fall short both times. He lost to Leo Leite in the weight division finals and to newcomer Rodrigo "Comprido" Medeiros in the Absolute semifinals. Comprido went on to submit Roleta in the finals of the Absolute with a vicious foot lock, denying both three-time world champions, Sperry and Roleta, a chance to repeat again. Roberto Traven took the Open division for the second year in a row.

Fabio Gurgel confounded critics to take another world title.

Mondial 2000

For the 2000 championships, there were simply too many great players in each division and only one place at the top. The event was fantastic with tremendous fights in every class. Attending the competition was virtually every important name in the sport. Besides the regular competitors you could see Reyson, Relson, Carlson, Ril- lion, Carlos Jr, Rolker and Royler Gracie, Ze Mario Sperry, Alexandre Paiva, Leo Castello Branco, Joe Moreira, Aloisio Silva, Andre Pederneiras and many others.

ose and the Blue Belt Adults started, the tremendously, and this was shown by

been competitive in the Adult division.

In the Blue Belt Adult division one of the stars was Roger Gracie. The 18-year-old resident of Florida won his Medium Heavyweight division and got second in the Absolute division with a great display of technique and maturity. In the finals he met Australian wonder kid Daniel Cherobin, who submitted all three of his opponents via triangle choke prior to meeting Roger. Also in the Blue Belt division was Fabricio

te divisions. He had to fight ten matches n Europe.

B.J. Penn showed nearly flawless form.

2000 Day Two
In the second day of competition the purple belts went at it. The higher the belt, of course, the higher the level of skill. The most impressive thing about the purple belts is that they almost have the skill level of most black belts. There were several great matches and Daniel Moraes was one of the big names. He dominated all his opponents on his way to his title.

2000 Day Three—Brown Belts
The third day was comprised of the Brown Belt and the Absolute Black Belt divisions. The Brown Belt competition had two Americans in the Super Heavyweight class, Garth Taylor from Santa Cruz, California, and Kai Garcia from Hawaii. They both had very difficult fights but managed to keep winning and got to the semifinals. The two were denied an all-American finals, though, when Kai lost by two points on a sweep and Garth lost by advantage. Later on, Kai told me, "How can I get swept on a move that we practice all the time?" He was still happy with his performance and he continued, "Next year I am going to come here sooner and get into better competition shape. You have to get the latest techniques down in order to compete for the title."

Marcio "Pe de Pano", who has a very offensive, submission-oriented style and Alexandre Ribeiro were the big standouts this day. Pe de Pano won his weight division easily while "Xande," had to fight against arch rival Gabriel Vella on the second round. Xande had the fight of his career against Vella and after that the title fight was anti-climatic. The match was a sequence of near scores with both Gabriel and Xande almost achieving guard passes and sweeps from the half-guard—but in the end Ribeiro got the nod by advantage. Xande then scored a competition-record 26 points in the semi-finals and won the finals convincingly. Alexandre has a style similar to brother Saulo, very technical and with great competition sense and tactics. The other big winner was Gustavo Correia. Each of Gustavos fights were difficult, including a semifinal win over US star David Camarillo, who won his first two fights via

Comprido in perfect position.

Flavio Almeida in control.

submission (knee bar and arm lock) and had a lot of momentum going into the match with Correia. The two exchanged controlling grips the entire match with Camarillo almost losing his temper in the end—but Correia got the nod.

2000 Day Three—Black Belt Absolute

The big story of the competition, however, was the Black Belt Absolute division. Carlos Gracie Jr. made the great decision to have the Absolute on a different day than the regular weight division, and this caused the top stars to enter. The Absolute Black Belt was the stuff dreams are made of, and the list of names was a *Who's Who of Jiu-Jitsu,* including Leo Dalia, Marcio Corletta, Alexandre "Cafe" Dantas, Flavio "Cachorrinho" Almeida, Antonio "Nino" Schembri, Rodrigo "Comprido" Medeiros, Leo Leite, Fernando "Margarida" Pontes, Jose Mario "Esfiha", Renato Ferro, and others.

Margarida showed that he meant business early. He submitted Francisco Mello and Cafe by arm bars in his opening matches. Esfiha submitted Renato Ferro by kimura and then defeated Marcio Corleta by points. Comprido, on the other side of the bracket, advanced over Leo Dalia, and then met up with one of the favorites, Nino, in the quarter-finals. The entire stadium stood up and cheered when Comprido and Nino stood there in the middle of Mat 2. Comprido opened up with a quick takedown, but Nino responded by placing him in the guard. As Comprido stood up to open Nino's guard, Nino started to make his move and somehow was taking Comprido's back while the two were still standing. Comprido kept his cool and avoided the danger and managed to get Nino down and tried to take Nino's back almost immediately as things happened in a very fast and furious sequence. As Nino defended a choke by Comprido, he managed to escape and get to Comprido's side and attack the arm with a kimura lock, Comprido quickly reversed with a kimura lock of his own now and was more successful, forcing Nino to tap.

The next match was the best match of the night, Margarida vs. Cachorrinho. Margari- da still had a bad taste in his mouth from his defeat the prior year and was ready for revenge. He pulled guard and kept attacking Cachorrinho constantly. Cachorrinho, on the other hand, was trying to get base to pass the guard. Suddenly Margarida got him in an arm bar, the same position as the year before, and it appeared that the fight would be over quickly, but Cachorrinho again managed to pull a series of Houdini moves and somehow escaped the sure submission. The fight continued with tremendous velocity and positional changes until Cachorrinho got to Margarida's side and tried an arm attack of his own. Margarida defended it well and ended up on top. The failure to get the submission seemed to take the air out of

Cachorrinho and give new life to Margarida. He quickly passed guard, put his knee on the stomach, and sunk-in a choke for a submission with only a minute left in the match. Cachorrinho just had nothing left in the end and could no longer keep up with the speed and technique of Margarida.

Comprido then disposed of Esfiha with a foot lock and Margarida mowed down last year's super heavyweight champion Leo Leite, with a series of unstoppable moves that are now considered Mar- garida's style. Leo Leite, the Brazilian national class judoka, who last year beat Mario Sperry for the world title, started attacking Margarida on the feet, but Margarida didn't back down and fought stand-up for a while without giving much ground. He then pulled guard and defended Leite's attacks. After a while Margarida started to take control, he swept Leite and then worked on passing the guard and got cross-side and attempted knees on the stomach and other attacks until time ran out.

Margarida would meet Comprido in the Absolute finals. Comprido, who was last year's Absolute champion, was looking to go back-to-back, while the hungry up-and-coming Margarida was looking for another dragon to slay. Comprido is a very smart competitor and he had already seen that movie before, however. He had fought Margarida a few times in the Sao Paulo state circuit and knew what to do to be successful. The book on Margarida has been to pass his guard to the left, and after an early take down, Comprido stayed with that strategy. Margarida, however, had other ideas and was threw everything he had at Comprido. After a while, when the game seemed established and Margarida was beginning to make successful counterattacks, Comprido changed course 180 degrees and went back to the traditional right-side pass. That seemed to catch Margarida off-guard and throw his game off for a little while, and it was enough to allow Comprido to control the rest of the match to gain the title of World Absolute Champion for the second consecutive year.

Comprido needs to be given special recognition as one of the all-time great fighters now that he is a two-time Absolute champion. Although he has the humorous habit of calling people that he likes "Uncle," he loves to fight and his amazing accomplishment at the tender age of 24 is noteworthy. After the win, Comprido said, "I want to dedicate this win to...my teammates and to Uncle Jacare. Tell Uncle Tahnoon that I hope he invites me back to Abu Dhabi to achieve the only title that I don't

Marcio Corleta is always a crowd favorite.

have yet. I love to fight and want people to watch me fight and see a person that has fun doing it." It seems that with this victory, that Comprido has stamped his passport to the ADCC championships.

2000 Day Four—Black Belt Preliminaries

The final day saw the most complete line-up of black belts ever to fight in a single competition. Despite the absence of Royler Gracie and Ze Mario Sperry due to injuries, and Ricardo Liborio and Murilo Bustamante withdrawing, both still grieving from the tragic death of a teammate the day before, the line up was stacked. All the athletes from the Absolute entered, plus quite a few more name fighters. The competition was so tremendous that many times, there were great fights going on at the same time in all four rings. It was hard to follow the frenetic pace of the action. Just when you thought it was not possible for this tournament to get any better, it did. It was just fantastic, with the place packed full of people including the different academies' organized fan sections. Alliance, Nova Uniao, Gracie Barra, and Gracie Humaita had full-on cheering sections with giant flags and drums to support the fighters and also to annoy the opposing academies, chanting all the time when one of their fighters was competing. There were so many great fights that an entire magazine could be written about this day alone.

Nino vs. Charuto: Nino pulled guard and immediately started pulling his leg over Charuto's head for an *homoplata* (shoulder lock), Charuto rolled out to escape and Nino simply took the arm bar. Less than one minute and the fight was over. Shaolin defeated Leozinho via a takedown, while on the opposite mat, Leo Santos, the Pan American lightweight champion, and Marcio Feitosa, the reigning world champion were locked in battle. The two butted heads for the entire match with Feitosa taking the decision by advantage. Then Ze Mario "Esfiha" defeated Rigan Machado 5-0 by takedown and guard pass. Rigan looked like he lacked the sharpness that only comes with regular competition.

American B.J. Penn was now into his run for the world title, and he defeated Soca Carneiro, then continued his unprecedented march by eeking out a win over Fredson Alves, and then defeating Edson Diniz in the Featherweight division final by a sweep. B.J. is the first non-Brazilian to win a world title as a black belt.

The fight of the tournament occurred in the Medium Heavyweight division, and once again it was Margarida against Cachorrinho. Cachorrinho came back with a different strategy this time. He controlled Margarida's hips and managed to pass the guard for an early lead. Margarida would then reverse and either pass the guard or almost do it. He got Cachorrinho in an arm bar and the fight

appeared to be over—but Cachorrinho managed to escape one more time and had new life. He proceeded to attack and got to Margarida's side after a guard pass. The fight ended with Margarida ahead on points in one of the best fights that anyone has ever witnessed.

2000 Day Four Black Belt Title Matches
Super Featherweight—Robinho def. Parrumpinha
Before the fight begin, they looked as if they were in a NHB fight, staring into each other's eyes, almost nose to nose. The crowd went wild until the match finally started. After few moments standing, Robinho pulled Parrumpinha to his guard. Parrumpinha started to pass Robinhos guard, but Robinho did one of his sweeps and Parrumpinha went down for a 2-0 disadvantage. Parrumpinha didn't like that situation and at the first opportunity stood up. Robinho then immediately pulled Parrumpinha back into his guard. Robinho almost got another sweep but Parrumpinha prevented it. Parrumpinha continued trying to pass Robinho's guard until the end of the match.

Featherweight—BJ. Penn def. Edson Diniz
When the referee said "Fight!" they both tried to pull guard at the same time. Edson decided to go on top and attempted to pass BJ.'s guard. He got the early advantage by rule but that move proved to be a grave mistake. Edson tried to pass the guard for a while and all of a sudden BJ. went for a sweep and had Edson on the ground for the 2 points. BJ. was went on top, attempting to pass Edson's guard. Edson has an excellent guard, however, and even tried a choke for a 2nd advantage. BJ. got to the half-guard and got an advantage. He then proceeded to work Edson and eventually passed the guard. After that, he controlled the fight. Edson managed to get a good foot lock in, but B J. escaped and won. He became the first non-Brazilian to ever win in the black belt division.

Roleta showing his championship form.

Lightweight—Shaolin def. Feitosa

This was the most controversial match of the entire tournament. Feitosa scored several advantages and seemed to stall a little at one time. Referee "Toco" warned him to move, then he stood the fighters up. The fight went to the ground again with Feitosa in Shaolin's closed guard. Feitosa got warned again and advantage was given to Shaolin. This repeated several times. Not to take anything away from Shaolin, who is a great champion, but both he and Feitosa stalled at the same time and the general consensus was that the referee erred by punishing Marcio as he did.

Mediumweight—Terere def. Nino

After a great tournament, Nino ran into Terere in the finals. Nino's game is on the ground and he tried to stay with Terere in the stand-up game and got taken down for points and that seemed to throw his game out of sync. Terere is certainly one of the top young stars and controlled the rest of the fight for the title.

Medium Heavyweight—Roleta def. Margarida

Roleta pulled guard and used his entire arsenal to keep Margarida off balance. Margarida attacked Role- ta's feet and knees several times and Roleta used those opportunities to reverse him. At one time it seemed that Margarida had Roleta's foot for sure, but Roleta managed to somehow escape. Roleta won 6-0.

Heavyweight—Fabio Gurgel def. Ricardo Arona

This match pitted the current ADCC under 97 kg champion against a former world champion. Gurgel has been around for quite a while and Arona is one of the young lions, but Gurgel used all of his experience to take this fight to Arona. He did a takedown and then controlled the younger Arona. He then methodically worked his way into passing Arona's guard for a complete and undisputed victory. With this surprise victory, Gurgel has established himself as one of the all-time jiu-jitsu greats at any weight.

Super Heavyweight—Saulo Ribeiro def. Daniel Simoes

Once again, Ribiero showed everyone why he has so many titles and is considered the best jiu-jitsu competitor in the World. He gained half-guard on Simoes and started to squeeze and gain position inch by inch. Simoes, feeling the pressure, exploded to escape and Ribeiro took advantage of the explosion to gain better position. After another exchange, Ribeiro placed Simoes into his guard, and then controlled the arm and the opposite leg and went for a traditional Ribeiro sweep. He had just about completed the sweep when Daniel based to avoid the points, Ribeiro was like a lion going for the kill and quickly took Daniel's back and tried to work on a choke until time ran out.

Overweight—Leo Leite x Aurelio Fernandez

These two judo guys going at it in an a typical final. Leite won on aggressiveness as the fight ended without any points.

Conclusion

There were many great fighters at the 2000 Mondial. Robinho and Omar are almost guaranteed winners every time they compete. They both overshadow the competition in their respective weight classes. Omar has been the class of the rooster division for the last two years and Robinho's domination of the Super Featherweight division with five world titles (one as purple belt and four as black) is undisputed. BJ. Penn showed that he belongs in the Black Belt division without a doubt, having just graduated to that level and winning his first competition as a black belt—and the world title, no less (as Robinho did his first year). Other notable included Terere, for having defeated the incredible Nino in the Middleweight division; Roleta, for stepping back on the top and defeating Margarida in the finals; and the incredible performance by Fabio Gurgel. Gurgel had been so sick that he couldn't train for ten days prior to the competition, and yet still managed to defeat ADCC Champion Ricardo Arona.

The Best of the Best

There were three fighters, though, that stood out above all the rest. **Rodrigo "Cumprido" Medeiros,** won the Absolute for the second year in a row! He is one of the nicest people you will ever meet and a great champion to boot—a technical, powerful fighter who is also a masterful tactician. **Saulo Ribeiro** has now won five different world titles (the first was shared) in the Light, Medium, Medium Heavyweight, Heavyweight, and Super Heavyweight divisions. He is the best competitor out there, no doubt. His fight strategy is flawless and when the opportunity presents itself, he moves like a tiger to the kill. This year he had a major set back in Japan, losing to Yuki Kondo in Coliseum 2000 and had many injuries. Many doubted him. But he went up one a weight division again and simply ran over everyone. And consider the fact that he broke two fingers on his right hand about two minutes into the first fight! Despite the fact that he ended up with two seconds, **Fernando "Margarida" Pontes** he has to be the story of this tournament. He took-on everyone and went for the finish every time, without regard for points most of the time. He submitted many and beat several of the top guys in the world all in two days. Not bad for a 21-year-old!

Frank Shamrock's Ultimate Training and Fighting System

Train harder? Frank Shamrock, who has, in a few short years become THE no-holds barred fighter against whom other fighters are judged would like to change that tired old bit of advice to "Train smarter."

John Steven Soet

Beginning with the first Ultimate Fighting Championships in 1993, martial artists of all different styles, backgrounds and weight classes were able to pit their skills against each other in the ring. It was a rude awakening for many. A horde of martial artists who considered themselves invincible was soon tapping out. And these events answered once-and-for all, questions being asked by martial artists and fans for decades.

The first question answered was, "Do martial arts work?" The answer was a resounding YES. Martial arts training was touted as being able to give a person the ability to overcome a larger, stronger opponent. Many doubted that this was true. Yet when the world watched 155-pound Royce Gracie continually humiliate and defeat opponents outweighing him by as much as 50 pounds, the public had no choice but to become believers.

The second question answered was, "What is the BEST martial art?" The answer was again indisputable: NONE. Martial artists from a myriad of different backgrounds and styles fought in these events, and it was clearly demonstrated that there is no superior martial art; there are only superior practitioners.

The next question was, "Did Bruce Lee know what he was talking about?" The answer was: You betcha! More then 30 years ago, Lee incurred the wrath of the martial arts community by insisting that it was a mistake to rigidly adhere to the teachings of a single style or system. Lee insisted throughout his adult life that martial artists should take advantage of opportunities to train in many different styles and ultimately develop a personal style as a form of self-expression.

This was quickly proven by the experiences of the early fighters in mixed events. Suddenly, it was not uncommon to see a tae kwon do stylist grappling, or a grappler delivering a Thai hook kick. Martial artists who were highly trained in one style were quick to learn the weaknesses inherent in their system, and fill in the gaps by training in other martial arts. Practitioners who were highly skilled in their respective arts realized they needed to familiarize themselves with other systems so they could defend against them and develop effective counters. Fighters also immediately understood the need for cross training, such as weight training for strength, stretching for flexibility, and drills for speed and precision.

In short, the martial arts community got a much needed reality check. And the ultimate result was the birth of a new martial art. In fact, this martial art is so new that it has yet to be given a name. The public refers to this art variously as "no-holds barred fights," "ultimate fighting," and "mixed martial arts." And in no single individual is this new martial art more embodied than in Frank Shamrock.

Birth of a Legend

Born Frank Elisio Juarez, Shamrock owes his good looks to his Mexican/ Native American heritage. He grew up in Northern California and ultimately took the name of his adopted father, Bob Shamrock. Fascinated by martial arts his entire life, he began training in a variety of styles at a very early age.

"Let's face it," says Frank. "We live in a world where there are unprecedented opportunities to train. A fisherman in Okinawa had to train with whatever karate master lived near him. He couldn't go to a karate lesson one day, a jiu-jitsu lesson the next, and a boxing gym the day after. We can. And we have fighters who are constantly testing and refining their skills. We have an unlimited pool of knowledge.

Frank quickly swept the world of mixed martial arts. With five UFC victories and a score of dazzling no-holds barred championships to back him up, he quickly became "The Man." Wherever there were butts to be kicked, Frank Shamrock came riding into town and kicked them all. And according to Frank, he has one, and only one secret. Training smarter.

Frank Shamrock's "Smart Training"

"First," Frank insists, "I want everybody to forget that tired old piece of nonsense, 'Without pain there is no gain.' If it hurts, it's bad for you. Pain is your body's natural way of telling you that something is bad for you. That saying was originated by bodybuilders, and I guess they're right if you don't mind tendonitis, sprains, and walking around like you're an old man by the time you're 30.

Frank quickly swept the world of mixed martial arts. With five UFC victories and a score of dazzling no-holds barred championships to back him up, he quickly became "The Man."

"Let's take stretching for example. When you stretch to the point of pain, you're tearing down muscle fibers. When the recover, they grow back harder, and less flexible. You're impairing your flexibility, not improving it. The trick is to stretch to the point where it just begins to hurt, then back off."

Frank is also a believer in daily training. "It's okay to take a day off every so often, but only through training every day do you constantly improve. I train every day of my life, and I haven't reached my peak yet. I'm not saying you should lift weights every day without giving your body a chance to recover, but you should alternate your various forms of training; weights, stretching, car

dio, calisthenics, practicing your martial arts. They're all part of your training regimen.

"For example, I lift weights three days a week. I keep my workouts simple, and I don't use really heavy poundages. I keep it light, fast, and maybe do three exercises for each bodypart. That's it."

The Importance of Diet

Frank also believes that diet is an important part of a fighter's regimen, but, like everything else in his training philosophy, he believes this should be practice in moderation too. "You have to keep away from the fad diets, the so-called latest discovery in diet technology that's going to turn you into a lean machine overnight. Hello! People have been eating since day 1. There aren't any new discoveries or secrets out there. There's nothing any doctor or scientist can tell us that we don't already know.

"The trick is to eat cleaner. We know what's good for us and what isn't. It may be fashionable to start your day with the latest state-of-the-art meal supplement, but what's wrong with a chicken breast and some white rice, or a bowl of oatmeal and a couple of eggs? We know that's good for you, we don't need to be told."

Frank also believes that, from a psychological standpoint, it's important to cheat. "I eat a lot of junk. Burgers, pizza, stuff like that. Your body can handle it, just don't overdo it. If you eat healthy stuff, lean protein, vegetables, fruits, stuff like that, you can have two 'cheat' days a week to keep you honest. If you pig out two days a week, then it's not like your bound to this restricted diet your whole life."

He laughs when the discussion turns to fad diets or "secret weight loss techniques." "Again," smiles Frank, "there's no substitute for good-old common sense. People are always asking me, 'Frank, how can I lose weight?' I tell them to stop drinking sodas for a while, and switch to bottled water or a sports drink. There's as much sugar in a soft drink as there is in about two-and-a-half candy bars. And if you wanna lose weight, try this one: stop eating bread. Just try it for a week, no bread. You could lose up to seven pounds.

The Ultimate Training System

With his busy schedule, Frank soon realized that he had to become an innovator in the interest of saving time. With that realization, he quickly set out to create what may be the most ingenious training system ever devised. "What I did," he begins, "was to combine my exercises with fighting moves. That way, you're not only getting a great workout; you're practicing moves that you'll use in fights.

"It programs the mind, similar to kata. You do something thousands of times your subconscious mind takes over and you just do it instinctively. And if it's a physical exercise, you get the physical benefit.

"An example of this would be the humble squat. It works all of the muscles in the lower body. But then, when you drop into the squat, you can pivot around when you come back up. So it duplicates a move you'd use when someone tries to put a lock on you or attack you from behind. You squat down, pivot and step around, and when you come back up you're in back of the guy who attacked you."

Frank has designed an entire workout program based on exercises that duplicate standard, effective body exercises, and incorporate fighting moves. The exercises utilize motions that include escapes, reversals, evasions, etc., virtually everything a fighter would use in a match. The workout takes about 45 minutes to complete, and can get the fighter into top condition while programming the subconscious mind to respond to actual combat situations. Once this automatic response becomes natural, the body moves instinctively in a situation, responding to an opponent's attack without conscious thought and reacting instantaneously.

"This can make all the difference in the world in a fight," says Frank. "The fraction of a second it takes to think about what you're going to do is all your opponent needs to finish you off. When you react automatically, on instinct, you eliminate that little window of time that can make the difference between victory and defeat.

Visualization

The final aspect of Frank's training system is visualization. "I can't emphasize the mental aspect enough," he insists. "A fight looks very physical, but with two equally-strong, equally-fast and equally-trained fighters, it's more of a chess game. They both know what works and what doesn't. They both have experience, and neither one has the advantage over the other. This is when the fight goes to the mental level, and the fighter with the better mind will win.

"I use visualization constantly. I relax completely, and create a mental image of the fight in my mind. I see myself against the other fighter, and I see him coming at me. I mentally visualize myself in every conceivable situation, and winning in every conceivable situation. In the real world, I've been in many, many matches, it's true. But in my mind I've been in literally thousands of matches. In my mind I've been through it all, every move, every attack, every type of fighter, and every situation. I hold these images in my mind, let my instincts take over, and I win.

"One of the questions a lot of people ask me, in personal conversations and interviews is, 'Frank, what was the biggest surprise you every had against an opponent.' And the truth is, I've never been surprised. No one's attack or strategy or technique ever took me by surprise because I'd been there before, if not in the real world, in my mind. I can honestly say a fighter who doesn't use visualization is not a complete fighter.

What Lies Ahead

So what's next for Frank Shamrock? Like Alexander the Great, does he weep because there are no worlds left to conquer? Hardly. For starters, Frank recently appeared in an episode of "Walker: Texas Ranger" with Chuck Norris. "I'm definitely going to pursue an acting career," he laughs. "I know every martial artist says that, but I really am. I'm studying constantly, and putting as much effort into making myself an actor as I did into making myself a fighter."

He also wants to share his knowledge with the world. He recently relocated to Southern California, where he teaches in his own school, and completed a set of videotapes in which he reveals his Ultimate Training and Fighting System to the world. "Face it," he says. "People are always looking for the real thing: the best way to train and the best fighting and self-defense techniques. I learned the hard way. Now everybody else can learn without taking the hits," he adds with a laugh.

I train every day of my life, and I haven't reached my peak yet. I'm not saying you should lift weights every day without giving your body a chance to recover, but you should alternate your various forms of training; weights, stretching, cardio, calisthenics, practicing your martial arts. They're all part of your training regimen.

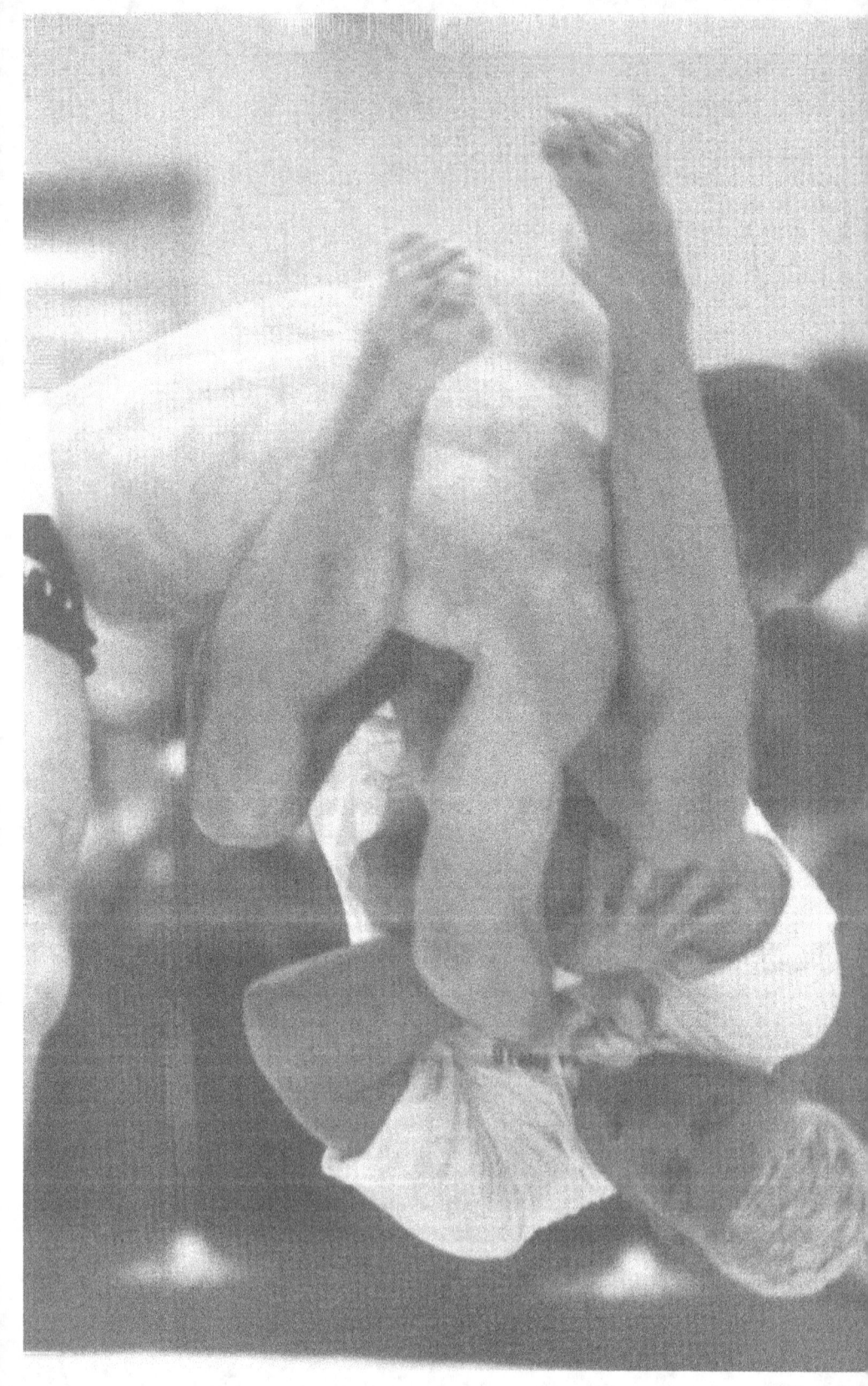

Notes written from under the bleachers at the

Abu Dhabi 2000 Submission Wrestling World Championships

We're Not in Kansas Anymore, Toto

John G. Keating, MD, photos by Bill Curry

It's a fight fanatic's dream come true. Some billionaire angel throws open his pocketbook to put on a freewheeling event to pick the best submission grapplers on earth. Agents are sent out to scour the planet for the best fighters on the planet to meet in an exotic location for a week-long single elimination tournament for bragging rights as the best on Earth against the toughest competition in history—with hundreds of thousands in prize money thrown in for good measure. It's Jean Claude Van Damme's *Lionheart* times ten.

Enter the Prince. The prince is, of course, H. E. Sheikh Tahnoon Ben Zayed, a Bedouin royal who went to San Diego to study finance and came back enamored of the UFC and Gracie (now unfortunately called "Brazilian") Jiu-Jitsu®. Imagine what you would do if you had more money than a horse could jump over and you wanted to immerse yourself in something—to master something. Well, that's what the prince did. He brought Professor Nelson Monterio, Brazilian jiu-jitsu black belt, to Abu Dhabi and set him up in the Abu Dhabi Sports Center (which morphed into the Abu Dhabi Combat Club) and began intensive private lessons, eventually bringing in sambo fighters and Russian wrestlers to build his own private competition team. By all accounts His Excellency, the sheikh, is an accomplished student who has ascended to the rank of genuine purple belt in Brazilian jiu-jitsu.

But that's not really enough, is it? I mean, if you're a real fanatic and you've collected all the video tapes available, and you've watched and re-watched all the fights from around the world, you've got to step up and do your own thing—and in 1998 that's exactly what the prince did—he held the first ADCC championships.

Except, of course, you are not finding the best submission grappler on Earth; you're finding the guy best at mastering the rules for this particular contest. Keep in mind that this is not a no-holds-barred event. It's a sporting event with special rules. And for those who leave the United Arab Emirates complaining that the best submission grappler didn't win, I offer this advice: it's the prince's country, it's his city, it's his house, it's his table, it's his deck of cards, all the chips belong to him, and he makes the rules—and, by God, if you don't like that idea stay in Kansas with Dorothy and Toto.

First of all, it's not easy to get there. If you're a competitor, you've got to go through a hellishly tough obstacle course to qualify for the tournament and the trip. If you're not one of the seeded fight-

VIP central

/ou've got to fight your way through
·ld to compete in the Prince's House.
ɔu get an invitation. Remember, it's

ure lounge of Kennedy International
east of

Long Island, and they damn sure aren't on the political menu in the UAE. But my trusty photographer and I decided that this was the place we needed to be, so away we went.

After battling our way through the Frankfurt Airport, where we had an eight-hour layover and a snarling lecture from a German customs officer on the moral, technical, and aesthetic superiority of Germany over the United States (how *did* we manage to win that war?), we arrived in Abu Dhabi in the dim predawn hours. Anybody who confuses the experience of passing through visa control there with getting off the plane in Topeka, Kansas just isn't paying attention.

Once you're through the x-ray machines and surly

Jean Jacques Machado

Looking for the heel hook

Ricardo Morias

customs officers—no more surly than those at Kennedy (but then the average US customs agent can hold his own with Saddam's Republican Guard on a bad day)—it behooves you to remember that the UAE is a devoutly Moslem country. Do a little research, figure it out before you get there, and behave, and you'll have a good time. But don't for one second think you have any rights. You have whatever rights the Royal Family feels like giving you—or not.

Ditto for the fighters in the competition. The guys who end up feeling cheated are the ones who weren't paying attention when they stepped off the airplane, and promptly got braced by a veil-wearing harpy who never heard of the NCAA and couldn't care less that you were an All-American. The guys who do alright and have a good time are the guys like Tito Ortiz and Matt Hughes who understand the purpose of the exercise: the prince wants to see some good fights and have a good time. Those type of guys show up with a sense of adventure and fun and enjoy themselves, and don't take themselves too seriously. Interestingly enough, this attitude bears fruit, and both of these guys did extremely well. In Matt's case, there was some confusion about which weight class he was going to enter, and they jumped him up *two* divisions. Instead of throwing a temper tantrum and whining about getting screwed, Matt kicked a bunch of ass. As a result, he'll be back next year with a nice sponsorship and fighting in whatever class he chooses.

The idea behind the rules is to make things as fair as possible for everybody—in other words, don't slant the playing field for the jiu-jitsu guys or the wrestlers. Toward that end, the first five minutes are pure submission—there are no points for anything: near submissions, passing the guard, take downs, nothing—you submit your guy or you don't. That encourages the fighters to go for it—you don't have to worry about losing points for a technique that fails and lands you in a compromising position. The next five minutes, however, have some fairly arcane rules. Takedowns score points (advantage wrestlers); putting somebody in your guard costs you a negative point (advantage wrestlers); passing the guard gets you points, getting the back gets you points, getting the mount gets you points, sweeping gets you

Mark Kerr dominated the action.

Jean Jacques Machado in a typical position—choking someone out.

Kerr took no prisoners.

points, and the knee on the opponents stomach gets you points (good for everybody); stalling in the guard costs you a negative point (advantage jiu-jitsu). In fact, it seems to me that this system slightly favors the wrestlers. The wrestlers tend to stall for the first five minutes, then shoot for a takedown and use their athleticism and balance to hang on to the point advantage from the takedown.

The bottom line is that this is a private function the prince is throwing—at a huge personal expense—for his own amusement. He can make any rules he wants to, and he can enforce them any way he chooses. If you don't like it, stay at home.

Barkalev loses his cool—
and his job at the Abu Dhabi.

Sperry outdueled Travern in the superfight.

A textbook naked rear choke.

With the exception of the Russians, who were to the man a group of churlish louts, the fighters were generally good-humored. Anybody who loses a decision, of course, thinks he got shafted—a couple of them may have, but most of them didn't.

The first fight of the tournament—one of the best of the whole week—was a case in point: Royler Gracie vs. Baret Yoshida. You don't have to be a big Gracie fan—which I unabashedly am—to recognize Royler's greatness. Hell, he submitted every opponent he fought en route to winning the 1999 ADCC championship. On the other hand, Baret is a kid from Hawaii who fights out of the Egan Inoue camp. Baret and Egan are both great guys, but nobody was giving Baret much of a chance—until he caught Royler in an arm bar. I've watched the tape 10 times and I still don't know how Royler got out of that arm bar. Royler went on to get the decision and Baret felt cheated. I don't think he was, but I understand his frustration; it was a phenomenal effort, and it was close. He was, however, cheerful and good natured about it.

On the other hand, there was Mark Robinson. Nobody's ever really gotten the story about his leaving the tournament last year. One story has it that he was paid to leave to clear the way for another fighter more favored by the prince. Another was that he was threatened. This year his first match was with Ricardo Morais, one of the prince's favorites. Well, by any account this was

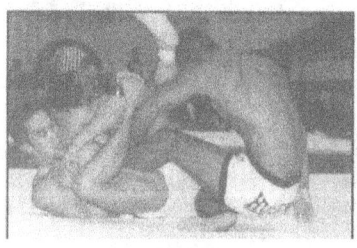

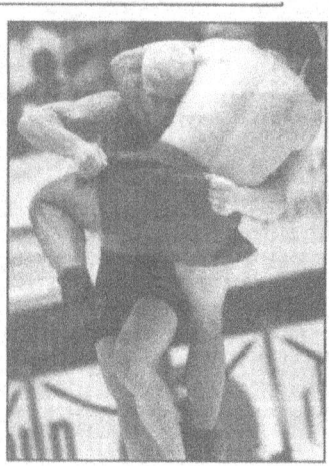

Escape from an ankle lock.

an interesting match-up. Robinson, a former world amateur sumo champion, is six feet tall, weighs 315 pounds, trains with Obake (Tim Catalfo) and is one of the strongest men on Earth. Morais is a Brazilian giant, standing 6'5" tall, weighing 295 pounds and having the shredded physique of a body builder. These leviathans battled back and forth, crashing around on the mat like a couple of tsunamis. In my opinion, Robinson has the edge when they go to the edge of the mat, and are stopped to be dragged back to the center of the mat in the same position. Except they aren't in the same position; Morais has substantially improved his position in transit and when they return to action, he has Robinson in an ankle lock—match to Morais. Screw job? Well, yeah—but I see worse every month in Don King promotions, and King is nowhere near as likeable as the prince. Robinson is the ultimate gentleman—and he shrugged, grinned, and enjoyed the rest of the tournament from the sidelines with an ice bag on his ankle.

Jean Jacques Machado battling Renzo Gracie.

Just when you think this is a fairly benign form of despotism—the subtle shading of decisions, the unexplained overtime in a fight seemingly dominated by one fighter—along comes Kareem Barkalev, one of the Prince's imported Russian fighters. Kareem is a nasty, unlikeable piece of work who you would expect to get favoritism because he fights for the prince out of the ADCC. One of his favorite nasty tricks is to crack his opponents in the side of the neck in a putative attempt to grab the posterior cervical region in the traditional wrestler's hold. Ricardo Arona, newly minted BJJ black belt, responded to the third such mastoid jarring slap from Kareem with one of his own, only this one wasn't disguised. It sounded like a cow being smacked in the ass with the flat part of a banjo—paayooww! At which point Kareem went totally berserk—literally insane. He came shrieking across the ring, punching and kicking. Which was interesting in the sense that for years when boxers actually "came to blows" outside the ring (Ali-Frazier, for example) they would invariably end up rolling around on the ground. And here are grapplers, punching and kicking. Go figure. At any rate, the zebras swarm the mat, holding the fighters apart. Arona immediately calms down (if you can imagine a Brazilian being the cool head in such a situation.)

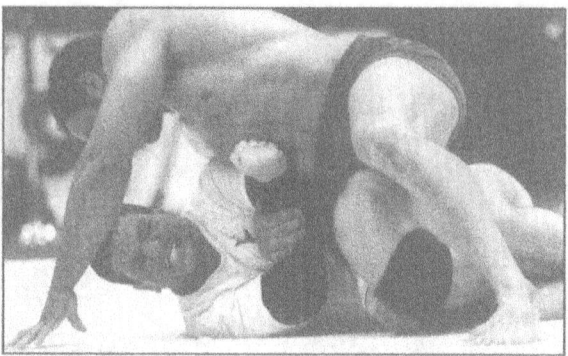

Rigan Machado trying to survive Kerr's power.

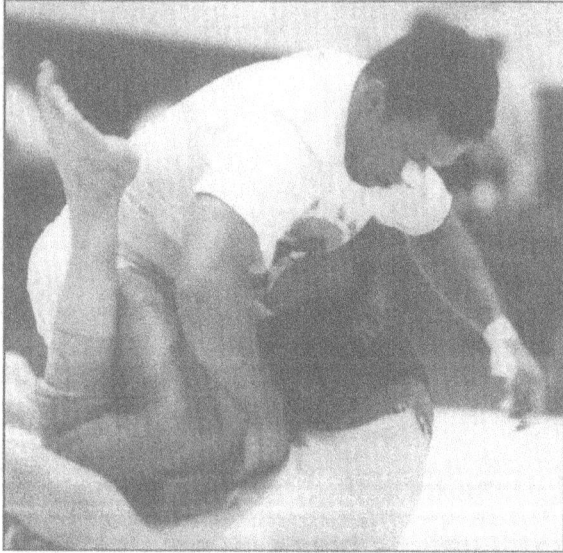

Barkalev, on the other hand, continues to scream and thrash like a wolverine who's gotten a bad hit of LSD-25 and a Three Stooges hotfoot at the same time. Down comes Nasyr, ADCC Health Club Manager, from his seat by the Prince, to urge Kareem to calm down: *he is embarrassing the Prince.* After another five minutes of spitting on the mat, and giving the finger, Kareem allows himself to be coaxed into finishing the match—but not before completely embarrassing His Excellency.

After the fight, he spits at the jeering Brazilians in the stands, gives them the finger *again,* grabs his crotch, and walks over to the post-fight interview area—where he is greeted by machine- pistol toting, blue-berets wearing commandos, who escort him out of the building and directly to jail where he sits in his shorts until 4:00 a.m. Then is put on an airplane back to whatever godforsaken part of the collapsed Soviet empire he came from—end of Kareems Abu Dhabi career. One day he's making big bucks teaching a couple of kids' classes a week in a plush sports complex and training to represent the ADCC, and the next day he's sitting in a jail cell in his shorts waiting to be deported. Face it, Toto, you are not in Kansas anymore—you're not even in Abu Dhabi anymore.

Sometimes the benign despotism takes the form of looking the other way during a rules infraction. To wit, Brazil's Liborio vs Japan's Oyama. Mr. Oyama, apparently unimpressed by Liborio's reputation as one of the greatest jiu-jitsu fighters ever, began the match by twisting a couple of Liborio's fingers and breaking them. Small joint manipulations are clearly illegal, but before anybody could do anything about all this, Liborio, in his understandable pique, got Oyama's back, clawed his eyes to get his chin up, sank in a deep, deep rear naked, and choked the Japanese judoka completely and totally unconscious. Nobody said squat. They just patted Liborio on the head and passed him and his broken fingers onto the next round.

And there are, apparently, limits. In the most fun match of the entire week, Mark "The Specimen" Kerr, and Leo Vieira, a 19-year-old Brazilian phenom and the most likeable kid in the sport, went at it in the Absolute division. Here's a kid outweighed almost 100 pounds putting Kerr, a world-class wrestler and the 99 kilogram and above champion, to a hell of a test. Leo's slick as snot on a door knob, and it's a great fight, back and forth, but Kerr's never in danger of getting tapped. The Texas Rangers have a motto: "Little man whip a big man ever' time if he's in the right and keeps acomin'." Well, maybe in Texas. But in submission wrestling the best you can hope for is a great fun match, and that's what this was.

At the end of the match there's a looonnngggg discussion among the officials, some of them maybe feeling that it would be good if Leo won. He didn't. Finally, everybody agreed that this was Mark's day, and he got the deserved decision. Texas Rangers not withstanding, it was the right thing.

Finally, at the end of a great week, we're headed back to the States, and we're passing back out through customs at 3:30 a.m., and everybody is just dog tired, and for the fourth time in 60 meters, we're stopped by yet another douanier martinet demanding in the typical brusque fashion to see (did I mention for the fourth time in 60 meters), our passports, tickets and visas, and my photographer just snapped. "No," he said. "Hell, no. That's enough! That's crap! You don't need to see my papers again! You've seen them three times already in the last two minutes." There was a moment of silence as this armed functionary began to wake up and focus his beady little eyes on this mini-rebellion—sort of like a lizard noticing a nice fat fly sitting an inch from his nose. With visions of Barkalev dancing in my head, I grab the photographers passport, visa and tickets, smile like a mule eating wasp nests, and in my most servile, obsequious fashion, gently thrust them at Mr. Customs Agent. "Forgive my friend," I murmur apologetically, eyes downcast. "He thinks he's still in Kansas."

After long, tense moment of silence, the official shrugged, glanced at the papers, stamped them, and we were allowed to leave—without the ignominy of spending the rest of the night in a jail cell in our shorts waiting for the next flight to God knows where.

ADCC 2000 Top Fighters
Courtesy Kid Peligro, ADCC Feature Writer

Under 65 Kg
(1) **Royler Gracie**, Brazil, (2) **Alexandre "Soca" Carneiro**—Brazil^ (3) **Joe Gilbert**, USA, (4) **Matthew Hamilton**, USA.

66-76 KG
(1) **Renzo Gracie**, Brazil, (2) **Jean Jacques Machado**, Brazil, (3) **Marcio Feitosa**, Brazil, (4) **Leozinho Vieira**, Brazil.

77-87 KG
(1) **Saulo Ribeiro**, Brazil, (2) **Ricardo Liborio**, Brazil, (3) **Alexander "Sacha" Savko**, Russia, (4) **Jorge "Macaco" Patino**, Brazil.

88-98 KG
(1) **Ricardo Arona**, Brazil, (2) **Jeff Monsen**, USA, (3) **Tito Ortiz**, USA, (4) **Matt Hughes**, USA.

98 KG and above
(1) **Mark Kerr**, USA, (2) **Ricco Rodriguez**, USA, (3) **Rigan Machado**, Brazil, (4) **Ricardao Morais**, Brazil.

Absolute Division
(1) **Mark Kerr**, USA, (2) **Sean Alvarez**, USA, (3) **Ricardo "Cachorrao" Almeida**, Brazil, (4) **Rodrigo "Comprido" Medeiros**, Brazil.

Superfight

Ze Mario Sperry, Brazil, def. **Roberto**

Shonie Carter—Semper Fi

Not willing to be classified as a wrestler, kickboxer, or submission grappler, Shonie Carter strives for flexibility, adaptability, and versatility.

Todd Hester, story and photos

One of the many talented wrestlers turned no-holds-barred fighters from the Midwest, Chicago-based Shonie Carter has no fear of mixed martial arts matches because he's already survived something much tougher—U.S. Marine Core Boot Camp! Joining the Marines right out of high school, Carter returned home from the Core with a new attitude of success, and the feeling that no accomplishment was beyond his grasp. Proving that his new goals were "more than a feeling," Carter quickly proved himself on the mat, becoming a two-time national tournament qualifier and an NJCA All-American. After attending the Olympic Trials in 1996, Carter "got into judo," and won several judo tournaments on the strength of his powerful wrestling ability. Coming back to Chicago from Tennessee after college, Carter hooked up with Master Robert Schirmer of Combat-do Jiu-Jitsu, who also had extensive experience as a boxer and kickboxer. Learning a wide variety of combat arts, Carter soon found himself turning to a new, fast growing sport which enabled him to utilize all of his new-found versatility—mixed martial arts. Thrown to the proverbial lions in his first match—a loss to MMA star Laverne Clark in Extreme Challenge—Carter emerged from the loss determined and focused. Rededicated to success he promptly reeled off "25 or 30 straight wins," including a victory over Dave Menne and two wins in the UFC. Still actively fighting and searching for new avenues of combative expression, Carter lives life by his own warrior's creed: "I don't fear failure and I won't give up—ever. I don't have dreams, I have plans."

Q: How did you get started in the martial arts?
A: I started off as a wrestler in the eighth grade and high school. I didn't do too well in high school—I did alright—at Proviso East High School in Maywood, Illinois. Then I went to the Marines after high school for four years then got back and went to the reserves and wrestled in junior college at Triton College in Rivergrove, Illinois. While I was there I was a two-time national tournament qualifier and an NJCA All-American. I also placed fourth in the nation, was a two-time World Team member, and went to the Olympic Trials in 1996. Then I started getting back into judo, which I had started when I was younger, but then didn't stick with it. I got back to judo when I earned my four year scholarship at Carson-Newman College in Jefferson City, Tennessee, where I wrestled under Don Elia. After I came back home I started working out and wrestling with some of the guys at Triton College just to stay in shape. Then I was introduced to Master Robert of the Combat-do Jiu-Jitsu School.

Training Strategy

"I do everything—running, weights, college wrestling, shidokan karate, judo, kickboxing, and boxing. I don't really have a percentage of kicking to punching to grappling that I strictly follow. Whatever I feel I need, I work on that week. A lot of my training comes from the classes that I teach at the Chicago Fitness Center and other places. I don't mind grappling with newcomers who are wild and out of control because in fights you get people like that—it teaches you to deal with pure, undisciplined aggression."

Then from there I started training mixed-martial arts under Master Schirmer. I started kickboxing and boxing and that's what really started my fight career. Each step of my training ended up being a progression to where I am now.

Q: What is Robert Schirmer's background?

A: Taekwondo, karate, wrestling, judo, jiu-jitsu, and founder and head instructor of the All-American Academy of Martial Arts. He was the all-marine karate team captain and the interservice boxing champion. He did just about anything you could do in the Marines. He was in Force Recon in the Third Battalion—and I hope I got that right for my sake. He has a very well-rounded base in all the major combat arts, striking and grappling. You can find out all about his style at www.combat-do.com.

Q: But when you started with him you were already an accomplished wrestler, weren't you?

A: Yeah, I was. I realized that being a wrestler, I had a strong foundation, but I wanted more. When I was in college I wrestled, but then I would go do judo—so even then I always wanted more. I was always looking for more knowledge and skills. My first judo tournament, as a matter of fact, was the state judo championships—and I took home two golds and a silver medal. I won the white-to-green division, the brown belt division, and took second in the black belt division—and all this as a judo orange belt. But of course I was a good wrestler. So all I did was shoot double-legs and then do belly-to-back suplexes on everybody. So I was able to adapt my wrestling pretty easily. Then I wrestled in Budapest and placed third or fourth, and then at the Grand Prix of Austria and placed sixth. So I had an extensive competition experience in wrestling which gave me an edge. I feel that wrestling skills are a very good base for many martial arts. But I wanted more, so with Dr. Stephan Terrell I started studying jiu-jitsu. It was more of a hybrid system because I'm not much of a traditional or conventional fighter. So I wanted to get a different type of jiu-jitsu that was similar to Brazilian jiu-jitsu but with differences. I didn't want to be a cookie-cutter type of BJJ fighter. I can say I know jiu-jitsu but you get in the ring with me and I'm not going to jump to my back and try to work an arm lock off the guard.

Q: What was your first exposure to finishing holds?

A: My first experience to those types of movements was in Tennessee when I was studying under Doctor Stephan Terrell. I gained a good understanding of submission holds, although I wasn't as versed as I am now because I was younger and less experienced. But it became more refined when I learned under Robert Schirmer.

control hold, then look for the submission finishing hold.

"I didn't want to be a cookie-cutter type of BJJ fighter. I can say I know jiu-jitsu but you get in the ring with me and I'm not going to jump to my back and try to work an arm lock off the guard."

Q: As a wrestler, was it easier to catch onto submissions?

A: Definitely. Wrestling is an art that teaches you to control your opponent— whether you're holding him down on the mat or throwing him. Its just different techniques that teach and emphasize control of opponents for points. So jiu-jitsu went to the next level for me. I used the philosophy behind freestyle or Greco-Roman wrestling to get the opponent down, under

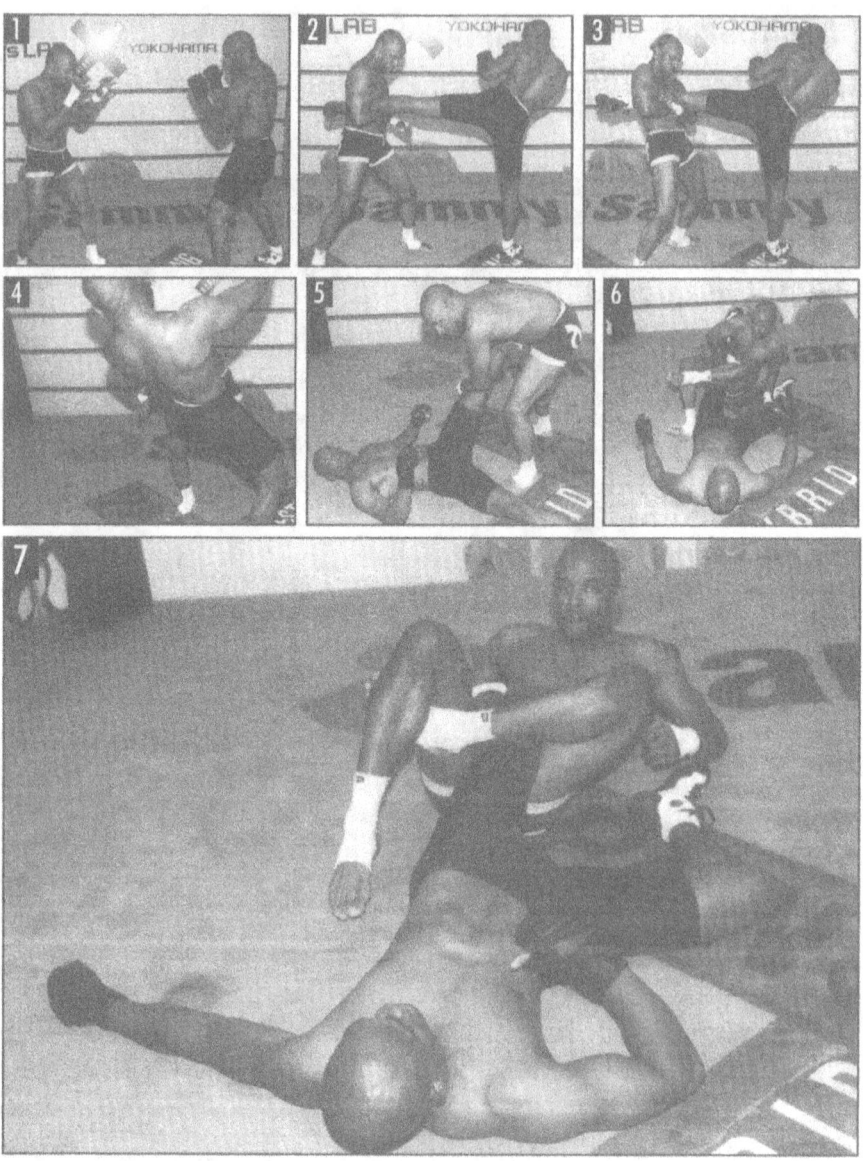

Facing opponent Brian Gassaway at the Pancrase Dojo in Yokohama, japan (1), Shonie Carter blocks the round kick by an outside arm wrap (2). Bringing his inside arm under the knee Carter lifts up to unbalance Gassaway (3), then spins him inside, taking him to the mat (4). Securing the leg with an over-under grip (S), Carter falls back and traps the thigh with his calf, keep Gassaway from escaping (6). Leaning back, Carter then hooks his foot under his own knee into a figure-four submission lock (7).

Q: At what point did you decide to move from sport competition to no-holds-barred fighting?
A: It was a challenge that I thought would be worthy of my time. I knew that there was more to this art of competition than just point grappling. I always knew that the end all or be all pinnacle of fighting was not the pure wrestling arts. However, you see that the grapplers, in general, tend to dominant this sport more often than not. It is mainly grapplers who have taken the art to the next level by putting submission moves on top of their wrestling skills. So I think that it is the most well-rounded, comprehensive fighter who prevails the most. But past a certain point of learning it is the person who prevails, not the art.

Q: Do you remember your first no-holds-barred fight?
A: Very well—a little too well, as a matter of fact. I lost in nine seconds to Laverne Clark. And I want a rematch. Laverne? You out there? Gimme another shot! Looking back it was a very tough first fight, but I didn't know any better. I was told by Monty Cox that Laverne was a boxer. So I said, "OK. I think I can handle a boxer." Man, I was doomed from the start. I found out after the fight that this "boxer" was an Iowa State wrestling champion. Thank you, Monty! So I go out there thinking that I would shoot in, take this guy down, not get hit, and then win the fight. Well, I shot in and he sprawled against the fence and popped me and out I went. Fight over. I looked at the tape later and saw that the punch wasn't all that hard, but I just had never been hit before and so it was a shock. Later in my career, I beat some guys who had beaten him. So I don't feel outclassed by him—just a little bad that I didn't get to show him my best side. I have a lot of respect for Laverne. He's 5-0 in the UFC and I'm 2-0, now.

So after that I went on to win 25 or 30 fights in a row because I took up boxing and kickboxing the day after the Laverne Clark fight and learned how to throw, avoid, and when necessary, take a punch. I realized the application value of being a well-rounded athlete and a well-rounded fighter.

Q: So that loss didn't end your career, but rather started it
A: Yeah, that's true. And I'm going to jump back to my time in the Marines and tell you why. In the Marines they taught you to overcome and adapt. To take a challenge head-on and don't ever give up. Also, my grandfather always used to tell me, "Shonie, its OK to give out, but its never OK to give up." So the next day I rededicated myself to my training. That was back when Extreme Challenge was very primitive. So after the fight Monty had an evaluation time afterwards with all the fighters who fought on that card. So I came in that day and I remember thinking that I'll be dammed if I let them think I'm a quitter or a loser. So we were all together and all working out—Pat Miletich was there, Dennis Reed, but Laverne wasn't, unfortunately—but a bunch of Iowa wrestling guys were. So I went through everyone. They looked at it like a training session but I had to prove to myself that I belonged with them after losing in 9 seconds. I didn't care who I faced—I just tore though everyone with takedowns and chokes and anything else I could get. So I let them know I wasn't a loser. But you know, you do get caught in this sport if you're out there looking for submissions. No one is undefeated and no one had never not been caught.

Q: So after that fight you went on a long winning streak?
A: Actually, it was after that training session. That was the beginning. That was when I knew what I was made of. I beat Dave Menne once and drew him once and I beat Andy Sanders out of Extreme Challenge, Phil Johns, Justin Wisniewski. I also did a lot of kickboxing and I beat a 9-time world kickboxing championship. Then I fought Miletich and that was what finally snapped my winning

Fighting Strategy

"My particular style is that I don't particularly emphasize any specific technique that I try to execute no matter what. I go into a fight extremely relaxed. I've been there before— more times than most—so I look to see what my opponent is doing wrong. I look to see if they're sitting back on their heels; If their hands are low; and are they tense and uptight? I like guys who try to psyche themselves up and try to bully me around and muscle me all over the ring—I'm like "Oh, good. Get tired. Please." I weather the storm, work off the angles, slip and move and frustrate them a little. So a kick or punch may come and you may see me directly clinch. I look for my opponent to make the mistake. I look to see what he's giving me."

streak. I was in Extreme Challenge 3, 4, 5, 16, 23, 27, and some more I can't remember off the top of my head.

Q: When was the first time you fought out of the United States?
A: The first time, outside of wrestling, was in Beijing, China when I kick-boxed against the All-Asian San Shou Team. And I won the gold medal in that. San Shou is actually a mixed-martial art that not a lot of people know about, because it incorporates kickboxing with throws. No groundwork but a lot of throws. I really wanted to fight Cung Le, but never got a chance, and I still want to fight him. He recently fought a superfight in K-l against Muhammed Keita, who TKO'd me in a shi-dokan match. He's the bare knuckle USA champ and Cung Le fought him in a san shou match and beat him easily. But Keita is really good in bare-knuckle karate but anything with grappling involved he is lost.

Q: What was your next big fighting experience?
A: I'd have to say Pancrase. It was a little bit of a shock. I tell the guys back in Chicago—and there's a lot of mixed-martial arts fighting that goes on there—that once you take your act onto the international road it's an an exponential step up. My first fight in Japan was against Takafumi Ito and it ended in a draw. And that was one tough fight and it really woke me up to the quality of opponents that you meet in the Orient, but particularly in Japan. It really forced me to refocus my training and to raise my entire game to a much higher level.

Q: Is the fighting mindset more intense among fighters and fans in Japan?
A: I think the audience is much more knowledgeable and respectful than in the U.S. And I don't mean to knock the U.S. audiences, but the Japanese fans are more aware of what is going on. Maybe it's because judo is so much more an integral part of their culture than in the U.S. There are times that a fight is one the ground for a while—and if it was in the U.S. you'd probably have some booing—but the Japanese fans know what is going on. But I love American crowds for their energy. Some

Desired Opponents
"I'd like to fight Cung Le. I look at what Cung Le did in the KI against Mohammed Keita—he dominated him with wrestling throws and I don't think he could do that to me. I know how to stop those moves. I don't knock Cung Le—he's a very good fighter—but I would like to fight him. We both have an NHB-style of fighting that mixes up a lot of different types of techniques and I think it would be a good fight. Even though Keita beat me in bare knuckle karate, I think that I would have been the better selection to fight Cung Le because I'm much better in grappling situations. He definitely wouldn't have thrown me around like he threw Keita around."

of the funniest things you'll ever hear come out of a no-holds-barred crowd: "Poke his eye out!" "Kill him!" "Kick him in the Groin!" And I'm like "Oh, boy." You'd think that it is these caveman Neanderthals that are saying that but these are lawyers, teachers, accountants, and what you'd call normal people, who go to these shows and have no idea what mixed-martial arts is all about. They just know that they want to see action. Whereas a Japanese crowd is pin-drop quiet and they understand the submission attempts—they like to see the submission attempts. They want to see the punches and kicks but they also want to see someone with well-rounded skills. So I think they appreciate you more.

Q: You sometimes get accused of being a showman. Why?
A: Fighting is entertainment. So even if I'm winning or losing I want to make sure I'm looking good. If I'm losing I won't even know because I'm too busy looking good. If I'm winning I don't even know it because I'm too busy looking good. Seriously, some people say that I showboat or what have you, but its my way of staying loose and relaxed. The crowd wants entertainment and the judges want to see aggression. So I try to give a little bit of everything to make everyone happy. I want to give the crowd a show; I want to give the judges a show; and I want to give my opponent a hard fight. I may dance around a little bit more than most, but I think it's entertaining. I guess that I just don't fit into a category that most fighters do of being considered a grappler or a striker or a takedown artist. But

Facing Brian Gassaway at Pancrase Yokohama in japan (1), Shonie Carter blocks the left hook by trapping to the outside (2). Moving in, he clinches Gassaway to prevent him from punching (3), then throws him with a devastating backwards supplex (4), and goes to the side and prepares to mount (5).

that's OK because I don't want to be like everyone else. A big part of my mental flexibility comes from the time I've spent with Shihan Eddie Yoshimura at the U.S. Shidokan Headquarters at the Chicago Fitness Center. It is the bare knuckle karate Mecca, but Shihan Yoshimura also encourages a balanced and complete approach to combat and selfdefense. Check out www.ski-dokan.com and see for yourself.

Q: Do you feel mixed-martial arts is growing?

A: I most certainly do. And I'm really glad for it because it is gaining attention and people are becoming more knowledgeable of what we're doing. They used to call us brutes and troglodytes and Neanderthals. There are guys who look like Neanderthals who are some of the smartest people you'll ever come across—the name Jason Godsey comes to mind—Godsey is a science teacher but he's a tough, tough fighter. We have real estate agents in MMA, car mechanics, you name it. For myself, I've spent four-and-a-half years in fine arts school. I spliced fiber optic cable while being a fighter. I'm a Sunday School teacher and a father and I think I'm typical. No-holds-barred isn't populated by mindless brutes. It is a legitimate competitive sport that everyday, working people are getting into because it's a wonderful competitive outlet. There is a large amount of creativity that goes into being a fighter that most people don't consider. My father once told me that there are more potential moves in a single game of chess than there are stars in the sky. I think that in a wrestling match that there are more potential moves than there are in a game of chess—and that is even more true for mixed-martial arts.

Q: What has your martial arts training given you as a person?
A: I have gained a sensitivity that most people would never understand unless they took up a martial art themselves. I have a high sense of consciousness about who I am and what I do that someone outside of martial arts can never have. I understand how I react to anger, fear, uncertainty, stress and I don't fear those emotions. I get more stress in a single fight than most people probably get in a lifetime. Martial arts gives you the ability to deal with things inside you. I don't feel that I need to prove anything to anyone but myself. I understand myself better and so I understand others better.

Q: What do you feel makes a champion?
A: It's not how many time you get knocked down, it's how many times you get back up. If you believe in attaining something or reaching a goal then go for it without fail. And if you do fail try again. Don't be afraid of failure or success—learn to deal with them both. I'm glad to say that through martial arts, through the Marines, and through my grandfather's upbringing that not only do I not fear any man; but I also do not fear myself. I don't think there is anything that can stop me from attaining a goal that I've set, because I don't fear failure and I won't give up—ever. I don't have dreams, I have plans.

6 Attacks That Really Work from the Guard

Edward Lee Vincent, photos by Clenice Vincent

Let's be honest. Most grapplers who watch no-holds-barred fighting events have lost a sense of respect for the guard position. All we are used to seeing now are fighters who get taken down, wrap their legs around their opponent, and then take a good solid beating from the man on top who is in the supposedly "inferior" position. The days of the old UFC, where even a mediocre jiu-jitsu man could play with his kickboxing opponent from his back are long gone. If someone goes onto his back now the only thing there is to fear are the boos of the crowd, jeering a position that now just seems to lead to stalling, stalemates, and draws. The day of the effective attacking guard is over—or is it?

Guard Mystique Broken

There is no doubt that the mystique of the guard seems to have been broken. It is no longer a feared position and it seems that punchers and strikers who don't really know a lot about grappling seem to like this position and feel that they are safe there. But is it really the guard that is ineffective or are fighters just settling into a comfort zone? More often than not, they do not work the position actively, and look for the "silver bullet" submission—the chance to set up the perfect straight arm-bar and ignore other opportunities that come their way. Here's a little secret, fellas—everybody knows how to defend the straight arm-bar from the bottom. But it doesn't mean that you can't do something else.

Fighters Smarter

The fighters of today are much smarter than they were even five years ago. Everyone knows how important cross-training is in modern martial arts. Practitioners of any style should learn from this—if your art is limited in any aspect of fighting, then include training techniques that develop your area of weakness.

The Art of the Guard

Practicing the defensive guard and learning the offensive techniques that can be executed from the guard is an art unto itself. The following six attacks from the guard will hopefully present options to the lie-and-wait passiveness that has given the modern guard a bad reputation. My instructor, Walt Bayless, always instilled the idea to be proactive from any position, not reactive. Don't wait for the other guy to force you into something; make the first move and direct him to where you want him to be. No position fits this philosophy better than the guard. It is not simply enough to wait for an opponent to make a mistake. This mistake may never come, and you will end up getting a severe les-

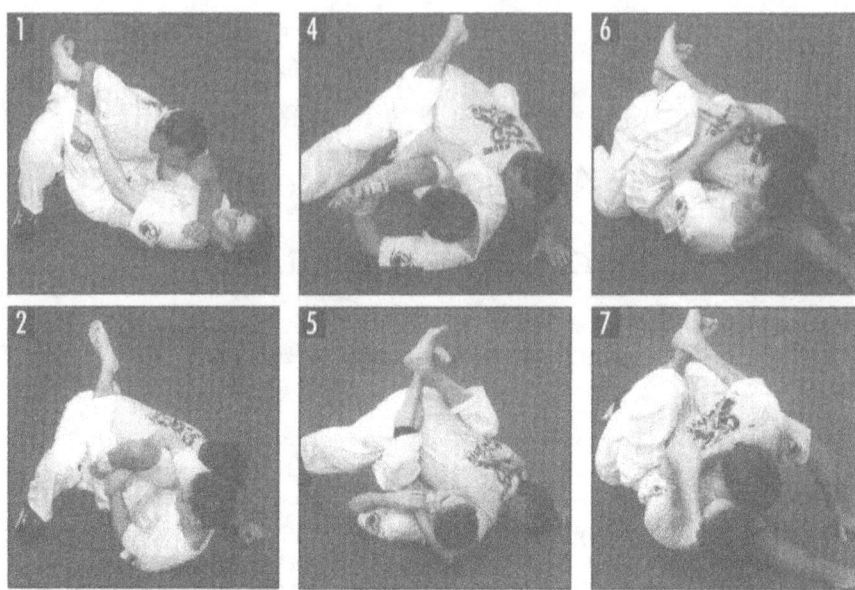

3 Kata-Game
As the man on top straightens out the arm to defend the key lock (4), the bottom man traps the arm with his head (5).

When the top man breaks the hold, the bottom man then clinches the arm and neck (6), and applies a powerful choke (7).

1 Ude-Garami
Fighting from the guard, the defender grabs the wrist (1), reaches over the top of the opponents elbow and grabs his own wrist (2), and then slides the hip out the applying the finishing force (3).

son in pain tolerance if you don't learn this quickly enough. I think that the most common submissions from the guard—the triangle choke and the straight arm-bar (also known as *the juji-gatame*)—are already in most fighter's arsenals. Therefore, I will present other attacks that can be used.

1 Ude-Garami

The ude-garami is the original name for what we Westerners call the key lock. It is a simple and easy attack to apply. Grabbing the opponent's wrist, you then loop the other hand over the opponent's triceps and grab your own wrist. It is important here to move the hips out to the side to leverage your strength and put more pressure on your opponent. If you want to get into the big debate of whether you should grab the wrist with the thumb or not, be my guest. If your opponent taps then you grabbed him is the right way. 'Nuff said!

2 Ude-Garami Variation

Progress to this move if the opponent powers out of the ude-garami. As he stretches his arm out to prevent you from locking him, bring his straightened arm out and around your own head. A key

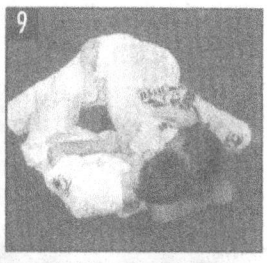

4 Sumi-Gaeshi
When the opponent doesn't tap, the bottom man hooks his leg under the top man's knee and sweeps him over with an "elevator" (8).

point here is to bring your head inside the opponent's arm—moving *to* him instead of making him move to you. Sometimes, the opponent will help you by gladly trying to wrap your head with a half-nelson. This is great because it is a sucker move. Just arch your back and push his wrist up to the ceiling for the tap. Again, the idea here is to keep moving your hips out to the side to add extra leverage and pressure to his shoulder.

3 Kata-Game

This is next technique in the logical progression of guard submission moves. Some opponents just don't want to give into the key lock, or they just have seemingly superhuman strength—or maybe they just had their Wheaties that morning. Whatever the case, continue sliding the hips out to the side the lock is on. Quickly execute a palm-to-palm grip and squeeze. Then bring the hand around the head to the bicep of the other hand and simulate a bicep curling action. This puts a little extra pressure on. Another good tip is to press your temple to his temple to prevent him from lifting his

arm and fighting off the choke.

5 Slipping to the Back
As the defender sprawls to avoid being overturned (9), the bottom man slides to the side and comes to a knee (10), goes to the back and puts in the "hooks" (11), and then finishes the fight from the dominant top position (12).

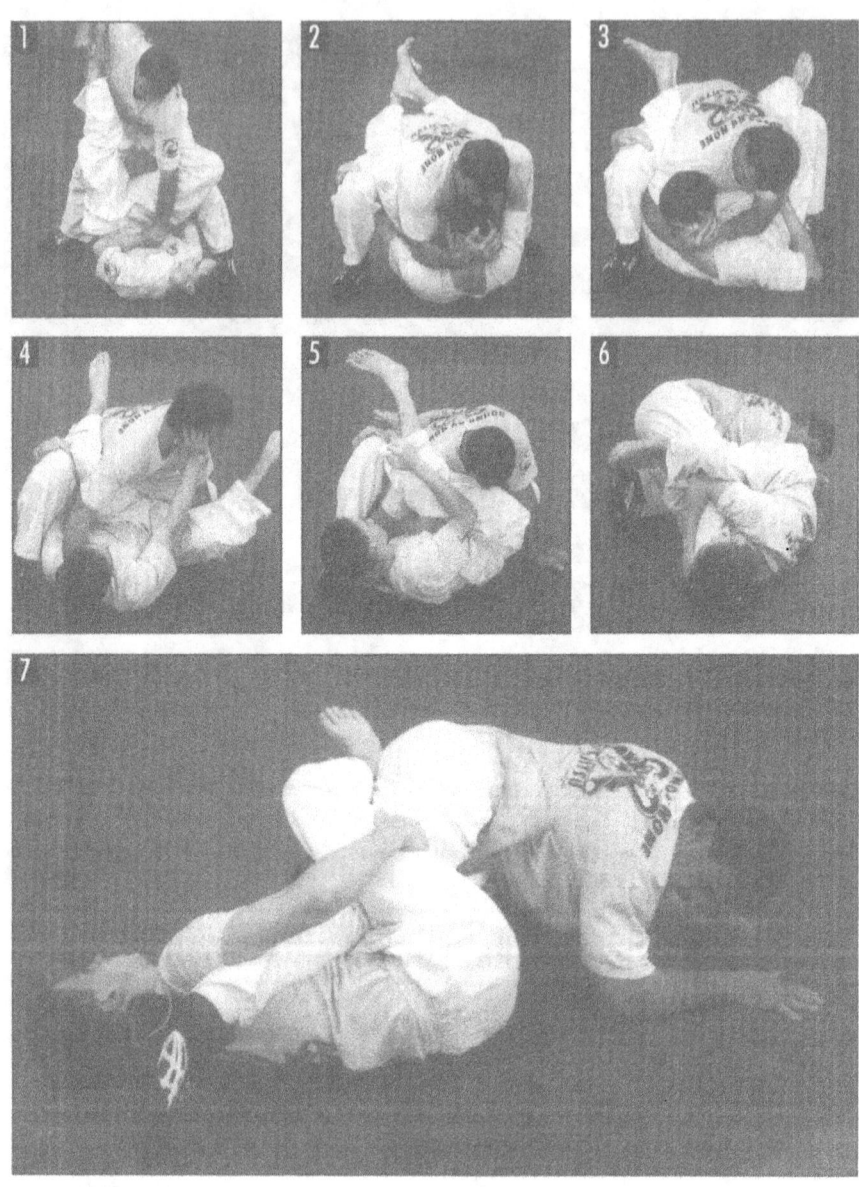

6 The Leg Bar
Defending against a dominant attacker (1), the bottom man pulls him in tight with the legs (2), and then hooks the outside leg with his arm to defend the neck crank (3). Pushing the top man's head away to create space (4), the bottom man slides his leg over the head (5), then slides down the leg (6), and applies the straight knee-bar for the finish (7)

4 Sumi-Gaeshi

Man, this guy just won't give up. If he continues his Herculean effort and is really battling the effects of your choke, he will sometimes drive his weight into you and get that old Mark "The Hammer" Coleman ground-and-pound going. If you let that happen then you will soon be nothing but "ground" meat. So as soon as you feel his weight drive up, slip your foot under his inside thigh. Then you must slide your hips underneath his body, pull him over you, and then elevate his leg. This has to be done all at the same time. In other words, you will flip him like a pancake but you must first get underneath him to do so. This technique is known to many as the "elevator."

5 Slipping to the Back

I think this move is self-explanatory. Before attempting to go around his back, try the reversal. This will give him something to think about other and distract him from noticing you moving to his back. Think of this as the left-jab feint before you use the right cross.

6 The Leg Bar

If all these moves don't work then you'd better think about getting out of the fight business and opening up a Starbucks (if only you could). If your opponent has fought off all your submission attempts, then slip back into the full guard while holding him tight. By now he is really angry and has had just about enough of all your wriggling around. A common move at this point is for the opponent to get up onto his toes and put pressure on you that feels like he's trying to crush the life out of you (just a good wrestling posture, actually). When he does this, reach under and around his knee. Spinning on your back (much like an '80s break dancer), bring your foot from the opposite side of his hip around to his butt. The knee that is on the inside slips between his legs. Wrap his leg up like you're hugging your favorite girlfriend in a time of need, and arch your hips. To really apply pressure, wrap your arm around his attacked leg and grab your hamstrings. This creates even more leverage and more pressure. Tap or die, sucka'!

Conclusion

Why only six moves, you might ask. Is that all that works? No, of course not. There are many more but these magazine guys won't give me any more space! Seriously, there are many variations of all these positions but they are all started by being proactive instead of being reactive. Learning to execute and move efficiently in the guard is an ongoing process of improvement. First of all, we are ingrained with the idea that being on top is the best. So with that idea built into our brains, it is sometimes difficult to get a real perspective on how truly devastating the guard can be. Find an experienced instructor and practice, practice, and then practice some more.

Edward Lee Vincent is a black belt jiu-jitsu instructor under Walt Bayless. He is currently teaching in and around the Pittsburgh, Pennsylvania area. For information on classes write the author at 2729 Lehigh St., Lower Burrell, PA 15068.

Erik Paulson
Training for a Fight

Erik Paulson is one of the most versatile and well-rounded teachers and fighters in martial arts today. He is not just someone who tells people how to train and fight, he speaks from experience and has taught, trained and fought all over the world.

Todd Hester, story and photos

ho rough," "complete," and "detailed" are all words that could be used to describe Erik Paul- ■ son's fight training methods. The Shooto World Light Heavyweight Champion for the past I five years, Paulson has fought against and beaten some of the world's top fighters. A Minnesota native who began training in judo and then moved into taekwondo, Paulson developed a wide repertoire of high kicks that served him well in the numerous traditional Midwest tournaments he competed in. Moving to Los Angeles in the mid '80s, Paulson began training in the Inosanto Academy where he was exposed to a variety of grappling arts under Larry Hartsell and Yuri Nakamura and immediately fell in love with the art of ground fighting. This eventually led him to Japan's Shooto fighting organization, where Paulson became the first Westerner to ever win a world title—a belt he stills holds over five years later. Continuing to expand his knowledge base during this time, Paulson also learned Brazilian jiu-jitsu under both the Gracies and the Machados, eventually becoming a Pan American Brazilian Jiu-Jitsu Champion. This well-rounded background has given Paulson wealth of training experience and knowledge from which to draw from.

Train Specifically

Paulson's philosophy for training for a fight involves a simple creed of hard work and dedication coupled with an extensive array of drills with and without partners in order to build up his overall expertise. Most of all, Paulson believes that if you don't go into a fight prepared, you shouldn't go into it at all.

"I start my training for a fight far in advance," Paulson says. "I like to have at least two months to properly prepare. But on last minute notification of fights you've always got to be ready, so you should never let yourself get too far out of shape. Stay healthy and stay strong and don't let your level drop. But you can't keep a peak at all times. You can over-sharpen your blade if you're not careful.'

Being as versatile as Paulson is, with many different types of events and opponents, he feels it is important to tailor your training to your challenge. "Each fighter that you fight has a different background therefore you have to hone and tailor your training to their specialties. So you have to watch

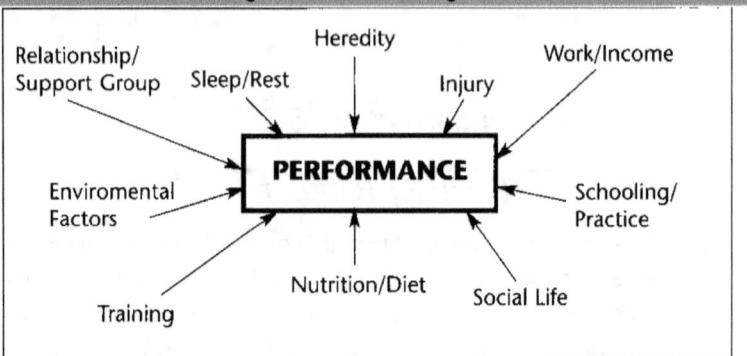

tapes of them and study the way they move and win, and also study the way they lose. For example, if I was going into a submission tournament I would practice my takedown skills and my general ground submission skills and then also my specialty moves. My specialty is the top game, so I try to stay off my back unless I absolutely have to or am forced there. I train the guard for three things: armlocks, sweeps, or chokes. If I have no luck then I'm back on my knees. I work a strong base, core conditioning, and my balance through different exercises and drills.

Every fighter has moves that they have come to rely on and that work for them. For example, Carlos Newton uses a lot arm locks; Jean Jacques Machado will generally choke people out from the rear sprawl; Royce Gracie will fight from the guard—so you have to know your game and then develop your game. Don't try to change your game at the last minute because you've had an epiphany—go with what got you there. Fighting is a game of percentages. All your training and moves should be based on development of high percentage finishes. By this I mean a move that you have used a lot in the past, that has finished people 80 percent of the time."

Training Time

For Paulson, the quality of time he trains is just as important as the quantity of training time. Consistency over a period of time is what Paulson considers to be the most important aspect of preparation. But with that taken into consideration, Paulson does believe in hard work, and his hours spent in the gym would qualify him as a "dojo rat" by any normal standard. "I would say that you need to train at least four hours a day, taking one or two days off per week, depending on how you're feeling. You have to listen to your body. It will tell you if you need rest or if you're getting mentally stale. This includes an hour-and-a-half in the morning of striking, then an hour of either running or lifting in the afternoon, then grappling and clinch work at night."

Training Fitness

While Paulson does get a lot of his aerobic fitness from his fighting drills, he also does traditional conditioning exercises to ensure that he doesn't "run out of gas" in the final minutes of a fight. "I like to run. It keeps my head clear and lets me know where I'm at and visualize my fight. I always wear a headset for motivation. There are two types of running: one is sprinting and I'll usually do a 50 yard dash, then a 50 yard slow jog and alternate that for anywhere from six to ten laps around the track. The other way is just jogging or distance running. Usually I'll jog 45 minutes at a moderate pace. You can't sprint

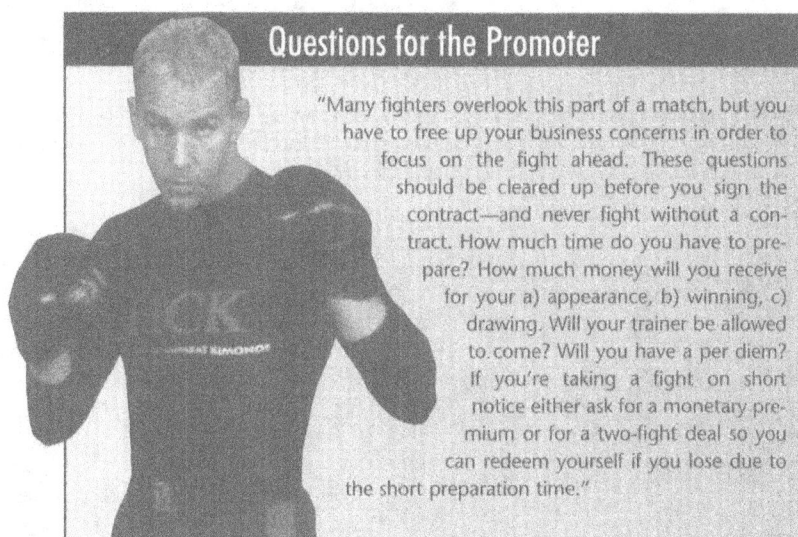

Questions for the Promoter

"Many fighters overlook this part of a match, but you have to free up your business concerns in order to focus on the fight ahead. These questions should be cleared up before you sign the contract—and never fight without a contract. How much time do you have to prepare? How much money will you receive for your a) appearance, b) winning, c) drawing. Will your trainer be allowed to come? Will you have a per diem? If you're taking a fight on short notice either ask for a monetary premium or for a two-fight deal so you can redeem yourself if you lose due to the short preparation time."

everyday because your body gets torn up. It conditions your heart but it tears up your lungs and tweaks your hips and thighs. Jogging is more to develop my mental motivation and also my overall endurance. Distance running also helps me in my footwork and helps me to be faster and lighter on my feet."

Ready to Rumble

Paulson feels that if you have to ask someone if you're ready to fight, then you're not. The mental discipline that it took to drive you to top condition will give you the mental attitude to *win*. "When you're ready to fight—you know it," Paulson insists. "You're pissy, ancy, you can't sleep at night, and you have too much energy. Your endurance is so high that you're going through everybody in submission training and making them tired—iron man training—one after another, after another. Mentally you feel strong, complete, balanced, confident, and a little nervous."

Despite the hardest training, though, Paulson acknowleges that sometimes, despite your best efforts, you just don't have it in the ring. "We're all human," he says. "When that happens, you just have to rededicate yourself to training and get them the next time. You can always tell when you go into the ring and you're off your game. Your focus is just not there—you're seeing the audience, you're seeing the corner men, and you're seeing people outside the ring talking. You're worried about everything other than the fight. That happened to me when I stepped into the ring against Carlos Newton. I wasn't focused, I was distracted, and despite my best efforts to ignore some destructive outside influences I just couldn't get my mind into the fight. I was just unfocused. And it showed in the result. So you've got to be into a fight in your mind as well as in your body."

Part of the mental training, Paulson says, is keeping away from destructive influences and petty distractions. While you don't need to completely isolate yourself, he explains, you do need to set yourself apart enough to insure that you can keep your mind on the business at hand. "For the month before the fight, all I do is train, relax and then spend most of my time at home. It is all about relaxation and mental focus. When you're training you're focusing on what you have to do; but when you're at home you're keeping your mind clear and not getting distracted."

Erik Paulson's Top Training Drills

The drills that Erik Paulson does are designed to give a complete workout in all areas of martial arts—this is essential in mixed martial arts competitions. "You can't neglect anything," Paulson says, "So all of my training routines work specific areas that integrate together to help totally prepare for a match."

Shadow Boxing
Warm-up with this for 15 minutes at the beginning of training. For the first five minutes go really light and just move. For the second five minutes three-quarter power—punching, kicking, kneeing, level dropping, and sprawling. Then for the last five minutes go full power, at full speed, with kicking and striking combinations.

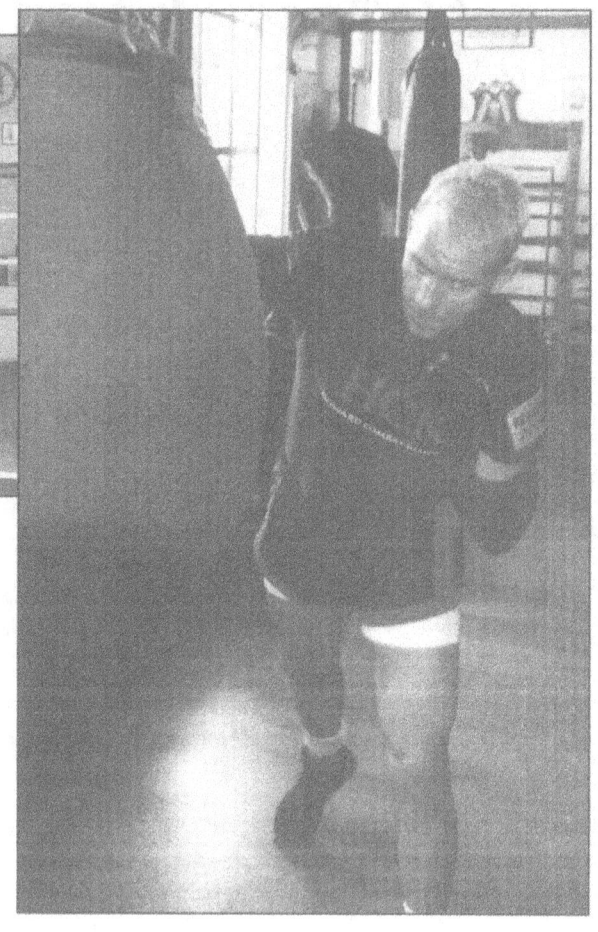

Heavy Bag
Don't throw more than five punches from any one place, and throw them in one to three punch combinations. These combinations include stepping off the centerline, clinching, elbowing, head butting, circling the bag, and then going in and out of range with footwork.

Best of Grappling, 2001

Glove Drills With Partners

Use realistic sparring scenarios. Have a partner that knows what they're doing and can attack in broken rhythm. You want to be defending and countering all possible attacks in the glove drills, and then use all your possible initial attacking combinations.

Focus mitts

Use these drill to "sharpen the tools." Do numerous vale tudo drills—punching, kicking, kneeing, head control, and hockey punching (one-handed), concentrating on speed, reaction, and retraction.

Thai Pads

Use this strictly for power and conditioning and focus on punching, elbowing, kicking, and kneeing. Go as hard and as powerful as you can.

Kick Shield

This training device is used specifically for punching-to-kicking maneuvers, as well as for chopping leg kicks. These are preferred over the Thai pads for leg kicks because they allow hard chopping and kicking.

Belly Belt with Thai Pads and Shin Guards

Use the belly belt for multiple counters and attacks, and combinations and setups. This drill allows you to practice counters to both punches and kicks, return strikes, and counter grappling tackles.

Focus Mitt with Kicking Shield

These joint drills are essential for developing hand/foot and foot/hand combinations and those should be the focus of the drills.

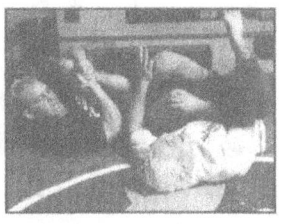

Sparring

Sparring sessions should be against a variety of opponents with various skills and should include boxing, kickboxing, shootboxing, clinching and hitting, takedowns, takedowns to submissions, submissions, submissions with striking, and then mixing it all up.

Jump Rope or Running

Do immediately after the end of training before your heart rate drops. Run for one-and-a-half miles or do five minutes of jump rope/running in increments of 30 seconds jumping, 30 seconds jogging, and 30 seconds sprinting.

Get a Grip!
Four Can't-Miss Defenses
Against the Standing Grab

The defense against the standing grip is one of Brazilian jiu-jitsu's least practiced skills. However, once mastered, it can give the defender a big edge in tournament competition.

Todd Hester, story and photos

ccording to Beverly Hills Jiu-Jitsu instructor Marcus Vinicius, Brazilian jiu-jitsu players have historically neglected practicing attacks and defenses, with and against, the standing grip. Part ■ of the reason, says Vinicius, is that BJJ sparring traditionally starts from the knees, so the students get used to simply clinching from a knees-down position and initiating all moves from there. Another reason is that because BJJ is oriented 80 percent towards mat work and 20 percent, at best, on standing throws and sweeps, it is not a skill that is emphasized. Perhaps yet another factor is that BJJ has always been associated with *vale tudo,* or "anything goes" matches, and the punch was considered the best defense against a close grab.

Sport Jiu-Jitsu Replacing Vale Tudo

"It used to be," Vinicius says, "that because of Royce Gracie and the UFC most people in the United States identified and practiced Brazilian jiu-jitsu almost exclusively for street combat, self-defense purposes, or for *vale tudo* fighting. However, since the explosion of popularity in the United States of BJJ, numerous Brazilian black belts have moved north, set up schools around the country, and started having and emphasizing sport jiu-jitsu tournaments. Tournaments afford normal, working students, who train jiu-jitsu to stay in shape and for fun, an outlet to test their skills that doesn't involve trading head butts with Tank Abbot! Whatever the reason, standing grips are definitely a weak part of the BJJ game. This is especially true when compared to Kudokan or Olympic judo."

Judo's Standing Advantage

Vinicius maintains that judo attacks typically start on the feet, and while mat work is involved, the judoka's primary goal is to go for an *ippon,* or "full point" throw—the judo equivalent of a boxing K.O. Because of this emphasis, judo has a wide variety of attacks, counters, and defenses against standing grips, all designed to off-balance an attacker, thus opening them up for a throw. Vinicius

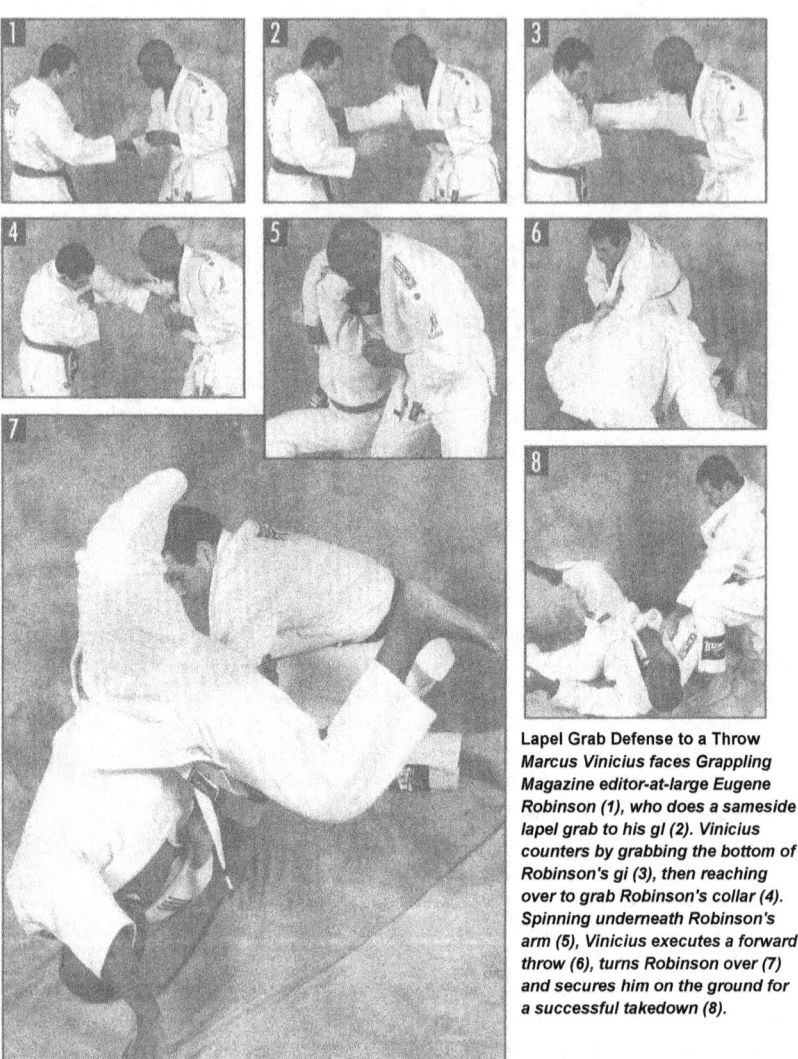

Lapel Grab Defense to a Throw
Marcus Vinicius faces Grappling Magazine editor-at-large Eugene Robinson (1), who does a sameside lapel grab to his gi (2). Vinicius counters by grabbing the bottom of Robinson's gi (3), then reaching over to grab Robinson's collar (4). Spinning underneath Robinson's arm (5), Vinicius executes a forward throw (6), turns Robinson over (7) and secures him on the ground for a successful takedown (8).

says that combing these standing grip skills with Brazilian jiu-jitsu's wealth of strong ground-control positions and numerous submission moves can give a Brazilian jiu-jitsu player a big edge in a tournament. "Standing skills," Vinicius points out, "can provide the top or mount position early on in the match (and substantial points) or can even lead to a quick submission."

Stand and Deliver
Contrary to most Brazilian jiu-jitsu instructor's experiences, Vinicius began his martial arts training in Brazil as a judo player, earning his black belt and several championships. He then "converted" to BJJ, earned his black belt, and became a world champion in that. This "backwards" approach which

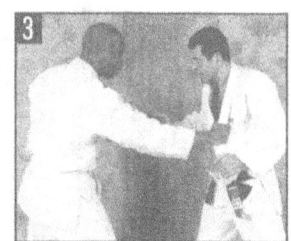

Same Side Lapel Grab Defense *Facing Grappling Magazine editor-at-large, Eugene Robinson (1), Marcus Vinicius is grabbed by the lapel (2). Reaching forward (3), he traps Robinson's wrist against his stomach (4), and twists his body inward, sending Robinson to the ground (S).*

helped him to learn the importance of the standing grappling game was also aided by the fact that he actually went to the Kudokan (the *honbo* or "mother" dojo) in Japan to study at the birthplace of judo. "I know firsthand how effective judo grips and throws are," he says.

Basic Principles
Early move recognition, quick response, good feet movement, and a strong base are all skills that will help jiu-jitsu players execute successful grip counters. While all are important, the most essential of these factors is early move recognition. When a grip is attempted, it is important to move or counter immediately. In judo, if you let your opponent get a secure grip on you, the next move is to go up, up, and away and get some frequent flyer miles. You can't wait to see what your opponent will do with the grip, you have to see it coming and then deny it.

Once the move is denied you have to have a quick response to move into the counter. There is a very small window of opportunity in which to attack. If you let your opponent move away, reset themselves, and then come in again to re-grip, then you're back to square one. Once you start the counter remember to move your feet and hips, not just your arms. Your feet are not nailed to the floor. Often, a half-step forwards, backwards, or to either side will be the difference between executing your move or missing it entirely. You have to be mobile.

The final aspect is your base. If you stay in base, even if you miss the counter, you can still recover, move away, and reset. However, if you attack wildly and let yourself get out-of-control, then your oppo-

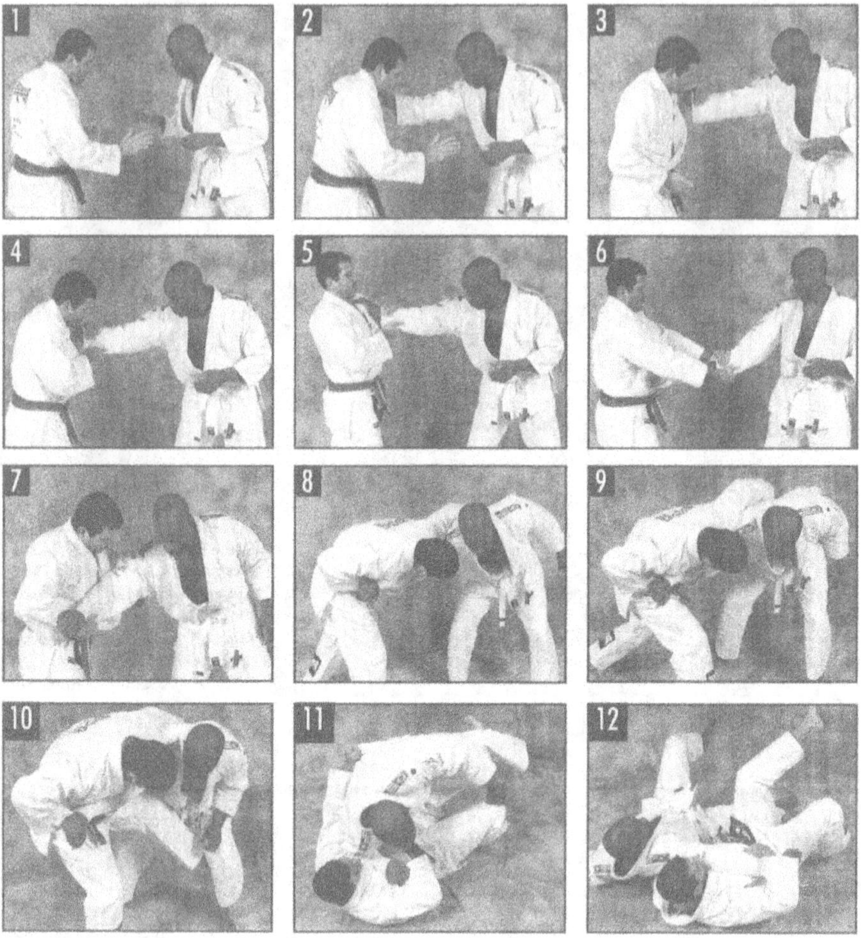

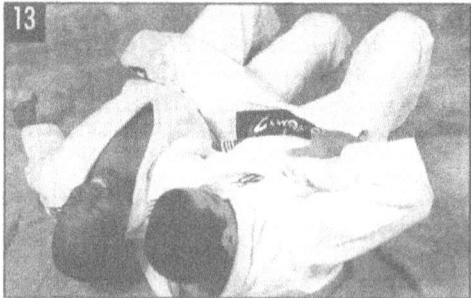

Lapel Grab Defense to an Arm Lock
Facing Grappling Magazine editor-at-large Eugene Robinson (1), Marcus Vinidus is grabbed by the lapel (2). Securing a single-hand top grip (3), Vinicius then moves his hand under the arm and grabs the sleeve (4). Straitening his back to create more distance and get better leverage (S), Viniclus thrusts his arms downwards and breaks the grip (6). Pulling Robinson forward to break his base and off-balance him (7), Viniclus then circles his off-arm behind Robinson's back (8), applies pressure to force him downwards (9), hooks his back foot Inside Robinson's knee (10), and then leans back throwing Robinson to his side (11). Releasing the hook and tightly holding Robinson's arm against his chest (12), Viniclus then throws his leg over Robinson's waist and raises his hips to apply a painful arm bar (13).

nent can throw the weakest attack at you and send you tumbling. What constitutes a good base? Keep your knees slightly bend, your shoulders over your hips, and your feet spread at least shoulder-width apart.

Practice

Plan on spending a lot of mat time in the studio or dojo if you want to master good stand-up counters. Spend time on your feet having your training partner come in and secure a grip. Once you go to the ground, then break, come back to your feet and then go again. Every sparring session doesn't have to end in a death match. You don't have to go to submission each and every time you grapple with an opponent. Go lightly and slowly, until you're comfortable with the move and then increase the intensity and the pace. Pair up with a training partner who wants to train not brawl—it is, after all, called "practice."

Conclusion

"There are no secret weapons in martial arts," Venicius says. "There are only so many ways the human skeletal frame can be bent, twisted, and jammed. For that reason, many martial arts have similar techniques—an arm lock is an arm lock is an arm lock." According to this judo man turned jiu-jitsu player, what will set you apart in the successful application of standup grappling defenses is your willingness to train consistently, pay attention to detail and position, and follow solid basic principles. Then the next time someone grabs you in a tournament and tries to give you a free ride on "Air Brazil," you'll be able to clip their wings and cancel the flight.

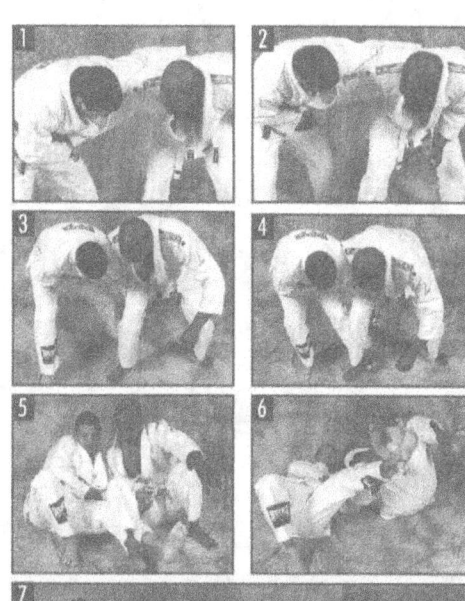

Lapel Grab Defense to Side-Control
(1) Vinicius circles his off-arm behind Robinson's back (2), applies pressure to force him downwards (3), then moves his arm off the back and reaches [inside Robinson's back and grabs behind the knee (4). Hooking his near foot behind Robinson's ankle (5), Vinicius sits back and throws Robinson's leg upwards to take him over (6), and then rolls inside to secure side control (7).

Black Belt Instructor Marcus Vinicius is the owner of the world famous Beverly Hills Jiu-Jitsu Academy in Los Angeles, California. A Judo and Brazilian jiu-jitsu black belt, he is 2000 World Masters Champion in his weight class. He can be contacted for Southern California classes or nationwide seminars by calling 310-854-3041.

Shark Attack!

Using an eclectic mix of striking and grappling arts specifically modified for no-holds-barred combat, Shark Tank fighters are "ready to rumble" on a moment's notice—anywhere and anytime.

Todd Hester

Becoming a championship team is never easy. It takes hard work, dedication and sacrifice to reach an elite level of expertise in any sport. In the new and growing sport of mixed-martial arts, the fighters and trainers of the California-based Shark Tank have definitely paid their dues. From taking fights on 12-hours notice to driving 14 hours in a van from California to make a fight in Texas, the Shark Tank has done it all and seen it all. While many might question their sanity, it has paid off for the Shark Tank in terms of their fighting successes many times over.

Fighting Record

As a team, the Shark Tank has notched over 95 wins in mixed-martial-arts competitions and has fought in almost every major event held throughout the world. This includes the Ultimate Fighting Championship, SuperBrawl, FutureBrawl, Extreme Challenge, Pancrase, Shooto, KI Japan, King of the Cage, Neutral Grounds, Universal Above Ground Fighting, and Rings Japan.

As many promoters have commented, and as is well-known in the industry, the Shark Tank is always ready to fight. As a group and to a man, the Shark Tank takes pride in their extreme conditioning program as well as their rigorous cross-training regimen. Refusing to be limited to any one style, their fighting mix includes techniques from Western boxing, kickboxing, Greco-Roman and freestyle wrestling, Shooto, Brazilian jiu-jitsu, muay Thai, and submission grappling. "Training is rigorous and painful," says top shark, Eddy Millis, "but it is also an excellent source of stress relief. We have a lot of fighters that train but also many people who work out with us just for that reason. The Shark Tank has an operational tempo that exceeds normal limits. This tempo allows people to push themselves past what they thought they could do. We're the original "Be the best you can be."

Origins

The Shark Tank is the brainchild of fighter and trainer Eddy Millis, who began training in karate when he was 8 years old, and developed an infectious passion for martial arts that would last a lifetime. In his early teenage years, Millis surprised his parents (and impressed his friends) by building a complete martial arts training center in his back yard. "I was punching and kicking plastic milk jugs filled with water and sand. I just wanted to be able to train the way I wanted to," Millis recalls. "I thought everything else was too easy." Seeing the need to balance his extreme fitness training with tra-

Phil Ortiz, Eddy Millis and Victor Hunsaker.

ditional combat methods, Millis also kept training at two local martial arts schools.

At 17, Millis enlisted in the U.S. Army and was stationed in Germany, where he continued to study karate and kickboxing and soon became captain of his military base's karate and kickboxing team. Wanting to apply what he had learned and taught, Millis began competing in full-contact karate tournaments as well as kickboxing matches, winning several of the tournaments he entered.

After his military tour ended, Millis returned to California and began studying jeet kune do, kali, Indian shoot-wrestling, and Brazilian jiu-jitsu. Liking the fast, aggressive style of the Japanese, he also began taking private lessons in Japanese submission fighting. With a natural aptitude developed from his childhood experiences of blending styles, Millis soon found himself mixing and matching the techniques of kicking, punching, and submission into a fighting method that was uniquely his own. Want to share it, he decided to start teaching.

Humble Beginnings

The Shark Tank began rather informally when Millis started training a few friends in martial arts at a local college. Soon, these "few friends" became 30 students. He taught kickboxing on the football field and submission grappling inside the gym. Training, however, without official college sanction, they often had to sneak into the gymnasium and practice inside the dance room where they would not be seen. As the number of students continued to swell, Millis' brother Steve, also a martial artist, started helping him with the training. After several months of clandestine training, the college finally caught on and told them to train elsewhere. Rather than bringing an end to the fledgling school, however, this rejection only increased the Shark Tank's desire to train. Seeing that his intensity was mirrored by that of his students, Millis decided to "keep their drive alive" and continue their progression in martial arts. "The fun was over," Millis smiles. "It was time for the Shark Tank to get serious and to have our own school—Combined Martial Arts was born." Millis rented space at a local gymnastic studio and began offering kickboxing and submission grappling classes several times a week. Due to demand from wives and girlfriends of his male students, a women's kickboxing class was also added.

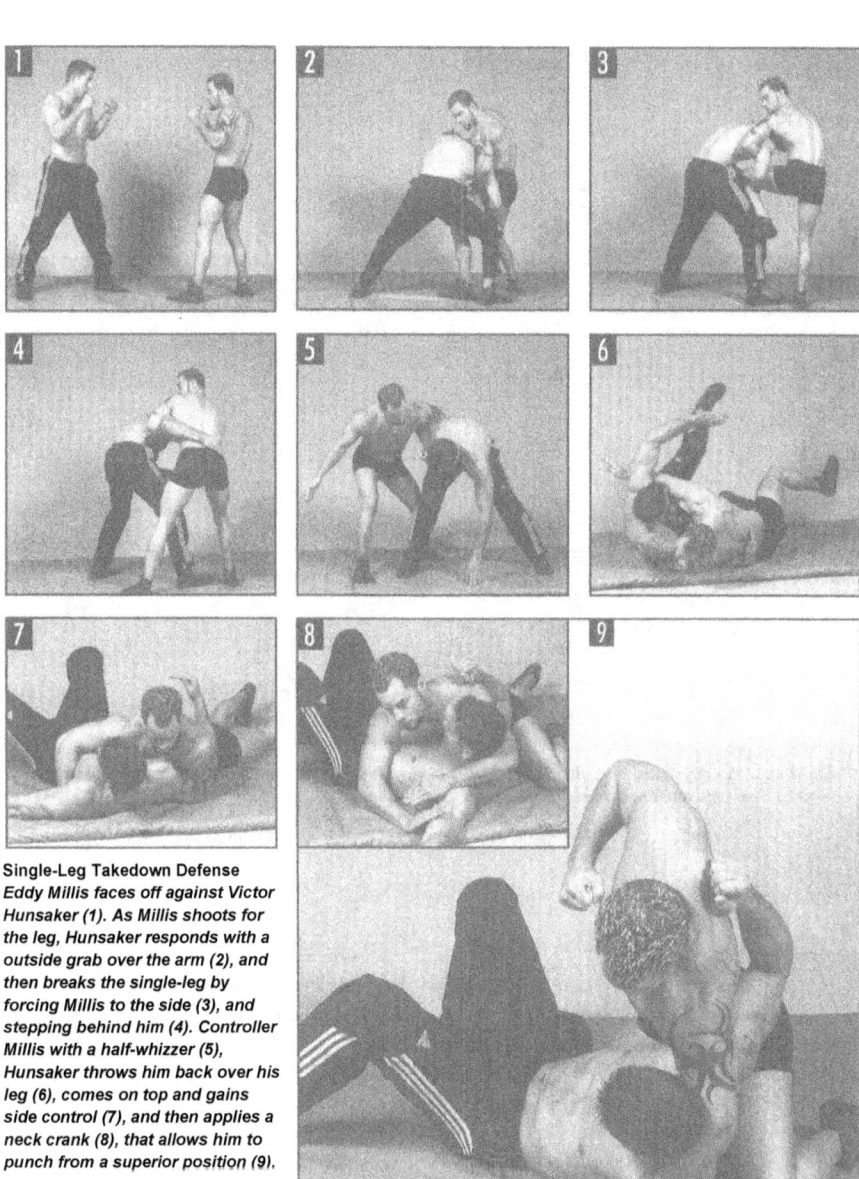

Single-Leg Takedown Defense
Eddy Millis faces off against Victor Hunsaker (1). As Millis shoots for the leg, Hunsaker responds with a outside grab over the arm (2), and then breaks the single-leg by forcing Millis to the side (3), and stepping behind him (4). Controller Millis with a half-whizzer (5), Hunsaker throws him back over his leg (6), comes on top and gains side control (7), and then applies a neck crank (8), that allows him to punch from a superior position (9).

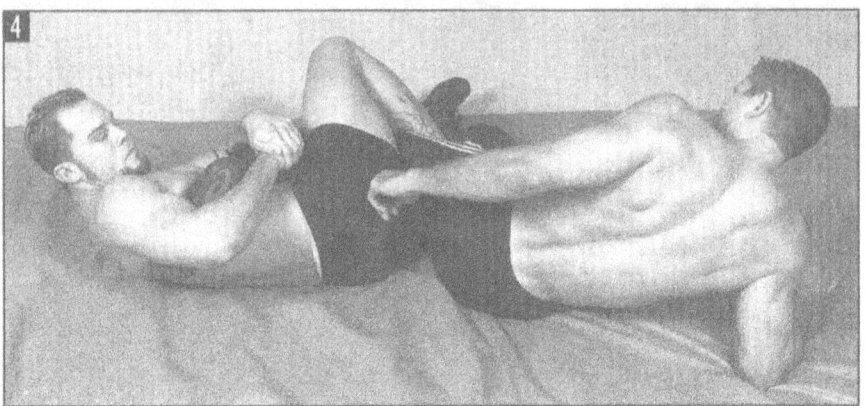

Heel Hook from a Clinch
Clinched up with Eddy Millis (1), Hunsaker falls back and scissors Millis' leg (2), takes him to the ground (3), and applies a finishing heel hook (4).

Ultimate Fighting Fever

Coincidentally, the UFC was just getting started around this time. Fueled by Royce Gracie's success, the UFC gained fame and popularity and caused no-holds-barred fever to sweep through martial arts dojos and schools around the country. Soon, several of Millis' students asked him when they could take part in a mixed martial arts fight. Always on the cutting edge of martial arts, Millis said, "Right now," and promptly took his team to several submission grappling tournaments, enjoying immediate success.

Millis' top student, Victor Hunsaker, emerged as the team standout, winning several big matches via leg and foot locks—soon to become trademark Shark Tank moves. Soon other students followed Hunsaker's lead—Ron Hernandez, Tony Covington, Matt Montecito, and Nathan Griego—also winning with foot locks. "At that time," Millis says, "most grapplers did not know a lot about leg and foot submissions. There wasn't a lot of people teaching them. But I love them, know them very well, and have a passion for them—so I passed that knowledge to my fighters. I really think that gave the Shark Tank a big advantage over our opponents in the early days of submission fighting. To this day, I still feel that it give us a advantage."

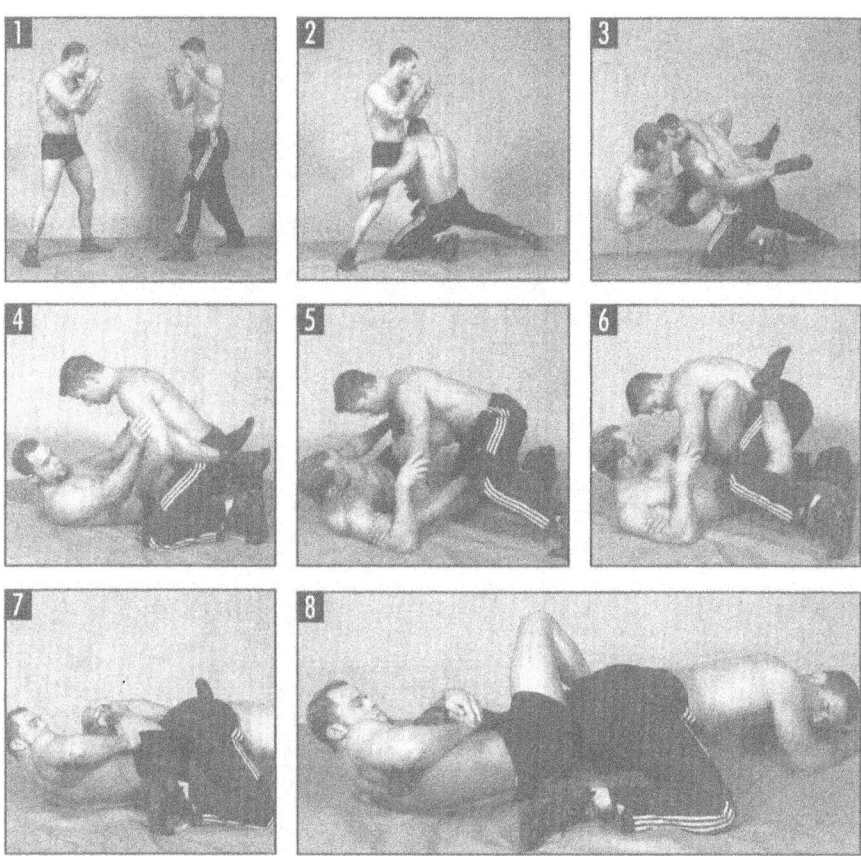

Double-Leg Takedown
Eddy Millis and Victor Hunsaker face off (1). Millis shoots the double (2), and then takes Hunsaker down (3). Keeping space to move, Hunsaker puts Millis into the guard (4), then puts a knee on the stomach (5), then hooks his other leg around Millis' leg (6). Turning inward, Hunsaker secures the foot (7), and applies the heel hook submission (8).

The Shark Tank

With Combined Martial Arts doing well in grappling events, Eddy decided to take the team to kickboxing "smokers," unofficial events held at individual martial arts schools. Again, the Shark Tank fighters were successful. Having shown promise in both grappling and kickboxing, Millis decided that the time was right to combine the two disciplines and enter no-holds-barred tournaments.

The team needed a name to fit their aggressive style—the name "Shark Tank" was born and the Shark Tank began fighting every month in local and out-of-state mixed martial arts events. "In the beginning we took anything and everything," Millis says, "just to get our feet wet. This was even

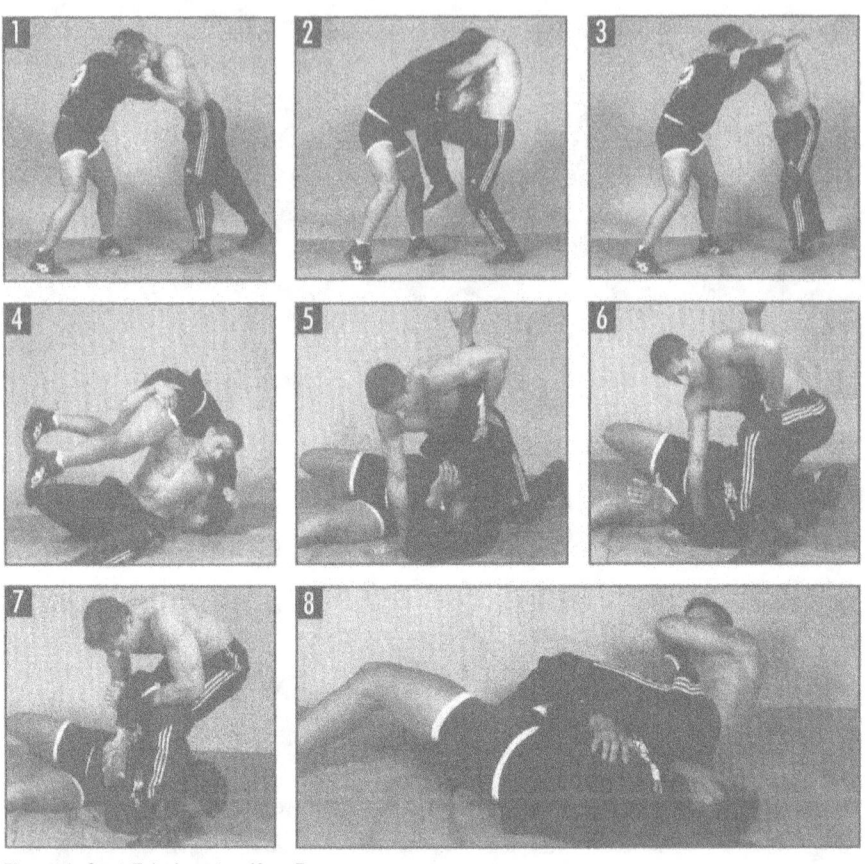

Fireman's Carry Takedown to a Knee Bar
Eddy Millis and Phil Ortiz collar tie (1). Millis knees Phil to the liver to open him up (2), then shoots a fireman's carry (3-4). Coming on top, Millis traps the arm and blocks Phil's hips (5-6). Phil counters and grabs his own arm (7). Millis then slides his right leg out to scoop Phil's right leg and finish with an option knee bar (8).

tougher when you consider that most of our guys work 40 hours a week at a regular job in addition to training and fighting. We're as blue collar as you get and never had the luxury of training full-time." Still maintaining a rigorous fighting schedule for the Shark Tank, Millis has become more discriminating about which events he sends fighters to. "My main concern is taking care of my fighters," Millis says. "Some no-holds-barred events are a little shady. I just want to make sure that my guys get paid now, and that they go into a situation where the judging is fair and impartial. I want my guys to know that I'm looking out for them and that they can depend on me to do the best for them."

Staying the Course
Today, Eddy Millis is considered one of the most well-rounded instructors in NHB as well as being regarded as a pioneer in the "team" approach to MMA fighting. His fighters, who are close to him on

a daily basis, back up the reputation Millis has of being a team player. "I have trained with a lot of guys," says Shark Tank fighter John Alessio, "but Eddy's blend of conditioning, submissions and kickboxing, combined with his passion for teaching are incredible."

In keeping with his original passion, Millis continues to travel and train around the world, having trained kickboxing in Amsterdam with KI great Peter Aerts, muay Thai in Thailand, submission fighting in Japan, and with the all-Army wrestling team. He also trains regularly with Shooto World Champion Erik Paulson, whom he considers one of the most technical all-around fighters and teachers in the world. Millis also recently expanded into the Hollywood scene, becoming a fight trainer and assistant stunt coordinator on the reality combat television show *Battledome*.

Future Plans

Not content to rest on his laurels, Millis is driving the Shark Tank to gain an even larger prominence in the martial arts world by having joint training sessions with the world famous Lion's Den of Ken Shamrock. According to Millis, "Ken Shamrock, Vernon White, and the rest of the Lion's Den guys are great to train with. If you want to become the best you have to train with the best. So I'm thrilled with the association we have with them."

But when all is said and done, it is his fighters which matter most to Millis. "The Shark Tank's spirit is kept alive by Victor Hunsaker, Yosh Hall, Tony Petarra, Brian Warren, Jay Martinez, and all the rest of the guys," Millis says. "If I've had any success it has only been because of them. I'm grateful for where we've been, where we are, and where we're going. With two schools open and excellent instructors to pass along our tradition, I think the Shark Tank will continue to grow into the new mil- lenium."

For more information on Eddy Millis and the Shark Tank visit their Web site at www. sharktankusa. com.

Tito Ortiz
Still Climbing

Tito Ortiz" meteoric rise to the top of the UFC has been due to equal parts of hard work and talent. But Ortiz knows it will take more than that to make the UFC appeal to mainstream sports fans.

Thomas Gerbasi

"I'm working my butt off to make it (mixed martial arts) credible as a sport," says Ortiz. "The UFC ■ made a big mistake by promoting it as the 'bloodiest sport around.' They made it a freak show. I But now, with all the great athletes involved, it's starting to be accepted as a sport."

Any budding sport has its growing pains, and even as middleweight champion, Ortiz has not been immune to such distractions. "There were lots of frustrations, but I take them as they come," he said, referring to contract squabbles with SEG. "I want to make this bigger and to do that I needed to make a stand for myself, which was great. I'm like the rusty penny in their pocket that turned out to be a gold coin. They needed to know it, and I needed to be treated as such. Now they know." Never was Ortiz' MVP status more obvious than during last December's UFC XXIX, when the Californian thrilled a Japanese crowd with a 1:52 romp over top contender Yuki Kondo, which the champion ended via a neck crank submission. For Tito Ortiz, it was a fight that almost didn't happen.

A Bermuda Nightmare

Six months ago, Ortiz and his new bride Kristin, on the second day of their honeymoon, took a moped ride in Bermuda. They were struck by a bus, and Ortiz' life turned upside down. "When I got in the accident, the doctor said me and my wife should have been dead," he remembered. "You could be the toughest man alive, and anybody could take your life." Ortiz, 25, suffered ligament damage to his ankle. Kristin's injuries were more severe. "Five months ago, I thought she was gone. It was the toughest thing I ever had to go through." His wife suffered three broken ribs and four fractured vertebrae in her back, but luckily, she has recovered nicely, and has given Tito a new lease on life as well. "We take a lot of stuff for granted, having someone to watch TV with, someone to yell at you for not taking the trash out. I'm here to make a mark in this world. I got a second chance when I got in the accident. I took that thought into consideration, and said 'Wow, God gave me another chance on this Earth, and I'm going to make the best of it.'

Mentally and physically, Ortiz was on top of his game against the talented Kondo. And he owes it all to preparation. "I watch all the guys I fight," he said. "I make sure I get at least six or seven other

A lot of guys use their brawn when they fight, but you've got to use your brain in this type of fighting. It's like a boxing match, a wrestling match, and everything all put together.

fights on tape. I take the scientific side of it; taking people apart, picking their brains, their weaknesses. I see what their strengths are, and I make a game plan. And I try to fulfill that game plan while I'm fighting. A lot of guys use their brawn when they fight, but you've got to use your brain in this type of fighting. It's like a boxing match, a wrestling match, and everything all put together. So you've got to take it that way."

Into the Octagon

Before the Kondo fight, Ortiz had no trepidation about stepping into the Octagon for the first time since the accident. "It has all been put behind me now," he said. "I've had about five and a half months to heal and recover. My cardio is better than it's ever been. I've matured as a fighter. I've been in this game now for three years, and in each one of my matches I get better and better. So in this one, I expect for it to be over quick or it's going to be a long brutal one." It was over quick, and now all eyes turn to the possibility of a 2001 rematch with Frank Shamrock.

Shamrock defeated Ortiz in an epic battle that many consider to be one of the greatest UFC matches ever. And while both now share a mutual respect for each other, Ortiz would undoubtedly like a shot at redemption against his fiercest rival. Shamrock or not, at 25, Ortiz has already made a mark on the world of mixed martial arts, in and out of the Octagon. A two-time state junior college wrestling champion in California, "The Bad Boy" got his chance at the big time when he was enlisted as a sparring partner for the UFC's original bad boy, David "Tank" Abbott. "I was a wrestler in high school, I wrestied in college, and then I started training with Tank Abbott," said Ortiz. "When ultimate fighting first came out, it caught my eye right off the bat. Plus, I watched a movie called *Bloodsport*. There was always a dream in the back of my mind of being somebody, and being one of the best martial artists in the world really intrigued me into doing something about it."

But to be competitive in the UFC, Ortiz needed more than wrestling. "I noticed that people need a lot of technique," he said. "In ultimate fighting, you need to be an ultimate fighter by putting everything together. All of a sudden I started seeing guys who were winning belts and becoming champions, and they had everything in their game. They had the ground game, the standup, the cardio, and so I said, 'I've got to take this sport seriously.'" Tito made his debut at UFC XXIII, and as an alternate, he defeated Wes Albritton in under a minute. An injury gave Ortiz a shot at Guy Mezger in the main draw, and though a controversial loss followed, the California native was hooked.

Straight to the Top

"I automatically made $19,000 in my first fight," he said. "That kind of paid the bills. I also had sponsors that were helping me out. Stanky's XXX, an adult bookshop, was one, and another sponsor was Speedwear. Those guys took care of me. I got my rent paid for, and everything was taken care of. I really didn't have an extracurricular job, so I was able to put myself full-time into fighting. And I knew I could win a world title. That's when I set my dreams of being a world champion. On April 26th I won my first title. I plan on winning a few more. Frank Shamrock has five world titles, and I plan on getting six. One of my goals is to be the best mixed martial artist that ever graced the Octagon. My dreams are high, and I think that I can achieve these dreams."

Ortiz has scored victories over Kondo, Mezger (in a rematch), Jerry Bohlander, and Vanderlei Silva. But to many, Ortiz earned the respect of the hardcore fan with his participation in the Abu Dhabi World Submission Wrestling Tournament. "I just did it for the competitive side of it," said Tito. "Once I got there and started submitting people and stuff, they were like, 'Wow, Tito Ortiz knows submissions.' It was an honor for me. Going back to the *Bloodsport* thing, I was an invite. They invited me to come. They noticed me as being one of the best guys in the world, and they wanted to see what I could do. The Prince came up to me a few times and said, 'You're a tremendous athlete.' And each time I made sure I went up there and tried to entertain him as much as I could. I ended up taking third in my weight, fourth in the absolute, and I stepped back and I said 'Wow, I'm actually pretty good at this type of martial art.'"

Life With Tank

But to be a star, you need an image. Was it tough for Ortiz to break free of the connotations of being associated with Abbott? "It was real easy to get along with Tank," said Ortiz. "But once I went out with him in public, it was a different story. He was not really a sociable person. Once in a while he would meet somebody he liked and he would talk to him. But most of the time he would see somebody and be like, 'The hell with you!' or 'What the hell you lookin at?' and try to start fights with people for no reason at all. I don't need to go out and fight people on the streets. I know what I can do in the ring, and it's better for a person to look up to me and say, 'That guy's kind of cool.' To talk to someone and tell them what it's like to be in the Octagon, and just be friends with people, I have no problem with that at all. Trying to distance myself from Tank, that was no problem at all. All I had to do was just push it aside and say, 'Whatever. I'm me and Tank is Tank. That's who he is. No one is going to change him.'"

"I got a second chance when I got in the accident. I took that th'ought into consideration, and said 'Wow, Cod gave me another chance on this Earth, and I'm going to make the best of it.'"

It's obvious that Tito Ortiz is cultivating a fan-friendly image to the public. Why the "Bad Boy" moniker then? Are there two sides to the UFC middleweight champion? "That's the whole point," he laughed. "You're catching on. A lot of people ask me that. Once I get locked in that cage, there has to be something in my body to trigger me and make me want to go out and inflict pain on a person. The money and everything, that's fun, but at the same time the competition can work wonders for somebody to win. The feeling of losing, there's no worse feeling than that. There is a difference between Tito Ortiz in the ring and Tito Ortiz outside the ring; because once I get in the ring, the light switch turns on. It's like a red light and it's time to go as hard as I can and try to break this guy. Break him mentally, physically, his arms, his legs, because that's what his job is, to take me out. Each and every time that I do it, it's a job for me to do, and I'm going to take the strategic way of putting things together with a game plan. But once I step out of the ring, I'm all smiles. My job is over, and hopefully I did my job. And each time I step out I make sure that I feel satisfied that I pushed myself as hard as I could, and that I took myself to that second level."

A Fan Favorite

As a fan favorite (Ortiz received the biggest ovation of the night at UFCXXVII in Atlantic City without even stepping in the Octagon), he is well aware of the importance of the public to the long-term survival of the sport. This awareness is no doubt due to his love of pro wrestling, an area that Ortiz has hinted at engaging in. Is MMA about to lose one of its most marketable stars? "I'm going to hold out on that right now and see how far this sport will go," said Ortiz. "I went to Wrestlemania a while back and I saw the brutality, the pounding those guys take. And they do it every day. People say those slams are fake, wrestling is fake, yada, yada, yada. But when you see the punishment those guys take, it's not fake. I'd rather step in a ring where I know I have a chance to stop anybody slamming me or to stop them from punching me. There you don't. The punches are pulled, yes, but getting slammed every day, getting hit by tables and chairs; all of that stuff takes a toll on your body. I think those guys are tremendous athletes, every one of them. They still inspire me. I watch WWF all the time. I learn little things from it because people look up to them so much. People don't understand what they go through, mentally, physically."

Role Model

Like one of the top pro wrestlers, Ortiz has done everything right outside as well as inside the ring. He stars in the UFC video game, has his own clothing company (Punishment Clothing, available on titoortiz.com), and has gone on tour with Limp Bizkit to promote the game. But admirably, Ortiz' main goal is much more lofty. "To be a role model for kids is my main goal right now," said Ortiz. "Showing kids that once you set your mind to something, you can achieve anything at all. For some people, as soon as something negative enters their minds, they quit. Well, they didn't try hard enough. You've got to try and try and try until you either conquer that or you just don't do it anymore. My philosophy is go hard or go home'. You go all the way with something or you don't do it at all. I'm living my dream each and every day. The harder I work, the easier things come. The reason I'm different from everybody else is that I'm a real person. I care about my fans, I care what they think about. It means a lot to me, and I want to be something more than just a fighter. I want people to know what I'm like on the outside of the ring."

He continues, "I get E-mail from kids on my Web site all the time, saying 'you've been such an inspiration to me.' It's not a point of me being an inspiration to them, it's more of them being an inspiration to me, by writing and telling me this stuff. It makes me work harder. I wake up in the morning and run harder, box harder, wrestle harder, so kids could look up to me and say 'Wow, there's a person I could be like when I get older.' But at the same time, you

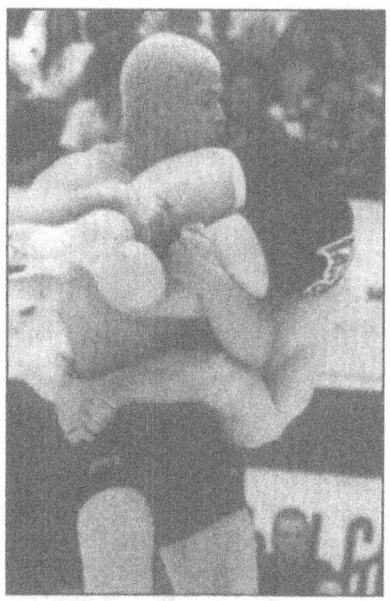

"One of my goals is to be the best mixed martial artist that ever graced the Octagon. My dreams are high, and I think that I can achieve these dreams."

could be anything. You don't have to be a fighter. You can be President. I never let any roadblock get in front of me that's going to block my way. That goes to every fan or friend—just achieve in life, and be a good person. I'm not really a religious person. I don't go to church every week or anything, I just believe in being good people, and treating people with the respect that they need. In the long run I want to help abused children, and kids in gangs."

Positive Energy

"When I was in college, and I was wrestling and trying to get my degree in teaching for physical education, special education teaching was my minor. So I want to help the kids who have problems with their parents and stuff like that. It's the negative people that try and bring them down, because there's something wrong in their own lives. You need to push those people aside, get rid of the negative energy, and turn it into positive energy. That's an everyday idea. Any negative energy I have I just turn it around and make it something better. When I say I can't do that, I turn it around and say I can do that. I'm trying as hard as I can to do that. The negative things I try not to think about so much, it's mostly positive things every day."

And he owes a great deal of those positive thoughts to his wife. "She's my best friend," Ortiz said. "We've been together nine years. We were best friends first and we didn't even start dating until after high school. It took a lot of hard work. We're the perfect team, and we're lucky to have each other."

Tito Ortiz has come a long way. And he's still going.

Estima (bottom) and Jeff Monsen.

Comprido attacks Ivan Fanton.

Wander Braga (bottom) sweeps Yasushi Miyake.

Royler Gracie (bottom) and Anthony Hamlett.

Saulo   Comprido   Dean

Royler Gracie submits

'Twas the Tournament Before Christmas
The 2000 International Pro-Am of Grappling

Raleigh, North Carolina isn't exactly a hotspot of the international grappling scene—so what was Royler Gracie, Saulo Ribeiro, Rodrigo "Comprido"Medeiros, Luis "Limao" Heredia, Jeff Monson, and other world-class submission fighters doing at the Dorton Arena three weeks before Christmas?

Kid Peligro, photos by Koichi Kawasaki

The International Pro-Am of Grappling was spawned by the visit of promoters Frank Mullis and Billy Dowey to the ADCC World Submission Wrestling Championships in the United Arab Emirates. The two were so impressed that when they returned home they immediately put the wheels in motion for their Christmas present to the submission fighting world—to have the best grapplers in the world compete on U.S. soil for prize money, championship trophies, and a lot of prestige.

They began by contacting some of the best fighters in the world and seeing who was available and interested. With potential names in hand, they decided to have three 8-man grappling divisions: under 170 lbs., 170-200 lbs., and over 200 lbs. Wanting to attract the world's best they offered $19,500.00 in prize money which broke down to $5,000 for 1st, $1,000 for $2^{n\wedge}$, and $500 for 3rd. Additionally they secured the services of four-time world Brazilian jiu-jitsu champion and two-time ADCC champion Royler Gracie to compete in a superfight against AMC Pankration star Anthony Hamlett, who had taken 4th place at ADCC 2000, and who many predicted would give Gracie all he could handle and then some.

The Buzz
As the preparations for the event began to be released to the general public, the promoters realized they had stumbled upon a winning formula. Fighter interest from around the globe was intense and the international media began contacting the event for information and sending in credential requests. All of a sudden the event took on a life of its own. As more "name" fighters were announced, more interest was raised by the press—which prompted still more "name" fighters to enter. In the end, 24 top fighters were selected for the 3 divisions, along with 16 fighters competing in 8 superfights.

Lightweight Brackets
Matt Serra (Renzo Gracie Team) v **Naoya Uematsu** (Shooto Japan) **Leo "Leozinho" Vieira** (Alliance Team) v **Scott Schultz** (Tai Kai JJ) **Vitor "Shaolin" Ribeiro** (Nova Uniao Team) v **Sean Dunn** (Team Rival) **Fernando "Terere"** (Alliance Team) v **Wander Braga** (L.A.Jiu-Jitsu Club)

Middleweight Brackets
Sean Williams (Renzo Gracie Team) v **Phillip Smith** (Alliance Team) **Saulo Ribeiro** (Gracie Humaita) v **Jamie Levine** (Team Rival) **Rodrigo "Comprido" Medeiros** (Alliance Team) v **Ivan Fanton** (Team G.Machado) **Mark Laimon** (Nova Uniao Team) v **Dean Lister** (Fabio Santos Team)

Heavyweight Brackets
Ze Mario "Esfiha" (Alliance Team) v **Wade Rome** (Team Rival) **Jeff Monsen** (AMC Pankration) v **Rhadi Ferguson** (Lloyd Irvin/Bid Dogs) **John Rallo** (Renzo Gracie Team) v **Marc Robinson** (Team Rival) **Garth Taylor** (Claudio Franca Team) v **"Bull" Shaw** (Alliance Team)

Superfights
Luka Dias (Team Megaton) v **Kathy Brothers** (Machado Team)
Luis "Limao" Heredia (Rickson Gracie Team) v **Mario Aielo** (Gracie Humaita)
Cleber Luciano (Luciano Team) v **Francisco Neto** (Team Yamasaki)
Wander Braga (LA Jiu-Jitsu Club) v **Yasushi Miyake** (Japan Greco-Roman Team)
Wellington "Megaton" Dias (Team Megaton) v **Gustavo Machado** (Team G.Machado)

Featured Fight
Royler Gracie v Anthony Hamlett

But nothing goes smooth when it comes to NHB or grappling events—injuries occur frequently as fighters train harder than usual to prepare for competition. Among the notable casualties were Carlos Barreto, Rodrigo Minotauro, Marcio Feitosa, and Sean Alvarez. However, this still left stars Vitor "Shaolin" Ribeiro, Leo Vieira, Wander Braga, Saulo Ribeiro, Rodrigo "Comprido" Medeiros, Jeff Monson,

Leozinho (top) attacks Shaolin.

Matt Serra (left) taking Naoya Uematsu's back.

Garth Taylor, Luis "Limao" Heredia, Magaton Dias, Cle- ber Luciano, and Yasushi Miyake to compete.

Day One

On Saturday, the stage was set for the best grappling event ever seen in the U.S. outside of the Pan-Am games. Entering Dorton Arena, you could sense the excitement and tension in the air. Despite a low public turnout the arena was filled with press, including representatives of *Grappling Magazine, Gracie Magazine, Baseball Magazine, Gong Magazine, Submission Fighter Magazine,* ADCC News, Eddie Goldman's Eyada Sports Radio, and Sport TV from Brazil. Additionally, no-holds-barred booker Koichi Kawasaki and shooto reporter Manabu Takashima were there as photographers to capture all the action. Also in attendance were the North Carolina boxing commissioner, a world kickboxing champion, and instructors Matt Hume, Pedro Sauer, Relson Gracie, Pedro Valente, Romero "Jacare" Cavalcante, Fabio Santos, Carlson Gracie Jr., Steve and

Mario "Esifha" celebrates.

D.C. Maxwell, UFC referee Mario Yamasaki, and promoters Brian Cimins and Kip Kollar.

The event was supposed to start with two superfights. However, Kathy Brothers and Mario Aielo did not show up to face opponents Luka Dias and Luis "Limao" Heredia, leaving them to claim their titles by default. Heredia, a world-class black belt instructor and the number one fighter on the Rickson Gracie Competition Team was understandably disappointed. "I trained very hard for this and came to fight. Of course, I feel I would have won anyway, but I still wanted a chance to show my

Serra (top) passing Terere's guard.

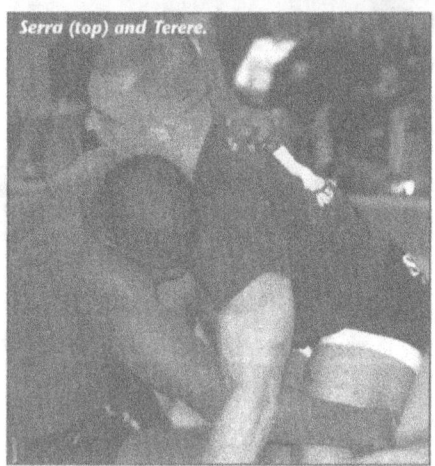

Serra (top) and Terere.

skills and test myself." As it turned out, however, this was not an omen of things to come. From that point on the event went from good, to better, to great.

Cleber Luciano vs. Francisco Neto

In the first contested superfight of the night, the California version of the Tasmanian Devil, black belt Cleber Luciano, went toe-to-toe with the New York's Francisco Neto, the "Beast from the East." Both fighters have had tremendous success against top-level competition from their respective areas, and it was only fitting that they would square-off in this event. During the 1 0-minute regulation time, the two fighters exchanged positions and showcased their tremendous stand-up skills with neither gaining a clear advantage. As overtime began, the wily Luciano feinted a shot at one leg and went for the other, completing a beautiful takedown for 2 points. The match continued on the ground with several leg attacks from Neto while Luciano attempted to pass the guard. When time finally ran out Luciano had a two-point advantage and was awarded the title.

experienced Japanese fighter Uematsu. After an intense exchange submitted him with a rear naked choke. Next, Leo Vieira mounted ibeiro then completely dominated a game Shawn Dunn 21-0, who st- minute replacement for an injured Paul Rodrigues. Fernando L.A. Jiu-Jitsu's Wander Braga 2-0 in a close match.

itions and attacks for ten minutes with Smith emerging the victor. me world Brazilian jiu-jitsu champion and current ADCC world ked for this match-up and had spent a month training hard for this live with the Rival Team in order to maintain top focus, shape and going at Ribeiro 110 percent—like no one has ever gone at him before." However, reality quickly set in when the match started as Levine quickly learned that Ribeiro didn't accumulate all his titles by chance. In a masterful sequence, Ribeiro surprised and confused Levine with a series of submission attacks never before seen, going from a crucifix, to an *omoplata* shoulder-lock, to a reverse *omoplata* with an opposite leg shoulder-lock. The exchange was so fast that Levine couldn't keep up and ended up submitting with a scream of pain. Afterwards, the shell-shocked Levine said, "I thought he was going to get my right arm, when all of a sudden I felt the pain my left are. I couldn't move so I had to yell. I'm mad! Not at Saulo—but at myself because I wanted to stay on the mat longer." Levine is a warrior but he learned first-hand that Ribeiro is head and shoulders above most grapplers in the world.

Next, Comprido submitted Fanton by a foot lock to move into the semifinals, and then Marc Lai-mon and Dean Lister locked up in one of the best battles of the tournament. Battling hard for 10 minutes, the two ended up in a 4-4 tie. They had already faced each other a few months back in Grapplers Quest West, with Laimon coming out the victor, and Lister was looking to even the score. However, as overtime began Laimon went ahead 8-4 by taking Lister's back. But keeping his head, Lister didn't give up, kept up the pressure and evened the score just prior to the end of the 5-minute overtime and then got the referee's decision—and a measure of revenge.

Heavyweight Preliminaries

These were not small people—the lightest weighing in at a svelte 260 lbs. In the first match 1999 ADCC champion Jeff Monson faced USA Olympic judo alternate Rhadi Ferguson. After a beautiful takedown by Ferguson, Monson used all his experience and skill to come back and win by the score of 5-2. Then Ze Mario Esfiha submitted Wade Rome via a kimura lock. The heavyweights continued with 325 lb. WEF champion Marc Robinson besting John Rallo by a score of 9-0. Rallo put up quite a fight but the power and experience of Robinson was just too much. The final match saw California's Garth Taylor defeating Bull Shaw by a takedown.

Semifinal Matches

The lightweight semifinals opened up with Serra taking on Vieira. In what can arguably be called one of the best grappling comebacks ever witnessed, the effervescent Serra started by two scoring two quick takedowns on his way to taking Vieira's back. Down 4-0 and facing the threat of a submission, something inside Vieira clicked on. In a dazzling display of technical jiu-jitsu, Vieira proceeded to execute five successful takedowns on Serra, including a beautiful throw that launched Serra 6 feet into the air. The acrobatic Serra, however, somehow did a summersault and landed on his feet. But Vieira was just too much and won a clear 10-4 decision. In the other lightweight semifinal Vitor Ribeiro beat Terere by a score of 6-4.

The stadium was still buzzing from the lightweight matches when the middleweights went to work. Saulo Ribeiro quickly submitted Smith via foot lock, while Lister battled Medeiros hard for ten minutes before losing a heartbreaker by just a single sweep. In the heavyweight semifinals Robinson defeated Taylor 5-0 via a takedown and guard pass, and Monsen edged Esfiha by a lone takedown.

Day Two
Wander Braga vs. Yasushi Miyake

The second day started with a match between L.A. Jiu-Jitsu Club instructor Wander Braga and Yasushi Miyake, an Olympic Greco-Roman wrestler from Japan. Miyake had defeated the famous shooto fighter Rumina Sato not long ago and was considered the overwhelming favorite. Braga, though, had other ideas. In a highly contested match, Braga made effective use of his half-guard game and swept Miyake and then took his back for the points and the win. With this huge upset, Braga caused quite a stir in Japan and several fighting organizations are reportedly said to be very interested in negotiating a fight deal with him. Has a new star been born? Only time will tell.

Consolation Matches

In the third place matches, Terere swept Serra for the close lightweight win, Lister submitted Smith by foot lock in the middleweight match, and Esfiha out-pointed Taylor in the heavyweight division.

Lightweight Finals

Vitor "Shaolin" Ribeiro vs. Leo "Leozinho" Vieira

The match between Vitor Ribeiro and Leo Vieira did the impossible—it surpassed the excitement of the Vieira-Serra match. The two athletes let it all hang out, left nothing on the mat, and showcased all their skills. Ribeiro attempted two beautiful suplexes on Vieira, but Vieira somehow managed to twist in the air and land on all fours. Next Vieira got position on Ribeiro for a beautiful takedown, but Ribeiro contorted his body, wriggled away, and escaped from the jaws of defeat. The crowd was very excited and vocal during this entire match, yelling encouragement to both fighters when their mouths were not open with amazement at the skill of both men. After an incredible amount of sweep attempts and other highly technical maneuvers, it was tied at the end of regulation. Overtime produced more incredible displays of athleticism and techniques by both fighters and at the end of the overtime they were still scoreless. It was up to the referee to make a very difficult decision, but Vieira got the nod due to the fact that he initiated more of the action.

Middleweight Finals

Saulo Ribeiro vs. Rodrigos "Comprido" Meideros

This was a Brazilian jiu-jitsu dream match: the five-time world champion, Ribeiro, against the two-time world absolute champion, Meideros. Both fighters entered the finals in less than optimum condition. Meideros had a bad knee and Ribeiro was suffering the effects of a bad nights sleep and severe jet lag. The fight began with the two champions feeling each other out. When the stand-up game ended up being a virtual stand-off, Riebiro put Meideros in the half-guard and, after some adjustment, went for a sweep. As Comprido's back hit the ground, one could see in his face a look of resignation—as if to concede the match. Ribeiro was now on top, ahead 2-0 and in Comprido's half-guard. That would be a position most fighters would want to avoid like the plague, because of Ribeiro's methodical and relentless attacking style. But this was not Ribeiro's day. As he began a guard-pass attempt, he carelessly left his arm in an exposed position—that was all Meideros needed. Attacking the arm with a kimura, he forced Ribeiro to give up a two-point reversal which tied the match 2-2. Ribeiro was startled by the move and in haste tried to stand-up—without noticing that Meideros had his foot in control. Meideros tripped Ribeiro, who landed with his back on the mat. In that single moment, Meideros had changed the complexity of the match in a matter of seconds and went ahead 4-2.

Ribeiro, sensing the tide had turned against him, attempted several half-guard moves but they were well defended. It became apparent that Ribeiro had nothing left in the tank. The effects of his long travel, along with Meideros' pressure and solid positions, had exhausted him and the match ended 4-2 with Meideros on top, surprising many doubters who had predicted that Ribeiro would dominate him.

showed himself to be a classy and gracious winner: "This is a aulo defeated me in the Rio State Championships and I want-

Saulo (top) getting to Comprido's side.

ed to even the record. He is one of the top competitors in the world and I am fortunate to come out the victor today." Ribeiro also showed a high level of sportsmanship: "Comprido is an excellent competitor, and at this level of competition one can expect these things. I wasn't feeling good today, I couldn't sleep last night, and he took advantage of the opportunity that was presented to him. Congratulations to him—but I'll be back."

Heavyweight Finals
Mark Robinson vs. Jeff Monson

As the heavyweight finals began, the certainty of Mark Robinson's victory seemed a given to most of the crowd. Robinson is a world champion sumo wrestler, a national judo and sambo champion in his native South Africa, and the current WEF super heavyweight champion—he also out-weighted Monson by 100 lbs. Pressing his weight advantage, Robinson spent most of the 15- minute regulation time attacking Monson's guard, and had the 1999 ADCC champion smothered and defensive. With only 15 seconds to go, however, Monson somehow managed to get between Robinson's legs for a half-guard sweep and score

Final Results

Lightweight Division
1) Leo "Leozinho" Vieira
2) Vitor "Shaolin" Ribeiro
3) Fernando "Terere"
4) Matt Serra

Middleweight Division
1) Rodrigo "Comprido" Meideros
2) Saulo Ribeiro
3) Dean Lister
4) Phillip Smith

Heavyweight Division
1) Jeff Monson
2) Mark Robinson
3) Ze Mario "Esfiha"
4) Garth Taylor

Superfight Champions
Luis "Limao" Heredia
Kathy Brothers
Cleber Luciano
Wander Braga
Gustavo Machado

Main Event Champion
Royler Gracie

Comprido and Saulo in a half-guard battle.

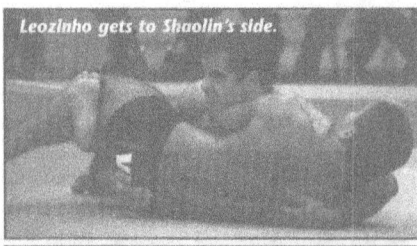

Leozinho gets to Shaolin's side.

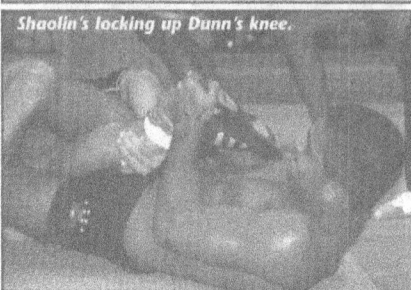

Shaolin's locking up Dunn's knee.

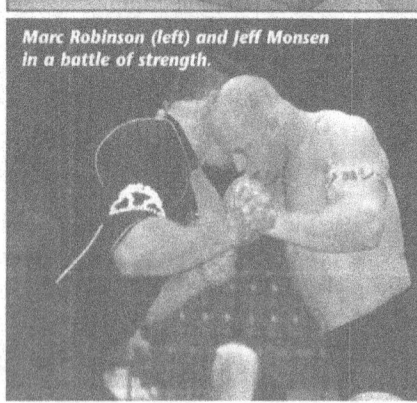

Marc Robinson (left) and Jeff Monsen in a battle of strength.

at the buzzer. Robinson, angry with himself and at losing the match in the final seconds, tried to start a fight with Monson, pushing him twice. Monson restrained himself, however, and Robinson quickly regained control of his emotions. Later, in a show of good sportsmanship, Robinson was seen apologizing and chatting amicably with Monson.

Featured Superfight
Royler Gracie vs. Anthony Hamlett

After a ho-hum superfight between an injured (two broken ribs) Megaton Dias and winner Gustavo Machado, the featured match took center stage—the rematch between Royler Gracie and Anthony Hamlett. The two had met once before, during the ADCC 2000 semifinals last March, with Gracie winning by points. Since then, Hamlett had been actively seeking a rematch. He stated many times that he hated losing more than anything and that he thought he was "out-strategized" by the much-more experienced Gracie, rather than physically beaten. Hamlett trained hard for the rematch. He had four months advance notice for the fight and with the help of coach Matt Hume, refined his fighting approach and devised what he thought would be a winning strategy. Royler also prepared hard for the match, wanting to prove to the Hamlett and the world that he was still top dog. Without the pressure of the ADCC tournament hanging on his shoulders, and with only one match to fight, he was confident he could unleash his fearless, go-for-it style that he felt Hamlett had not seen at ADCC. Before the match he said, "I am really well-prepared and I am going to go at him like a pit bull!"

The stage was set, with both fighters very determined and with a strong desire to prove their valor and skill. Both fighters wanted not only to win, but to destroy their opponent. But, of course, only one could succeed. As the referee signaled the start of the match, Hamlett snapped Gracie down and attempted to take his back. Gracie defended and the two stood up again. Hamlett again snapped Gracie to the ground, but this time Gracie put Hamlett in his guard and immediately attacked Hamletts foot. Hamlett responded by attacking Royler s opposite foot. Both fighters were not holding anything back, but Royler had a much better position and applied crushing pressure. In desperation, Hamlett tried to spin out of the lock but it was too late—the pressure was too much and he was forced to scream- out in submission. The referee stopped the fight. Royler Gracie, once again, had had proven himself to be the class of the field and perhaps the entire world.

Comprido (right) attacks Lister's arm and shoulder.

Middleweight champ Comprido.

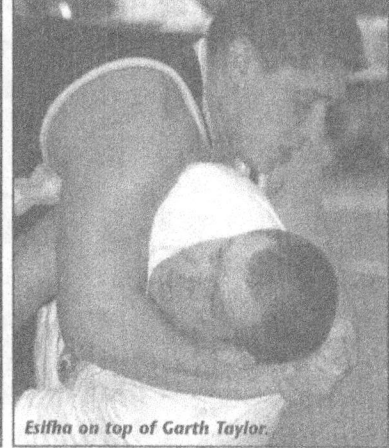
Esifha on top of Garth Taylor.

Final Words

The inaugural International Pro-Am was by most measures a resounding success—because great fighters make for a great event. If the promoters maintain the matchmaking formula next year, choose a hosting city that houses more grappling academies, and run the event during a more suitable time of year (anything but winter on the East Coast), then they will attract the spectators that the event lacked this year and thereby ensure a total and complete success. The vision, dedication, and hard work of promoters Frank Mullis and Billy Dowey is the kind of effort that will help push submission grappling to new levels of success in the United States, and help it to become a mainstream, accepted sport.

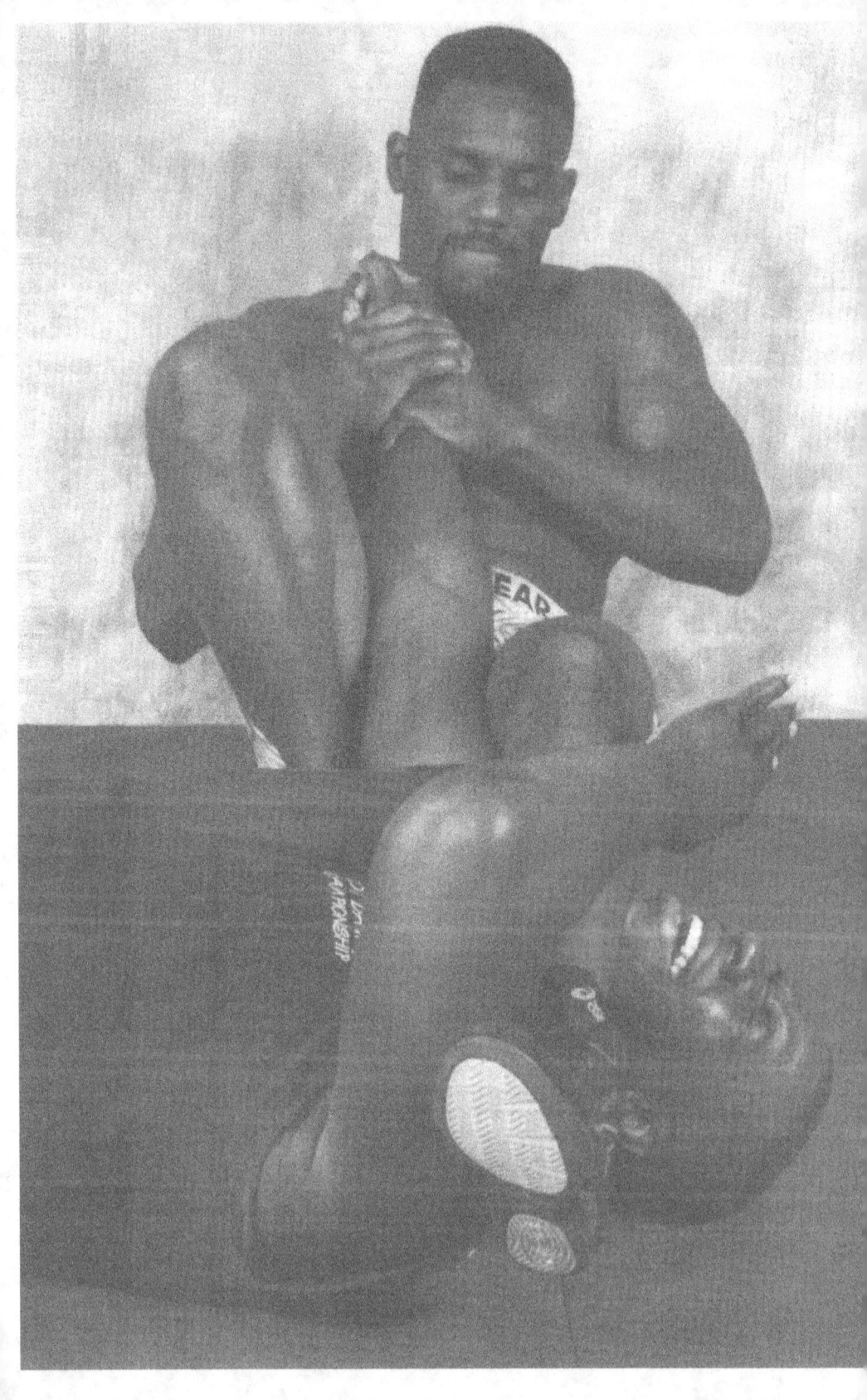

Antonio McKee
The Great Mandingo

Todd Hester, story and photos

"Mft fl andingo," is a nickname given to Antonio McKee by his wife that means "intelligent war- Iwl rior." The words "intelligent," and "warrior" are both terms which fit the 30-year-old ■ ■ wrestler turned no-holds-barred fighter like a freestyle singlet. A California state high school wrestling champion out of Long Beach, California, McKee also won two California state junior college titles while wrestling out of nearby Cerritos College. During his wrestling prime he was undefeated for five years, held a gaudy record of 112-0, and defeated Olympian John Smith in an exhibition match. After winning his second state JC title, he left wrestling for nine years to open up a chain of successful mobile communications stores—Crown Communications. But grappling was still in his blood and at the age of 30, after seeing the Gracie family and those who practiced their eclectic style of grappling win numerous events in the new sport of mixed martial arts, McKee came back. Showing the same competitive fire, skill and courage that made him a champion in his younger years, McKee has started in where he left off—resuming his winning ways and serving notice that he is a force to be reckoned with.

Q: Your no-holds barred record is 14-1, right?

A: Something like that. I started fighting in November of 1999. I've been fighting NHB for about a year or so. I started up after being away from wrestling for nine years then just decided to get back into wrestling through no-holds-barred. I was a three-time state wrestling champion which included one year as the California state high school wrestling champion and then two years as the California state junior college champion. During that time I was undefeated for 5 years. I guess what basically happened is that I got bored with it and just stopped. It stopped being a challenge for me so I moved on to other things. I went to Long Beach Polytechnic High School and then Cerritos Junior College.

Q: How did you get started in no-holds-barred?

A: I got interested in it because I went into a Brazilian jiu-jitsu school on a whim and ended up getting arm-barred three times—and I didn't understand it and had no idea what was going on.

Q: What made you go into a Brazilian jiu-jitsu school?

A: I was hearing about all this Gracie stuff and I had beaten up two Brazilian jiu-jitsu students before pretty easily. So when I saw a school locally, in Long Beach, I decided to just walk in and see what's up. That's when I met Mr. Francisco Bueno, and that's when I got arm-barred three times. I rolled

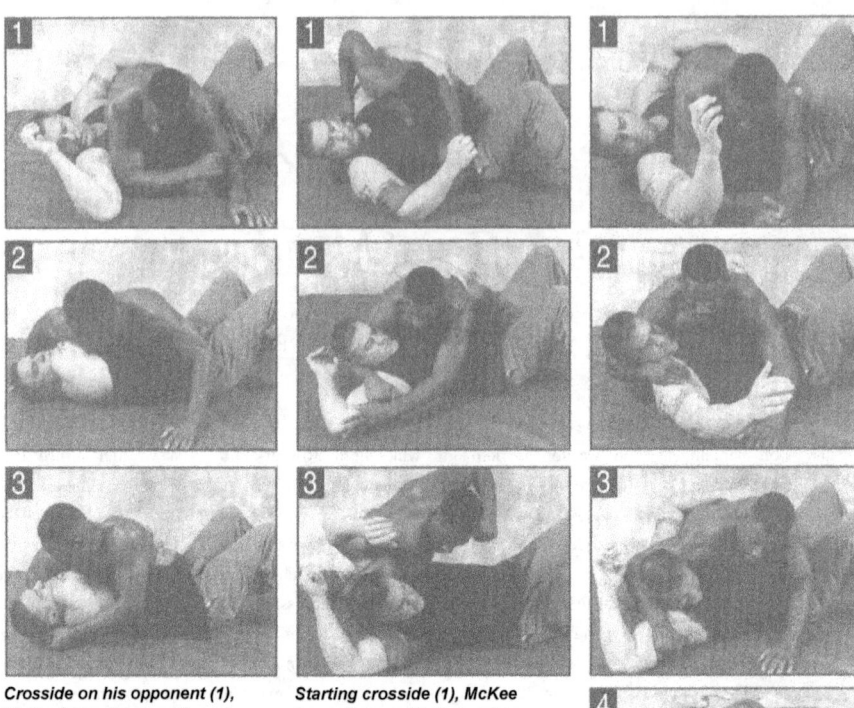

Crosside on his opponent (1), McKee traps the arm (2), and applies a choke (3).

Starting crosside (1), McKee traps the arm (2), then raises up to punch (3).

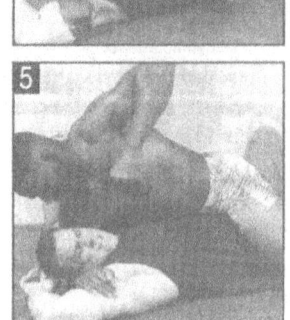

In crosside control (1), McKee traps the head (2), controls the arm (3), takes the mount (4) and prepares to punch (5).

with his students to begin with, but his students weren't having no fun with me. So then Francisco Bueno got on the mat with me, and then all of a sudden I wasn't having no fun. It was a whole different game with him. I saw the actual expertise of a real martial arts master. I mean, as a champion wrestler I had the base, the aggressiveness, and the good position but it didn't mean a thing against him. I was just shocked—completely puzzled. I didn't understand it for weeks. I kept thinking about it and wondering how someone could do that to me after I had been so dominating in wrestling for so many years. I mean guys couldn't even take me down—and then to get arm-barred three times in a matter of minutes was a total shock. I didn't even know what an arm bar was. But Francisco Bueno sure showed me.

Q: So after that what did you do?

A: I started doing some submission training with Joe Charles and his Dog Pound Grapplers school, learning positions and submissions—which are very different from wrestling. So I started putting things together with him, incorporating some of my favorite wrestling moves with joint locks and chokes. I also trained with Tedd Williams of Combat Grappling. Then things started coming together for me.

Q: How long was it from the time you walked into a Brazilian jiu-jitsu school that you had your first cage fight?
A: Four days. I trained for four days. I'll never forget because I found out about the fight on Saturday, started training for it on Sunday, and then had the fight on Wednesday—which I won. Some guys train for years before they fight. So I have to laugh when I think about it. My opponent was Shannon "The Cannon" Ritch, the guy who just fought Sakuraba in the feature fight in Pride. I didn't know anything so I basically just beat him into submission until he couldn't go anymore. All I knew how to do was punch in the ribs, punch in the ribs, and punch in the ribs—but it was effective. I guess five minutes straight of getting punched in the ribs did the job. But that's all I knew—take him down and punch

him in the ribs.

Q: What weight do you feel most comfortable fighting at?
A: I'm about 160 pounds and that's what I like to fight at. I like to fight bigger guys, though. I beat Shannon and he was Sakuraba's weight— I'd love to fight Sakuraba. I don't care, I've got nothing to lose. You put me with the best and I'm sure I'll step up and answer. I'll always rise to the level of my competition—that's just how I am. Give me a name and a date and I'll do what
I have to do. Like when I wrestled John Smith in a exhibition match in college. He hadn't been beaten in several years but yet I beat him. It was right before he lost to that Cuban in international competition. I felt that I rose to the occasion then, too. I've always had that knack.

> "I mean guys couldn't even take me down—and then to get arm-barred three times in a matter of minutes was a total shock. I didn't even know what an arm bar was. But Francisco Bueno sure showed me."

Q: Your only loss in no-holds-barred came in the King of the Cage?
A: Correct. To Chris Brennan. I was dominating in the first round, then I got caught with a kick that I wasn't expecting and I went down. Honestly, I still have questions about that fight. I did not feel like myself and even though I got caught with the kick, it wasn't all that hard. Before that fight I was training for an hour-and-a-half straight each day—just rotating guys in one after another. So for me to be sucking wind after only five minutes was very hard for me to figure out. I just didn't feel like myself in that fight—not to take anything away from Chris—but that fight did just not feel right. I would love to get a rematch with Chris in King of the Cage.

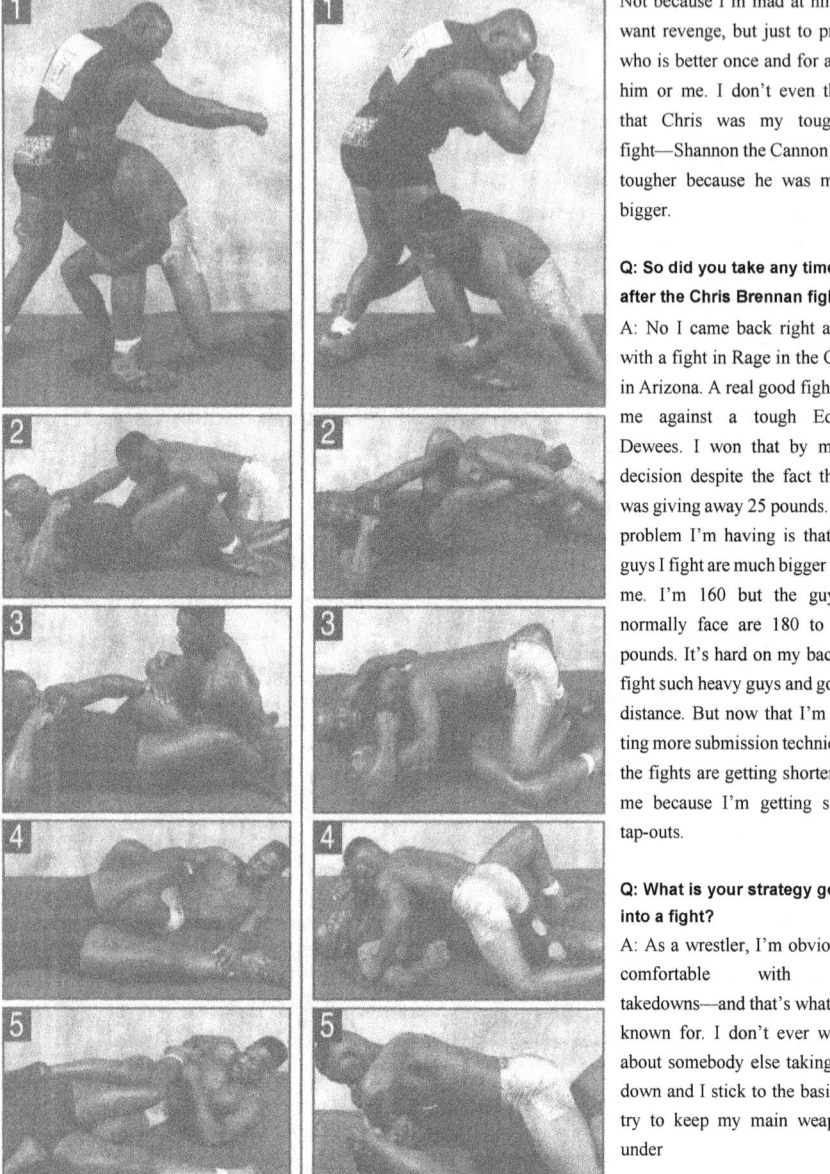

Facing Joe Charles (1), McKee takes him down (2), controls the knee (3), leans back (4), and applies a foot lock (5).

Shooting low (1), McKee takes Joe Charles down (2), passes his guard (3), gets side control (4), then mounts for the key lock (5).

Not because I'm mad at him or want revenge, but just to prove who is better once and for all—him or me. I don't even think that Chris was my toughest fight—Shannon the Cannon was tougher because he was much bigger.

Q: So did you take any time off after the Chris Brennan fight?

A: No I came back right away with a fight in Rage in the Cage in Arizona. A real good fight for me against a tough Edwin Dewees. I won that by major decision despite the fact that I was giving away 25 pounds. The problem I'm having is that the guys I fight are much bigger than me. I'm 160 but the guys I normally face are 180 to 200 pounds. It's hard on my back to fight such heavy guys and go the distance. But now that I'm getting more submission techniques the fights are getting shorter for me because I'm getting some tap-outs.

Q: What is your strategy going into a fight?

A: As a wrestler, I'm obviously comfortable with my takedowns—and that's what I'm known for. I don't ever worry about somebody else taking me down and I stick to the basics. I try to keep my main weapons under wraps because I want to save them for the big fights and the big paydays. There are a lot of questions like, "Does McKee have hands? Can McKee kick?" I don't really feel I have to answer that because right now people respect me for my takedowns. So I'll let them focus on that, let them study the tapes of my fights and expect me to come out and only do takedowns. Then they'll have a surprise when they don't meet a takedown. I'll open up another whole can of worms for them to deal with. I've got more game that I've let people see. Right now I'm just doing the bare minimum it takes to win. But when the right time comes against the right opponent then I'll let the dogs out.

Q: What's your training schedule like?
A: I love to train. I train in my sleep. I train from about 6:30 PM until about 9:00 PM. Sometimes I'll go until 2:00 AM, if I can find anyone to train that late. I just go until I'm tired—and it is hard for me to get tired. I would like to move into the upper echelon of fighting—get some fights in Japan and some in Europe—I've been working with Tedd Williams to make some things happen so I'm hopeful. I'm ready, you know. I'm 30 years old and I want to take on the world's best within the next five years or so, while I'm still in my fighting prime. I'm an intelligent entrepreneur so I want to make a name for myself, be able to say that I did it, and then move to the next level of life—whatever that may be.

Q: Do you have any fear of the Brazilian style of jiu-jitsu?
A: Oh, no. I love to fight the guys who do the Brazilian style because they have this idea that they can dominate anyone on the ground and so they will play around in my own backyard. I've fought some of the most effective jiu-jitsu players and I know that I've given them nightmares because of what I've done to them in their guard. So I don't feel any particular threat from Brazilian jiu-jitsu over any other style. I feel more threatened by a wrestler because I have so much respect for wrestlers that I might not go out as hard against them.

Q: You've got a successful line of mobile communications stores in Southern California. What is driving you to get back on the mat and into the cage?
A: I've got an ego problem in the sense that I always want to be the best at whatever I do. I've got a competition demon living of me and he's manifesting himself. Seriously, I don't know. I just like to fight and accomplish things. This goes for business, for being a husband, for being a father, and for being a fighter. Everything for me has been a fight to make it work—so this is just another expression of my personality to overcome whatever I'm facing.

Q: What makes the difference between the guy who wins in the cage and the one who gets carried out?
A: I think 90 percent of it is just having the belief in yourself that you're going to win—that you're not going to let your opponent impose his will on you. That's all that I think about when I fight— I'm going to win. There is no in-between or no thinking that maybe I'll win, or that I hope I win, or that I want to win—just that I will win. I put a lot of pressure on myself. I don't really think about the people who are watching. I just think about how I'm going to perform—because I'm a winner, you know? I've always been on top, so there's more fear of losing for me than anything else. I don't accept anything other than my best. I just have to go do it. I've talked to Michael Jordan and Dennis Rodman about this and they're the same way—they have a winner's mentality. Now I understand that other level of being good. Because I can relate to these people who just keep pushing themselves until they're eventually the best without realizing they're the best—because they're still trying to be the best. So mentally you never let up. You just keep going and going and going.

Heath Herring

*From Amarillo to Amsterdam—
The Odyssey of a Small-Toum Superstar*

Todd Hester, story and photos

Heath Herring has packed more down-home, honest-to-goodness, country wisdom into his twenty-one short years on Planet Earth than Andy Griffith, Jed Clampett, and the Duke boys did in their years on prime-time television combined. An apparent overnight sensation who emerged from nowhere to beat Tom Erikson and Enson Inoue in recent bouts in Pride, Herring is in reality a seasoned no-holds-barred fighter with 40-plus matches who has paid his dues, fighting on dirt rodeo floors for travel money, and in bars with ceilings so low that, "if you jumped too high you'd hit your head."

The youngest of all the current Pride gladiators, and the star of Amsterdam's Golden Glory team, Herring is a big-time fighter with small-town roots who has not let sudden success go to his head— far from it. He prefers to surround himself with people who will tell what he did *wrong* in a fight, will work him rather than praise him, and who don't mind giving him a swift kick in the pants when he slacks off—which isn't very often.

With his feet firmly planted in his solid Texas belief system of hard work, loyalty, and self-reliance, Herring seems like he'll be counted among the fighting elite for years to come. "You're always going to make mistakes," Herring says, "and you've always got to look at your mistakes and face up to them. Because when you stop looking at your mistakes and only look at what you did good, then your weaknesses are exposed. If you're looking for affirmation from someone else all the time, it means that you really have no self-belief inside yourself. And if you don't believe in yourself then no amount of empty praise will change that."

Q: How did you get introduced to no-holds-barred fighting?
A: It all started back in the USWF back in 1996 in Amarillo, Texas. I had just graduated from high school where I had wrestled. Steve Nelson was running some shootfighting shows in Amarillo and one of my really good friends from high school and I decided that we were going to start training together and enter it. So we both got into a show and I ended up getting into the finals against Paul Jones. My buddy made it to the semi-finals against Jones and then I got into the finals and lost to Jones. Going into the thing I thought that if I only won one fight in the tournament that I'd be happy. My friend and I were both wrestlers in high school but we'd never had any formal martial arts training of any kind. But we'd gone to a couple of shootfighting classes that Steve Nelson gave and he

> **"I surprised myself by making Jones work hard—
> he had to use one rope escape when I caught him in a key lock.
> He did finally make me tap with a choke, and it was the only time
> I've tapped, and it was the worst feeling in my life."**

showed us few very basic things—a choke, the Achilles leg lock, the arm bar, the key lock—just enough to confuse us.

I remember my first fight that night was against the Canadian national sombo champ. I was just out of high school and weight around 240, and he weighed something like 325 and was a one-time world bench press champion also who pressed something like 600 pounds. So he was huge. And the funny thing was that my Dad walked up to the ring with me, and when he saw the guy his eyes got real big and he tapped me on the shoulder, shook his head, and said, "Well, son, good luck."

And then, of course, after going into the tournament and making it that far I was happy with what I did. I surprised myself by making Jones work hard—he had to use one rope escape when I caught him in a key lock. He did finally make me tap with a choke, and it was the only time I've tapped, and it was the worst feeling in my life. But on the other hand, everyone was happy with the fight and I was happy that I had made it that far, so it gave me a lot of interest in continuing the sport and made me think that maybe this was something that I could be good at. So it just went one from there.

Q: Were you an exceptional high school wrestler?
A: No, far from it. I didn't wrestle until my senior year and I didn't really know anything. I played football—that was my main sport—I played the defensive line and I did get a scholarship to a local college in Amarillo, West Texas A&M. I was there for a while until I started to concentrate on my fighting career.

Q: So what happened after the first USWF?
A: After the first USWF, which was a big hit in Amarillo and sold out, the next show also sold out. And that was the first time I'd ever been paid to fight. Which was totally amazing to me that I'd get paid. It wasn't that much money, I guess, only $500 bucks, but it was a lot of money to me. And it wasn't a tournament either, just a single fight. So I was really happy about that. I won that one, and then football was going on and the football coach didn't want me to do it anymore. So I took another fight, though, but got paid a little less because they guy I fought wasn't as good.

Then I hooked up with a guy named Craig Kimberland, who is a really good submission instructor, and started training with him. That's really where all my submission skills come from. Craig had learned submission from a guy who had done a lot of self-defense stuff in the Army. So he came from a military self-defense, commando background. It's a lot like judo or jiu-jitsu. It's not real rigid and it's very adaptable. It's usable and it works. I really like Craig's style and a lot of what I do is still reflection of him.

What also really helped me in his training is that I never got used to training with a gi. I never got used to just wrestling without trying to strike. I was never into anything long enough to get really bad habits that might be good for sports but are bad for no-holds-barred.

Heath Herring Pocket Bio

Twenty-one years old, he is originally from Amarillo, Texas where he played football and wrestled in his senior year. While on a football scholarship to West Texas A&M, he saw the USWF and decided to try it out, making it to the finals in his first event. He then fought 20 or 30 shows before going to the WVC, where he fought in an 8-man tournament, losing to Cacareco in the finals in Aruba. He then fought in the Superbrawl Heavyweight Tournament and lost by decision to Bobby Hoffman in the semifinals. He then won the next WVC in Aruba, then got a football and wrestling scholarship to a college in Pennsylvania, only to leave before the semester started when he was offered a spot on the Golden Glory Team in Holland, training with Coors Hemmers. In his first fight with the team he lost in the Ultimate in Russia due to a cut forehead. He then got a contract with Pride, though the Golden Glory, and racked up wins against Willie Peters, Tom Erikson, and Enson Inoue.

Q: So what is your strategy in a fight? Punch-out your opponents or submit them?

A: I had absolutely no stand-up training at all until recently. I was usually bigger than all my opponents and I was usually stronger. So it was just bulldoze in there and see what happens. Usually I'd try to finish with a key lock or a choke—just whatever came up. Usually my fights would end up with a ground-and-pound situation. Before my last fights with Erikson and the Enson Inoue I was fighting at 280. I felt good at 280 but now I feel much, much better at 230—my conditioning is much better for one thing.

Q: So how long did you stay with the USWF?

A: I fought in the USWF off-and-on for a couple of years or so. During this same time I was also fighting in New Mexico shows that my father was promoting. He had hooked up with a guy from New Mexico, Eddie Deluca, and they put on shows there for a while. It was pretty okay working for my dad. I mean he didn't really feel obligated to pay me, but I got room and board so we had a good time out there. But at least we were fighting indoors in a real arena, which was much better than the USWF. We fought on a dirt rodeo floor in some of those early shows—you know, just brush the cow crap out of the way and start swinging. So I've came up through some tough shows and gone through some tough times.

Sometimes people look at how young I am and think that I really got lucky at an early age to hit it so big in Pride. But my biggest asset, actually, is that I have paid my dues. I have fought for no money plenty of times in the worst places you can imagine. I've had a ton of fights—probably 40 or 50—and I've gone against some bad men and never complained about it. I've fought in bars in Durango, Colorado, where if I jumped very high in the ring I would hit my head on the ceiling. You know, you kind of pay your dues so when you do get to a good show like Pride, you really want to do all you can to stay there—because you know what else is out there and it is nothing in comparison. I was a B-circuit fighter for around four years.

Heath Herring absorbs a kick from Dutch kickboxer Bob Shriver.

A: During that time I fought in Superbrawl, for TJ. Thompson, which is upper B-level. I really like TJ. so I have to give him a nod. I mean, it is in Hawaii. So even if it's a bad show you're still in paradise. It was the same way when I fought in the WVC in Aruba for Frederico Lapenda before I did Superbrawl. I got treated really good by the WVC. I got airfare, I got to eat whatever I wanted, I had a really nice hotel for a week, so that is another upper B-level show. The only thing that keeps it from being A-level is that they don't pay the fighters very much. But a lot of the other shows don't even pay your airfare, and you have to buy your own food. So the first time I went to Aruba for Lapenda that was like a miracle for me.

Q: So the WVC in Aruba was your first event out of the country after fighting in a lot of dub shows?
A: Yeah, it was. I had actually quit fighting for a year or so right before that. At around the age of 19 I just basically stopped fighting. I got married and had a kid, got a job—those things all take time. But one day Eddie Deluca called me up out of the blue and asked me if I wanted to fight in Aruba. So I went there absolutely by myself, no cornerman or anything—it was a little crazy. I was in a 8-man tour-

nament and I got off the plane totally by myself, wearing my camouflage hat, fresh from Texas, looking totally like a redneck—Ron Niquist, who was one of the producers of the show, still laughs about it. I actually can't even think what was in my head at the time. All logic dictates that was one of the stupidest things you can do—going to foreign soil all by yourself to fight in a no-holds-barred tournament. If I had been seriously injured, or hurt, or gotten into trouble no one would have known.

"But my biggest asset, actually, is that I have paid my dues. I have fought for no money plenty of times in the worst places you can imagine. I've had a ton of fights—probably 40 or 50—and I've gone against some bad men and never complained about it."

Q: But you made it to the finals, right?
A: Yeah, surprisingly I did. I didn't know anyone who was in the tournament. It was my first true no-holds-barred fight. You could head butt, elbow, kick on the ground—you could do anything. So I got through the first round okay against a pretty experienced cage fighter; then I went up against this crazy Russian who had won some extreme boxing event in Japan—and I had to knock his teeth out before he would tap. Then I got up against Cacareco in the finals and we went something like 35 minutes to a draw—and then he ended up winning by decision because he was so much lighter than me. It was wild—just crazy. So after it was all over with everyone went out drinking at the bar but I was so tired that I just went back to the hotel and went to sleep. I just took a shower and basically passed out.

Q: Was Cacareco your toughest fight physically so far?
A: It was my toughest fight mentally because I was so tired that it was all I could do to keep going and not quit. I had two tough fights before that. The first fight against Irwin Van Stien wasn't a super tough fight—I took him down to the mat and then ground-and-pounded him for about five minutes but it hurt my knuckles. Then the fight against the Russian in the second round was tough. I caught him in a key lock and turned it all the way over and ripped everything out. I wanted him to tap and told him to tap but he just wouldn't do it. So then I had to let it go and mount him and then just start punching him in the face. Those fights are tough on your body even if you win—my knuckles are still swollen up from that night and I still have trouble in my hand. Then, of course, with Caraceco we went 35 minutes basically trying to kill each other. Your body is just destroyed. You can't do that type of fighting in one night, on a regular basis.

Q: After the Cacareco fight did you think that if you could do that, you could do anything?
A: Well, that's one thing that I do remember thinking before I left Texas to go to Aruba. "This is a gauge. Is this something I need to keep pursuing or am I in over my head and should I start looking for something else to spend my weekends doing?" So I just went to test myself and I ended up doing really good by my standards. So I just decided to keep it up and see where it led.

After that I went to Superbrawl in Hawaii for TJ. in that big heavyweight tournament where actually there were a lot of good fighters who are all doing something now. Every time I think about it I actually get to laughing because everyone there was so tough. You had Bobby Hoffman, John Marsh, Ricco Rodriguez, Travis Fulton, Rocky Bastini, Josh Barnett, and me. So this was an all-star event. First guy I had was Rocky Bastini and I ended up choking him out in the first round. Then I got Hoffman in the second round. And to tell you the truth I've never even seen the video of the fight, but from what T.J. has told me it was just me and Hoffman beating the hell out of each other for the full 15 minutes. I caught Hoffman in a keylock and I heard it pop—it was locked in solid—after that fight I heard that Hoffman had to take off 6 months to heal. But he got the decision and went to the finals. That just shows you how tough Hoffman is because he went to the finals and fought Barnett after our fight with a messed-up arm for the full 15 minutes. The major fights in that tournament all went to decisions. It was me and Hoffman to a decision; then Hoffman and Barnett in the finals going to a decision, with Barnett getting it done.

But that was a great show when you look at it. Ricco and I fight in Pride now, Barnett is still undefeated, Hoffman is turning up in Rings and the UFC—he gave Maurice Smith a really good fight.

Q: Then from there it was back to Aruba and the WVC?
A: Yeah, I went to Aruba again a few months later and won the whole thing, beating Bob Shriver from Holland in the finals because Cacareco got hurt in the semifinals and had to withdraw. So that was a great win for me. Then I got another scholarship to go wrestle and play football at a college in Pennsylvania. Eddie set the whole thing up and then one day he calls me and says that I had an offer from Ron Niquist to go live and fight for him in Holland.

Pennsylvania was actually a very tough thing for me to give up, because I had everything there that I wanted. Everyone there was really, really nice to me and I could have finished my degree. But when the offer came to go to Holland to live and train I started thinking that I should do something with my life while the opportunity was there, rather than put everything on hold for 3 or 4 years and then try to pick it up later. So I decided to seize the day, and I packed up my bags and moved to Holland and signed with Ron and the Golden Golden Glory team. At the time I wasn't sure if I was doing the right thing. But 6 months later, with three victories in Pride, I know that it was the correct decision.

Q: So in a matter of weeks you went from Texas to Pennsylvania, and then to Holland. Was there a little culture shock?
A: Yeah, of course. I got to Holland in February, a year ago, and I'm thinking what the hell am I doing here? I didn't know anyone there. I knew Ron and I knew Bob Shriver and Gilbert Yvel and some of the other Dutch guys who'd fought in Aruba but that was it. So I started hanging out with Gilbert and training with him. This was around the time of the King of Kings tournament in Japan, which Gilbert ended up winning, so I went there with him, and that was my first time in Japan. So the whole thing was just a little bizarre to me. It didn't seem like reality.

Ron had the best of intentions in bringing me over but there wasn't anything solid for me. So by the middle of March I was just training on Gilbert's schedule—and Gilbert was in Amsterdam—so I had to travel an hour-and-a-half to do anything. So most of the time I was just sitting around by myself not doing anything. Then Ron hooked me up with one of the top stand-up trainers in Holland, Coors Hemmers. And then I started training full-time for real, starting in April.

Q: Did you do any fighting during this time?
A: I went to the Absolute in Russia, which was a total mistake for me. It was really one of the scariest things I have ever done and not because of who I had to fight. I got cut on the head in my first fight of the 8-man tournament and they stopped the fight. So I thought that I'd better get it stitched up because it was really long and deep. So I'm starting to go over there and Remco Pardo comes over and tells me, "Look, man, don't go. We'll go back to my room, I'll Superglue it shut, I'll put a butterfly on it, and

Heath Herring battling Michael Tielroy in Aruba.

then I'll take you to the hospital when we get back to Holland." I'm thinking, who the hell is Remco? In America when you get hurt you go to the hospital and that's that. So I left with a Russian trainer.

I found out that night that Remco is a very, very wise man—wise beyond his years—I will never doubt anything he tells me again. We get to the hospital and it is worse than any John Romero horror film you can imagine. *The Night of the Living Dead* was a light comedy compared to this place. There were dead bodies stacked in the corridors and lying uncovered everywhere. Blood was all over the operating room and they sat me down in a pool of warm blood—someone else's blood—on a table and stitched me up. I just wasn't sure I was going to make it out of there alive. If there was anything that made me appreciate democracy and Western civilization it was the Moscow City Hospital. And I was a VIP from America. I can't even imagine how they treat locals who go there. I think it is a place where life just isn't worth very much.

And I say that not to be mean. The event was well-run, it was promoted right, there was a big crowd, it was covered by the large newspapers, and there were even a lot of very high-ranking politicians there. So it was a good event. I think the plight of the Russian nation is mainly the result of their economic situation and how the general public was misused by the old political system for so many years. I mean the Russian people are friendly, the historical buildings like the Kremlin are beautiful, and they do the best with what they have—they just don't have very much.

Q: Did anyone else warn you about that fight?
A: Yeah, Coors Hemmers, my coach, also told me not to take it—told me that I didn't need it. Coors is a funny guy. Every time he has a new fighter come and train with him he says they always lose their

first fight. So actually, in retrospect, we both laugh about how it was good that I took that fight in Russia because I got that first loss out of the way and was then able to go into Pride and do well. Because my next fight was in Pride.

Q: Were shocked when your next fight was in Pride?
A: Yeah, of course. I had always dreamed about fighting in Pride, and I was coming off a loss, then all of a sudden there I am. It was really a result of Gilbert having won the King of Rings tournament. That gave Ron a lot of leverage and so he used the promise of Gilbert fighting to also get a fight deal for me. So I have to give a lot of credit to Gilbert and Ron for that. There are not a lot of fighters who make it to Pride and everyone wants to go—so for me it was a genuine honor.

Q: Do you feel limited by th41e small pool of fighters that you face in Pride?
A: Is it a limited pool or is it an elite pool comprised of the top fighters? I actually prefer it because you know all the fighters and you know what they've done and you know their tendencies. I think that's what helped me out in my first few Pride fights. I was the unknown factor and no one was really sure what I could do. No one knew that I could kick, for example, and that took Tom Erikson by surprise when I fought him. I lost so much weight from my first Pride fight against Willie Peters, that I think people didn't know what to make of it. I went from 260 pounds to around 230. It was really a transformation and people thought that they'd be fighting a jumbo-sized brawler and I came out as a stand-up striker and that threw a lot of people.

Q: How was your first Pride fight against Willie Peters?
A: Yeah, they brought Gilbert into fight Vitor Belfort and I was there to be the first fight of the night against Willie. Initially, I was supposed to be fighting Marcelo Tiger from Hawaii. But that didn't come through for some reason—and I'm not sure why to this day—but they got a replacement and it was Willie. It was a very good victory for me. I won by a choke in less than a minute. But I was bigger and stronger and I came in well-trained so I felt really good about it—especially since Willie is well-known in Amsterdam for being a tough, hard fighter.

Q: What was the general feeling in Pride about you fighting Tom Erikson?
A: Well, I know that Pride was a little worried about the way I looked. They didn't want this huge, sloppy fighter coming in, so I trained hard to come in really fit. Pride tries to do a total package show, to appeal to the mainstream Japanese fight fans—which I totally understand and support. They didn't want me to wear a wrestling singlet, they wanted me to wear fighting shorts, and they wanted me to try to change my look and also my ring personality—which I did. So I did the Heath Herring makeover.

It was true that a lot of people thought that Erikson was going to kill me. But I was surrounded by Coors, Ron, Gilbert and the entire Golden Glory Team who believed in me, which really helped me. They all told me that I was going to win, and then they told me how I was going to do it. So I started believing it myself. I certainly wouldn't have taken the fight if I didn't think that I could beat him—and I know that Ron and Coors wouldn't have done it, either.

Heath Herring Training Routine

On Monday, Wednesday, and Friday it's usually Thai boxing from about 10 AM to about 12 PM. It consists of jumping rope, sparring, techniques, and bag training. Then in the evenings, depending on if we have somebody coming to train with us, we can either do some grappling or some more Thai training.

Tuesday and Thursdays we go and train with Remco Pardo and some guys with Germany in grappling and submission in the morning. Mainly ground training and techniques—sometimes we do some sparring. Then in the afternoons we do some lifting.

Then Saturday is a free day—sometimes we train depending on what Coors thinks. But it is usually free. Sundays are always off. Sometime I don't get out of bed at all but just sleep all day to recover from the training. Especially if it's a hard week.

So I basically train about four hours a day.

Cardiovascular Training
On Tuesday and Thursdays we get up early in the morning and run 7 or 8 kilometers, about 5 miles or so. Then after that we go do circuit sprint training, running hills to a certain time. And that is really, really hard. That has really helped my conditioning a lot.

Diet
Not really. I'm a big guy and I train hard so I pretty much work anything off. Coors Hemmars, my trainer, really doesn't impose anything on my. I naturally eat pretty well anyway. I like to eat a lot of lean steak and salad and stuff like that. Now in America, when I'm visiting, I eat like an idiot. I eat a lot of hamburgers and fries and fast food. But when I'm training I do a lot better. In Europe, actually, it harder to get a lot of really fatty food. I've found that the worst food in the world as far as being bad for you is in the United States.

Training and Fighting Philosophy
The percentage split between stand-up and grappling really depends a lot of the fighter. But speaking for myself, what I've done is spend a lot more time on stand-up fighting. So initially with Coors it was probably 70 percent stand-up to 30 percent grappling. But now I'm training both areas with maybe a slight emphasis on stand-up, because they're both important. People have a tendency to do what they're good at. Of course I'm better at wrestling so I'd prefer to roll around on the ground with someone and play the position game because that's fun for me, rather that stand up and get bashed by someone who's trained muay Thai for 10 years and just uses me as a punching bag. The fact of the matter is that I like to be on the ground. But if I don't spend time 1 sparring then I might play punching bag in a fight, rather than in practice which would be worse. I've heard a lot of guys who say "Wrestler will take anyone down and dominate them." Well, as you've seen in Pride that just isn't true anymore. Stand-up guys who have learned to wrestle around on the ground are really starting to catch-up now. In my personal experience it was my stand-up that won the fight against Erikson, not my grappling. It's nice to know that if you have to, you can land some high kicks on the guy across the ring from you—I've never had that feeling before. So I really enjoy it. Being a well-rounded fighter is really the only way to go. Against Inoue, for example, after I couldn't get him to tap on the ground with the key lock I just let it go and stood up. I didn't want to give him a chance to catch me with something funky from the guard. Being comfortable from anywhere in the ring it the key—especially in transition. I think now, that most submissions come in transition. Most everyone knows the set, static positions and it's hard to catch people now when you're trying to force a situation. You have to look for your *best* situation and not try to force *just any* situation.

Heath Herring in full attack mode.

Q: Tom Erikson was considered nearly unbeatable by a lot of people. Why did you think you had a chance?
A: Well, we just saw weaknesses in his style, we saw openings. I firmly believe that nobody is unbeatable—everybody has something they don't do well. My advantage with Erikson was that with the exception of Kevin Randleman, he hadn't really fought someone who was fairly big and strong. Was Erikson bigger than me? Yeah. He's around 280 and for this fight I was only 230. He was 130 kilos and I was 106 kilos, so that's 24 kilos or over 50 pounds difference. So I knew he was bigger. I knew I would have to use my conditioning and my quickness on the ground. I had to move and could not let him get on top and just ground-and-pound me, like I knew he wanted to do. I've fought a lot of ground-and-pound guys—hell, I'm a ground-and-pound guy—so I've learned to not be static on the ground, but to move with the punch so you don't take the full power, otherwise you'll just get destroyed.

So as the fight developed I did really, really good in my guard. He took me down but I kept him low in my guard so he could never use his strength and size and get really heavy shots. He landed one or two shots on me that were really good, otherwise I was moving with everything else. I went for a knee bar and maybe could have gotten that. I should have had an arm bar but in retrospect you can always find things you could have done better. But in Pride they have a 10 kilo rule: if your opponent is more than 10 kilos that you, and there is no action on the ground, they'll stand you up. So also because of the time limit, if there is no clear winner then the lighter fighter will win.

So going into the fight I knew that if could keep him from ground and pounding me that I'd do okay. Because with Tom Erikson you're really not going to worry about an arm bar, you're not going to worry about a knee bar. So I knew what he was going to do but he didn't know what I was going to do. He didn't know anything about my standup—or even if I had a stand-up. I'm sure he knew that I was training with Coors Hemmers—I'm sure he'd heard something. And that was my advantage. When I got the high kick in I don't think that he was expecting that at all. But that advantage is gone now.

But he also was a little bit tired at that point and was not quite as aggressive as he had been at the beginning of the fight. He was winded, but that was normal. It was a long fight. It was seven-and- a-half minutes with action the whole time. Then when I stood up my breath was fine because I've really been doing a lot of aerobics with Coors and we really focus on that with a lot of up and down training and such. So everything just worked out for me in that fight. Sometimes it happens that way. It was my night.

Q: What about your most recent Pride fight with Enson Inoue? He knew about your stand-up game.
A: Well, Enson was a totally opposite fight. I went from being a lot smaller than Erikson, to being a lot bigger than Enson. I went from being faster and quicker to being bigger and stronger—so my whole game plan changed. With Enson what really surprised me was that we figured him to come out and try to throw some big bombs right off, because he's known for that. But he didn't do that. He came out and measured me and that kind of threw me off. Usually Enson comes running across the ring like a bull, just throwing shots. So my training really concentrated on keeping my hands up and trying to keep from getting my head separated from my shoulders by a big shot—one punch is all it takes from a heavy puncher like him. So when he caught me early on, that was because I wasn't expecting him to take his time—and he really caught me. Luckily, I was able to recover and then take the fight to the ground.

On the ground the biggest concern, of course, was the arm bar which he has caught so many people with. So on the ground I wanted to stay on top and not give him room to operate. Use the knees, use the punches, and keep him on the defensive and not allow him to get into his offensive game, where he is ferocious. So I actually ended up on top and got a key lock, which really surprised me, because I would have thought he would have been too quick for that. And I think the only reason I did get it was I just kind of fell into it in transition and took it. Neither of us had time to think about it. It was just there and I grabbed it. I wasn't trying to set it up or anything like that—I'd like to be able to claim I was that smart or that good but I can't. So I was telling him to tap, because I had the arm twisted all the way back and I could hear things cracking in his arm. I told him, "Tap, Enson!" But Enson has never tapped, and seeing as how this was his farewell retirement fight from Pride, there was no way he was going to tap. So he just said, "Break it if you have to, but I'm not going to tap." So he actually ended up getting out, and then I was able to get his back and land several shots to his head that he couldn't answer so the referee stopped it.

> "We get to the hospital and it is worse than any John Romero horror film you can imagine. The Night of the Living Dead was a light comedy compared to this place. There were dead bodies stacked in the corridors and lying uncovered everywhere. Blood was all over the operating room and they sat me down in a pool of warm blood—someone else's blood—on a table and stitched me up. I just wasn't sure I was going to make it out of there alive."

To be honest, I'm glad I won but I thought the referee stepped in a little soon. I mean, I don't think Enson was seriously hurt. I know that his arm had to be sore but those punches to his head weren't all that hard and I thought that he was just recovering on the bottom more than anything else. So I thought that he deserved to fight on a little and see what he could do. But you have to live with those types of calls, good or bad, and I was glad that it went my way.

Q: Was it hard for you to fight in front of such big crowds in Pride?
A: When you're in the ring it could be one person in the stands or it could be 100,000 people—you just don't hear them or see them. And if Pride, I don't think about it. Afterwards I think about it— how big it is and how far I've come. I think about the dirt bars, and the rodeo floors and the cow dung, and how I just fought in front of 50,000 people in the Tokyo Dome and also all the people on pay-per-view. It's kind of mind-boggling. But you can't let yourself think like that before the fight. It's too distracting. That's one of the reasons that I really like Pride, because the ring is white, white, white, and the light reflects off it and really blinds you to the crowd. Your whole world becomes the ring. Plus, the Japanese fans are really quiet. You can be in there with 50,000 fans but you don't hear 50,000 fans. During the fight it's almost eerie. But in America you can be in the ring with 500 people in the crowd and it's so loud and you can't hear a thing because it's so loud.

Q: So with three Pride wins, what do you think your next level is? Who do you want to fight next?
A: I'm not that concerned about that right now. I'm still young. I don't have to be number one tomor-

row, or even a year from now. I'd like to be, of course, but I'm willing to be patient and let my skills develop and let Pride develop who and where I fight. But I also can't sit back on my laurels and think how good I've done and then not try to go any further. If you're not testing yourself and going forwards, then you're going backwards. So right now I'm doing good by fighting whoever Pride gives me. They've given me really good fights and really good opponents. Mainly, I want to keep fighting exciting fights. I think the thing that's helped me out is that I'm not afraid to lose. With Erikson I wasn't afraid to lose. With Inoue it was the same thing. I just went out there to win, not to not lose. So I've got to keep that competitive edge and that fire so I'm going out there loose and active. I just can't get afraid to lose. I think that when you get afraid to lose that you start fighting boring fights because you're too cautious.

Q: With so many people around you now, telling you this and that—how great you are or whatever— are you ever afraid that it will go to your head and you will lose your way?
A: That's the kind of thing I try not to do. I listen to what Coors and my trainers say, and then I let Ron handle the business end. I have people around that are close to me, that I care about and that I know care about me. They don't say "You're the best." After the Enson fight, watching the tape, Coors was telling me, "You know, your hands aren't good here. You legs were to slow at this point." So that keeps my head on the ground. It wasn't so much, "Good job." It was more like, "OK, what did you do wrong." He doesn't need to tell me good job. I mean, we won the fight so I know that and I don't need him to stroke my ego and I wouldn't want him to. The fact of the matter is that the fight wasn't flawless. We're not there yet. When I have a flawless fight and there was nothing at all wrong with it, then maybe he can tell me, "Good job." But I think it's impossible to have a fight like that. You're always going to make mistakes and then you've always got to look at your mistakes and face up to them. Because when you stop looking at your mistakes, and only start looking at what you did good, then your weaknesses are exposed—mentally and physically. Because if you're looking for affirmation from someone else all the time, it means that you really have no self-belief inside of you. If you don't believe in yourself then no amount of empty praise will change that.

How to Beat a Black Belt

Todd Medina

Martial arts, from the very beginning, were designed to help smaller and weaker individuals defend themselves against larger and stronger opponents. In almost any martial art this basic precept was the reason systems of self-defense were developed and practiced. From Chinese kung-fu to Japanese karate, or to any of the Eastern-based grappling arts such as judo or jiu-jitsu their goal is the same—to allow a weaker defender to overcome a strong attacker. This is a very important concept to remember when faced with an opponent who is at a higher skill level than you.

While a blue belt in jiu-jitsu is at a definite disadvantage against a brown or a black belt, there is no reason to throw in the towel without even trying to compete against them. This includes facing a higher belt in a friendly competition in the dojo or studio, or perhaps even facing a higher level belt in a grappling tournament or a no-holds-barred fight. The key to facing a higher ranking belt is to remember what they were trained to do because of the entire martial arts mentality and development, and then try to do something different. Play your game, don't play their game.

Because martial arts were designed for the weak to use against the strong, most all of the moves are based on leverage and position, not strength and speed. This is especially true in jiu-jitsu, which employs a methodical sequence of varied attacks in order to put the opponent into a position where they can either be struck by blows without being able to return them, or they can be choked unconscious or submitted via a joint lock. The positions and moves that are employed are designed to work regardless of the opponent's size or strength.

What this means, is that if you, as a white or blue belt, go at a skilled jiu-jitsu brown belt or black belt with power and speed, hoping to overpower them, you'll be playing right into their hands and will most likely end up being submitted by a variety of chokes or joint locks. Many are the times that I've seen unskilled but yet powerful wrestlers come into a jiu-jitsu school and take on a high belt by powerful takedowns and thundering body slams. While these moves are painful, and can cause bruises, they are not match-ending. Eventually, the most common outcome is for the brown or black belt to wait out the initial attack, wait for the wrestler to get tired and to overextend an arm or to expose their neck, and then to end the match via a triangle or some other unexpected move. So when dealing with a higher level belt, this is definitely the wrong strategy.

The best thing to do is the unexpected and to come at your opponent with something that they don't expect that does not play into their strength of using martial arts to combat strength and aggressiveness. The best moves that employ this strategy are leg locks and knee attacks. The best thing about leg locks is that most BJJ schools do not focus on them. While most BJJ black belts know some leg locks, they are much more familiar with upper-body strategies and moves dealing with arms bars and various types of chokes. So while grappling with them, even the most experienced black belt will

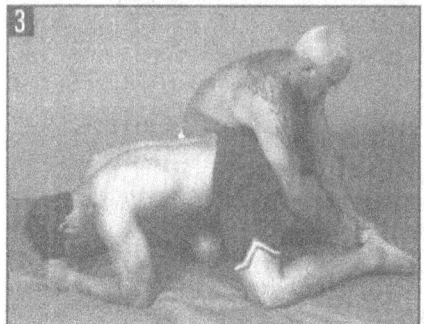
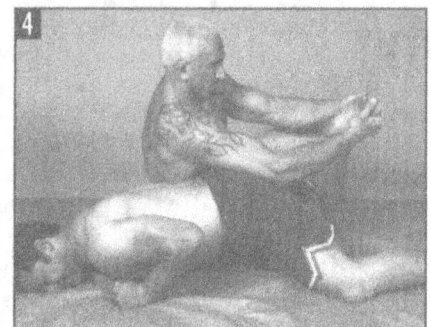

Todd Medina is facing a opponent who has "turtled up" (1). Medina slides to the side, confusing his opponent into thinking that he is trying to roll him to the side (2). However, Medina suddenly releases arm control and spins to the back, where he secures the ankle (3), and applies a painful leg submission (4).

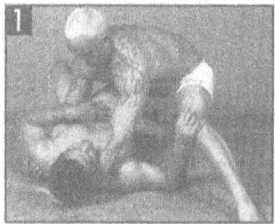
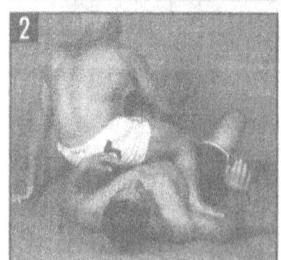
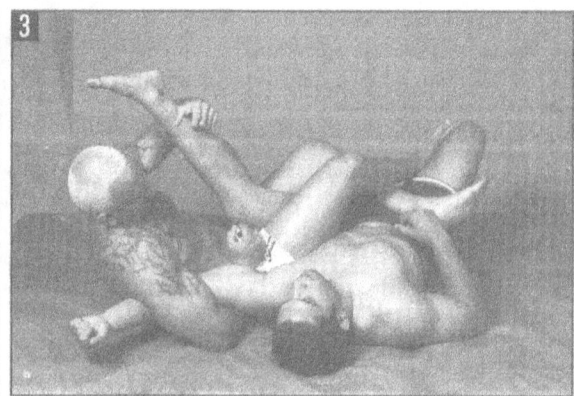

Todd Medina is in control of his opponent with his knee on the stomach (1). Instead of going for the expected and conventional mount position, though, Medina pivots on his inside foot and swings his outside foot over the head (2). Securing the ankle he leans back to the ground and traps the arm, and applies finishing pressure for the submission (3).

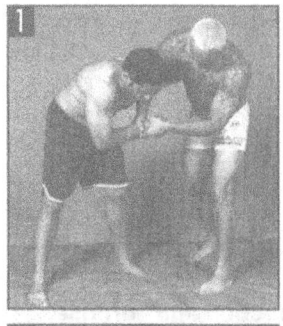
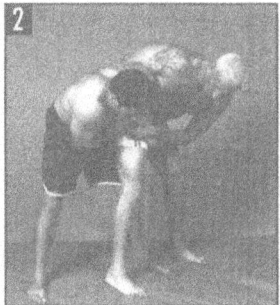
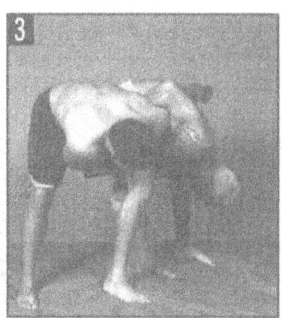

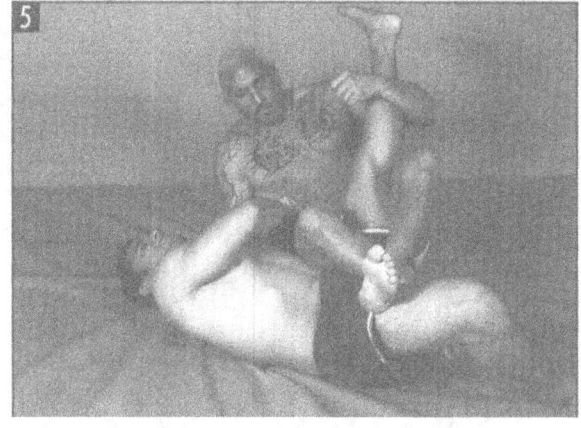

Todd Medina faces his opponent in a stand-up grappling situation (1). He steps inside with his outside foot (2), puts his weight forward (3), and then throws his opponent, rolling to the ground with him (4). Instead of trying to go to the conventional mount or side control, however, Medina keeps control of the leg, secures it with a figure-four, and then applies pressure for a successful leg submission (5).

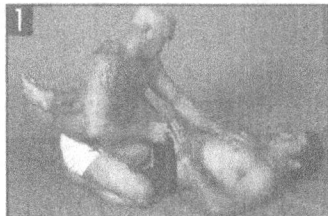
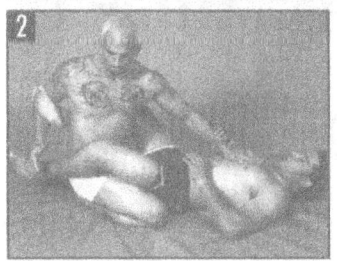
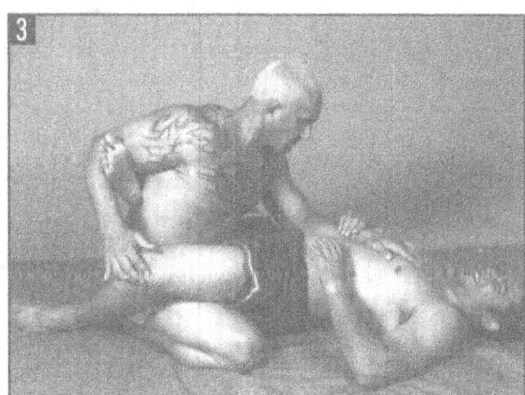

Caught in the guard (1), Todd Medina pivots outward and hooks the ankle (2), then applies forward pressure for the submission (3).

be thinking about defending the arm or the neck first, and will not be so worried about potential knee or ankle locks.

The second biggest advantage about using leg locks is that they are set-up out of a move that usually has a different attack focus, and so are very hard to spot until they are actually applied. This is especially helpful because it masks your intent and does not let the opponent know where the attack will come from. Because it also does not employ a lot of power, there is less danger that you are exposing yourself to a counterattack by exposing your neck or overextending an arm or an elbow.

Misdirection and surprise, not power and speed, are the keys to beating a skilled grappler who might be at a higher belt level than you.

The biggest key in successfully using leg attacks is to be mentally flexible. When you get to a point where you are on your opponent's back, for example, and are set up to attempt a rear choke (which a higher belt will usually successfully counter), consider other options. Don't get locked into an outcome or you will simply end up ignoring other possibilities to end a fight. Of course it is also necessary to find an instructor who knows and will teach you leg locks and leg lock set-ups.

If you can't find an instructor who will do this (and you'll be able to if you ask around) then there are many top quality instructional books and tapes available to gain this knowledge from. In particular, Russian sambo employs many effective leg locks, as does Japanese shooto and pancrase, or American catch wrestling. Don't be afraid to broaden your horizon and incorporate different submission methods into your training. After all, when you step onto the mat all you take with you is your conditioning and knowledge. And in competition or in a real fight, especially against someone holding a higher belt ranking, knowledge is power.

No-holds-barred fighter Todd Medina is a two-time UFC veteran, a member of the Carlson Gracie Competition Team, and the current European Heavyweight Cage Fighting Champion, a title he won in 2000 in Saint Petersburg, Russia.

Franco Columbu and Francisco Bueno
A Rock and a Hard Place

From opposite sides of the world, and a generation apart, two world-class athletes from different sports have found common ground in an uncommon alliance.

Todd Hester

Before Franco Columbu ever started working out, before the thought ever entered his mind about coming to America, partnering with an unknown Austrian bodybuilder with the unpronounceable name of Schwarzenegger, and appearing in a magazine called *Muscle and Fitness* for a dreamer named Joe Weider (who had the crazy idea of making it the world's number one fitness magazine), Franco was a martial artist—a boxer to be exact—who excelled as the lightweight championship of his native Italy.

Francisco Bueno, on the other hand, from the age of 4, was a judo player (good enough to win the Brazilian national championship) which in jiu-jitsu-crazed Brazil is highly respected because of its Olympic connection. After taking a break from martial arts, he then trained in muay Thai for nearly four years before finally moving to jiu-jitsu and adding boxing and wrestling to his repertoire of martial arts.

Franco Columbu, of course, parlayed his natural athleticism and his relentless drive to excellence by first becoming Italian, German, European, and world powerlifting champion. He then moved to bodybuilding where he won the titles of Mr. Italy, Mr. Europe, Mr. International, Mr. Universe, and one of the crowns of the entire sporting world—Mr. Olympia. Along the way he set world powerlifting records in the bench press, squat, and deadlift, and weightlifting records in the Olympic press, the snatch, and the clean and jerk. He is generally regarded as one of the most outstanding and versatile strength athletes of all time.

For Francisco Bueno the path to the top was different but no less impressive. Finding, in jiu-jitsu, an activity that made full use of his natural quickness, reflexes, and strength, he became an 11-time Brazilian jiu-jitsu champion, topping it off by becoming world champion in 1996. Wanting new worlds to conquer, he then embarked on a no-holds-barred fighting career which included wins in several prestigious no-holds-barred events including Japan's Pride. He also broadened his combat experience by going to the first Abu Dhabi Submission Wrestling World Championships in the United Arab Emirates in 1998, and making it to the final round (beating the Russian heavyweight Olympic champion in the process) before being forced to withdraw due to injury.

When Columbus bodybuilding career wound down, he followed an obvious path, using his competition knowledge of anatomy, nutrition, and exercise to become a doctor of chiropractic, and become a health, fitness, and exercise consultant. He authored numerous books on weight training, bodybuilding, powerlifting, women's fitness, and nutrition.

Bueno, known as no-holds-barred's "fittest and finest athlete" is a self-proclaimed "training demon" who spends hours in the gym training not only traditional lifting exercises, but also following plyometric routines designed to increase both tendon and ligament strength for speed and quickness, to help the striking and kicking aspects of his no-holds-barred fighting game.

Coming from two different cultures to settle in a third, the two shared common goals of hard work, focus, and a love of systematic, scientific training. But it wasn't until they were introduced by Frederico Lapenda, the CEO of the Rio Group, and both a Bueno fan and a Columbu admirer, that they both realized how much they had in common—and how much they had to learn from each other.

The First Meeting

"Like every other sports fan in the world I always admired Franco Columbu," says Lapenda. "I also happen to think that Francisco Bueno is the premier combat athlete in the world today. So when I met Art Birzneck, and found out that he was producing a movie with Franco's Westar Entertainment Company, and that he was looking for a martial arts expert to consult with him on some of the combat scenes in his upcoming action-adventure movie, *Ancient Warriors*, I immediately thought of Francisco." The rest, as they say, is history.

When the two met, Bueno was immediately impressed. "Of course I knew all about Franco from all his bodybuilding titles," he said. "What athlete doesn't know about Franco Columbu? What I didn't know was that he was involved in the production of so many movies, so of course I agreed to work with him. More than anything else, I didn't spend so much time on Brazilian jiu-jitsu techniques, but rather on how to carry yourself like a streetfighter, and how to do basic stand-up attacks and escapes from grabs and clinches—how to move against the thumb or against the elbow joint in order to create leverage. He catches on quickly, though," Bueno adds. "I guess he gets it from his years in boxing and from his knowledge of chiropractic bone manipulation."

For his part, Franco was also taken by the young Brazilian. "He is very strong," Columbu says. "Within a few minutes of meeting him I gave him a strength balance test, just to see if what everyone had been saying about him was true. It is a test that I administer to my patients that tests not only strength, but also the balance of the opposing muscles. He was a little out of balance between

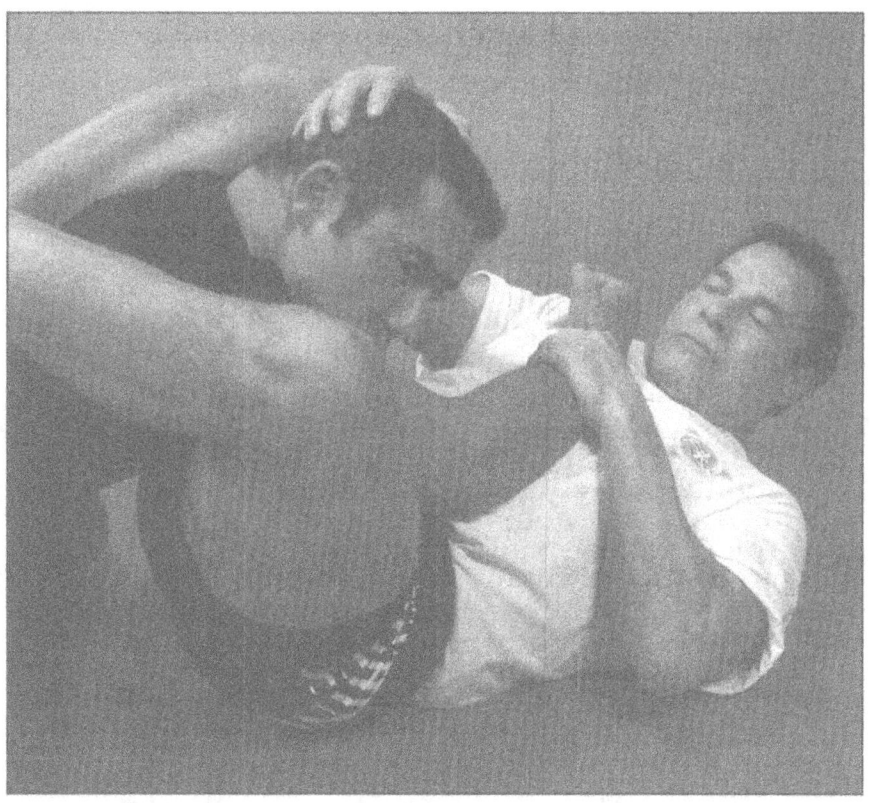

> **"Every time I showed Franco a move he would say, 'You know, you can do a special exercise to help develop the muscles that perform that technique.'"**

the biceps and triceps—but not much," Columbo recalls. "I remember that I had a tough time pulling his arm down from a curled position—and that's saying something coming from me, because I spent over a decade working-out with Arnold!"

Training for Combat

Once the two started working out for *Ancient Warriors,* Bueno quickly realized that their strengths complimented each other. "Every time I showed Franco a move he would say, 'You know, you can do a special exercise to help develop the muscles that perform that technique.' It was almost like he knew which muscles I was going to use before I used them! And he didn't just focus on heavy lifting, but rather mentioned many isometric and two-man training drills done without weights which will build both muscles and the internal joint, ligament, and tendon strength."

"That's correct," says Columbo. "Training the inside of the muscles in grappling is much more important than training the outside of the muscles. Because first of all, you prevent injuries because

Franco Columbu's Basic Strength and Flexibility Program for Grapplers

Time:
Avoid training too quickly after a meal, because this takes blood away from the stomach where it is needed for digestion.

Frequency:
Minimum of three and maximum of five days per week. Do all levels each training session.

Level 1: Warm-up and Conditioning Exercises
Hamstring stretches: 10 reps each leg; Standing side bends: 10 bends each side; Bent leg sit-ups: 3 sets of 15 reps; Bent leg raises: 3 set of 15 reps; Lying side leg raises: 3 sets of 20 reps each leg.

Level 2: Beginning Resistance Exercises
Push-ups: 3 set of 10 reps, strict and slow; Lunges: 3 sets of 10 reps each leg; Forward bends: 3 sets of 20 reps; Between door presses: 3 sets of 10 reps; Running in place: knees high like wind sprints; do as many intervals as possible with a short rest in-between.

Level 3: Weight Training Exercises
Seated Dumbbell Curls: 3 set of 10 reps each arm; One-arm rowing: 3 sets of 10 reps each arm; Triceps extensions: 3 sets of 10 reps with each arm; Squats: 3 sets of 10 reps; Lateral Raises: 3 sets of 10 reps; Bent-over lateral raises: 3 sets of 10 reps.

Nutrition Tips
Proper diet consists of a combination of a little special knowledge and a lot of common sense. Here's an example:

Special knowledge—"The body requires a minimum of 60-80 grams of carbohydrate a day, and about 1 gram of protein for every 2.2 pounds of body weight."

Common sense—"If you feel you are too fat and you want to lose weight, you should eat less and exercise more. The best body-fat measuring machine in the world is the hallway mirror."

when you're wrestling and doing submission you're really working the tendons, joints, and ligaments more than the actual muscles. In jiu-jitsu, the way Francisco explains it, the prime focus is on leverage and position. If you have muscles it's good—but only if you use them in the natural execution of the techniques and don't try to power through the positions. Muscles have to be a natural addition to the leverage of jiu-jitsu or any grappling sport such as wrestling or judo."

"I could really see what he was talking about," Bueno adds. "I've always been strong, but his muscle balance test was something I'd never seen before. I have trained weight lifting and I have bench-pressed as much as 600 lbs. before when training in the gym. I thought it was because of my power, but Franco explained that my ability to lift that much weight was more a factor of my balance and my muscle coordination that I had gained from jiu-jitsu over the years. I am very excited about training more with him in the future. I really think it will help me improve as a fighter."

Columbu seems equally pleased about meeting Bueno. "I learned a lot of things already from Francisco," he says, "that I think will help to make the fight scenes in *Ancient Warriors* and other movies very realistic. I'm really a stickler for detail and for realism. I won't do a fight scene in a movie unless it is something that I could use in real life. People can sense if something is real or fake when

they watch a movie—I know I can—so I'm very conscious about what I do. I've had many people offer to help train me in fighting—and I honestly could have chosen anyone in the world to teach me martial arts. But I knew that Francisco Bueno was the one when I met him—it was obvious to me that he was the real deal. He's just that good. For me, it was especially important to get everything right in this film because I'm very excited about it. I have wonderful costars in Daniel Baldwin and European supermodel Michelle Hunziger, there's a great plot, and a lot of action. For me it is the perfect movie." He laughs, "I even think Arnold will like it."

Dr. Franco Columbu is available for fitness, strength, nutritional consultation and chiropractic treatment by calling 310-477-8604. Francisco Bueno is available for private lessons, group classes, or seminars in Brazilian jiu-jitsu, submission wrestling, or no-holds-barred fighting by calling 310-801-1000 or emailing riosports@aol.com

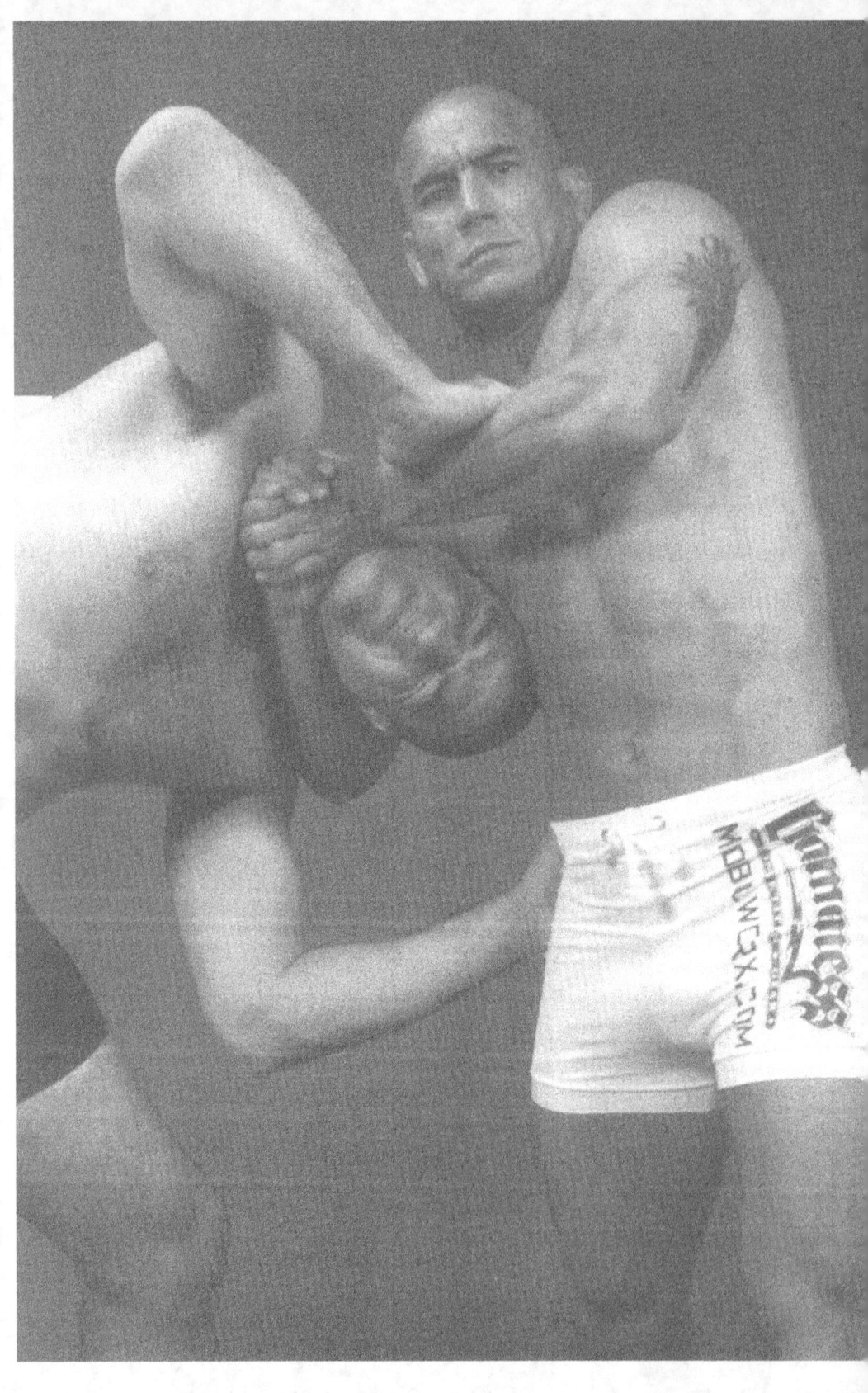

Fabiano Iha
The Brazilian King Midas
Every sport he touches turns to gold.

Loren Franck

Few athletes become a national champion in one sport. But when a superathlete becomes a national champion in six sports, all before age 25, you'd have to say he has a golden touch. Well, there is an athlete in mixed martial arts today who fits that description to a "T". You probably know this King Midas by another name: Fabiano Iha. If you're excited about no-holds-barred and the Ultimate Fighting Championships, you've seen him work his magic. One of mixed martial arts most affable fighters, the 30-year-old Iha vows to vanquish any opponent who dares to enter the Octagon with him.

Born and raised in Florianopolis, a picturesque city of about 250,000 people on the southeast coast of Brazil, Iha isn't the biggest grappler you'll ever see. But at a rugged 5'8" and 170 pounds, he's one of the toughest, most feared, and most respected. Ambitious? He wrote the book on the world. He wants everything—fame, glory, and cash—and he's willing to pay the price in blood, sweat, and tears to get them.

When you first see Iha in action, it's tempting to think his masterful fighting skills will eventually make him king of the ring. Resist that temptation. Although Iha is one of the most lethal fighters in the sport, the secret of his success is his mind, not his lithe, ultrafit body. In time, one can't help but believe that Iha *will* have it all simply because he wants it so badly. What's driving Iha to greatness? Why is he so determined to rule the ring? How did he became a Brazilian national champion in six major sports, including Brazilian jiu-jitsu?

Good questions. And there's no one more qualified to answer them than Fabiano Iha himself.

Q: When did you move to the United States?
A: Six years ago. Actually, it was in March 1995.

Q: Why did you move here?
A: For years I had dreamed of opening my own jiu-jitsu academy, but I didn't feel the opportunity was right in Brazil. So a major reason I came to the United States was to open my own school. However, I'm not one to remain satisfied with just one project, so I also planned to compete in no-holds-barred, and I wanted to work in the movies.

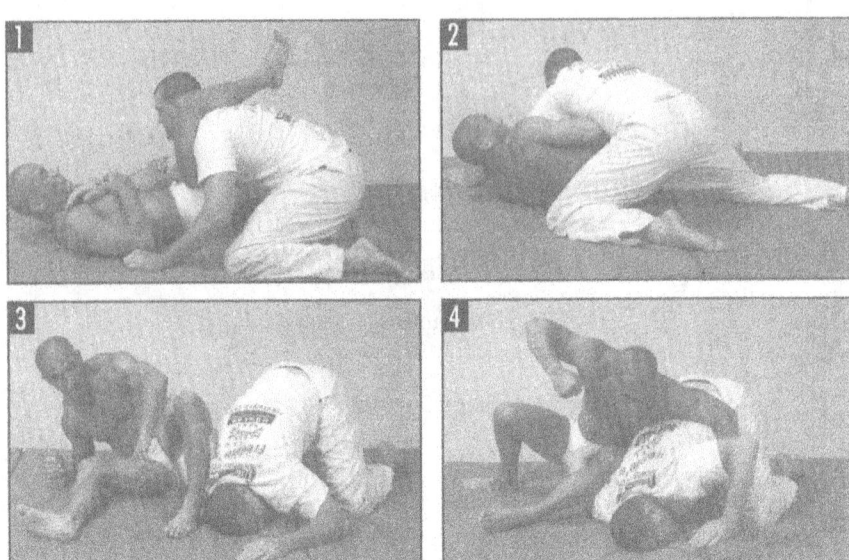

Half-Guard Reversal
Holding his opponent in the half-guard (1), Fabiano Iha slides to the side (2), sits up while maintaining arm control (3), and controls the waist while preparing to punch (4).

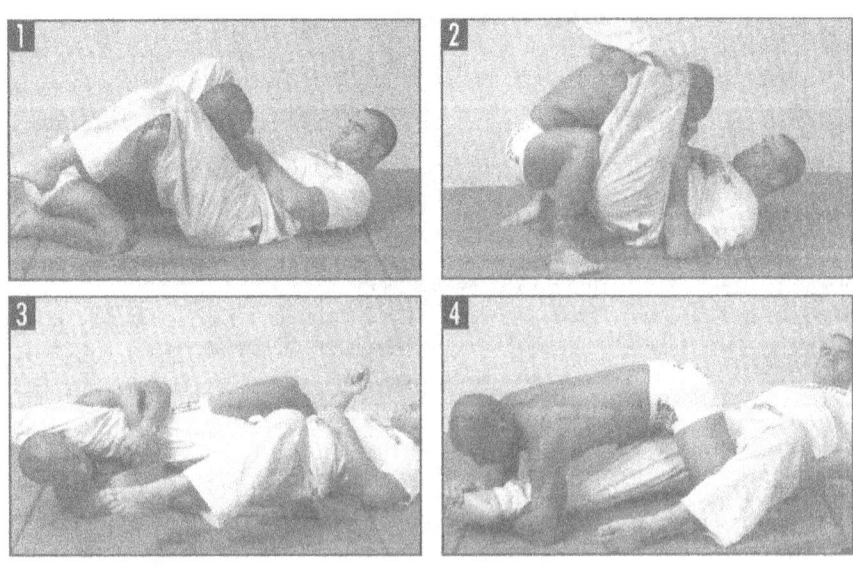

Triangle Escape to an Ankle Lock
Trapping in the triangle (1), Fabiano Iha straightens his back to create distance (2), slides to the knee (3), and secures the ankle for the finishing lock (4).

Q: Did you play many sports in Brazil?

A: Oh, yeah. But I'll tell you only about those in which I was a Brazilian champion. First, I competed in speed cycling. I was a Brazilian champion in speed cycling the first time I tried. The sport came so easily to me that I surprised myself. After speed cycling, I switched to motocross racing. After that, I surfed. I was a Brazilian champion in those two sports also. I took up car racing next, also becoming a Brazilian champion. Then I focused my efforts on paragliding and Brazilian jiu-jitsu. I set three long-distance paragliding records in Brazil.

Q: You were a Brazilian national champion in all six sports?

A: Yes, but not all at the same time. I was only 9 years old when I first became a Brazilian champion in cycling. At ages 10 and 11, I was a Brazilian champion in motocross, but I didn't become a Brazilian champion in surfing until I was 14.

Q: When were you a Brazilian champion in jiu-jitsu?

A: Two times, in '94 and '95.

Q: How did you get so involved in sports?

A: Through my dad. He was a well-built guy, a motocross racer, and he noticed that I was jumping from one sport to another. Whenever I won a Brazilian championship in one sport, I would get bored and change to another. But the new sport had to challenge me.

Q: You like challenges, don't you?

A: Definitely. I was never satisfied when I limited myself to one sport, so I always pursued something else. And I'm still that way.

Q: Why did you start studying jiu-jitsu?

A: As I said, I loved and played all kinds of sports, but I'd never done the martial arts. While in Brazil, I heard that jiu-jitsu was the best martial art to learn. So I said, "OK, I want to do that one." Also, it seemed that everyone in Brazil was learning jiu-jitsu. When I was 16, a friend began taking lessons, so I started at that time too.

Q: Do you compete in Brazilian jiu-jitsu sport tournaments now?

A: Not anymore. Instead, I concentrate on no-holds-barred and the Ultimate Fighting Championships. I have 14 fights now: 11

> "I want to make a name for myself in the sport, too. I want to be the best. Every organization has a belt, and I want to win the belts from all the organizations."

wins and three losses. That's my real record and I'm proud of it. Some people have imaginary records and like to say that they're undefeated. But I don't like to be fake or to make things up. My record has been compiled against some very tough fighters.

Q: Who was your toughest opponent?
A: There were two. David Menne and Frank Trigg—neither was easy. I faced off with Trigg about a year ago in Tokyo and I fought Dave Menne in February 2000. Unfortunately, I lost to both.

Q: Why were these two fights so difficult for you?
A: Dave Manne was a different body weight than I was, and he fought my game. He had a very good game plan. When I faced Frank Trigg, I was out of shape and he just dominated my physically. I don't blame anyone but myself for that loss. Trigg is a very tough fighter and I simply didn't train hard enough for him.

Q: You have a reputation for being very fit. How do you keep in shape?
A: My training has two aspects. I don't work out haphazardly. All of my training is carefully calculated to meet my needs. First, every morning, I do an overall conditioning class, mostly cycling. I also run as part of my conditioning program. In addition, on Mondays, Wednesdays and Fridays, a personal trainer helps me with weight training. The second aspect of my training is fight preparation. I train in kickboxing, including muay Thai, and then I do jiu-jitsu at night. It's great. Basically I train all day.

Q: How long are your workouts?
A: About 90 minutes each. One is in the morning from 7:00 to 8:00. I start the next at 10:00 a.m., and it lasts until 11:30. A third workout begins at 1:00 p.m. and continues until 2:30. Sometimes, I nap between workouts, and I usually do a fourth workout at night.

Q: Do you earn your living from the martial arts?
A: Yes, I make a living from fighting, and I teach at least one martial arts class a day at my studio, the Fabiano Iha Academy in Huntington Beach, California. I have about 150 students. My classes are in Brazilian jiu-jitsu and no-holds-barred fighting techniques. I do the NHB classes without the gi and BJJ with the gi.

Q: Besides muay Thai and Brazilian jiu-jitsu, do you train in any other martial arts?
A: I also train in kickboxing, western boxing, and wrestling. Nowadays, in NHB, you can't just be limited to submission moves. Everyone knows how to strike and to kick and you have to train in that if you want to be competitive. The days of grapplers dominating everyone is over. Even Kerr and Coleman, the kings of ground-and-pound wrestling, train in other martial arts now. You have to cross-train in fighting.

Q: Do you have belts in any of these arts?
A: No, belts aren't that important to me. I study these arts so I can use them in my fighting and so I can teach them to my students. I'm not into the theory or the philosophy associated with the martial arts. The martial arts are literally hands-on tools for me.

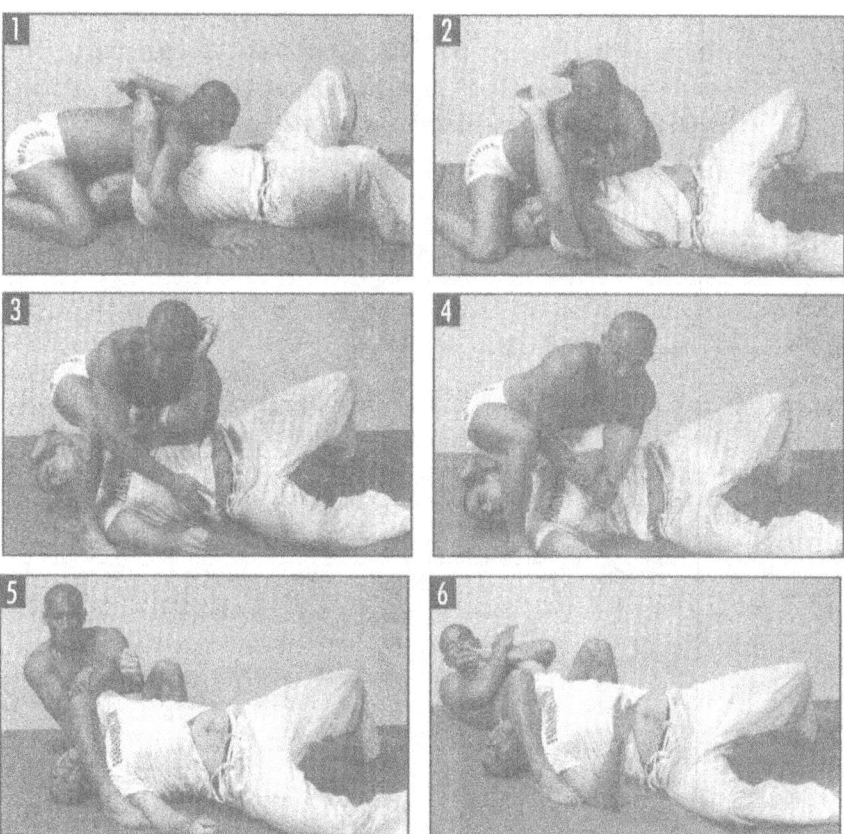

Chest-to-Chest Arm Lock
Held by his opponent in a chest-to-chest position (1), Fabiano Iha breaks the grip by raising up to the side (2). Securing the arm (3), he passes his leg over the head to prevent and escape (4), leans back (5), and applies the finishing arm lock (6).

Q: Which martial art helps you the most in the ring?

A: That's easy—jiu-jitsu. Although conditioning isn't a martial art, it helps me a lot, too. You know, it doesn't matter if you know a lot of jiu-jitsu by itself. Because if you're not in good shape, you won't be able to last long enough during a fight to defeat an opponent.

Q: Does the money you win make the fighting worthwhile?

A: Sure. But the money isn't the only reason I fight. I want to make a name for myself in the sport, too. I want to be the best. Every organization has a belt, and I want to win the belts from all the organizations. I'm trying to win the Ultimate Fighting Championship belt now.

> "People tell me I'm very persistent. And I am. I keep going, and I push myself hard while training and competing. Anyone who knows me will tell you I don't give up easily."

Q: And your weight class?
A: I fight in the lightweight class, which goes up to 170 pounds. I'm right at the upper bodyweight limit.

Q: Have you every thought about sharing you training methods?
A: I'm doing a video right now that I'm really excited about—it should be available very soon. Produced by Panther Productions, it will focus on jiu-jitsu without the gi. Martial artists of all styles who are interested in no-holds-barred and the UFC will want to check it out because I teach how to do my most effective fighting techniques. It's something that anyone who competes in any martial art will be able to benefit from. Even without competition, the techniques are very good for real-life self-defense because I only teach methods that have been proven to work—not just empty theories.

Q: You've also done some movie and TV work recently, haven't you?
A: Yes, I was recently featured on a local TV show here in Orange County, California, and I've done two movies so far. One is *Nowhere to Go*, and the other is in production right now with just a working title. Anyway, I just finished the film and had the time of my life. I wasn't a big-name actor with a lot of lines. I just reported to the set one day and did stunt work. The first stunt involved driving, but I also helped coordinate a stunt scene in which a guy hung from a wall and ceiling. It was a lot of fun to help put it all together, and it really taught me a lot about stunt work.

Q: With so many interests, what do you think you'll be doing in five years?
A: Teaching the martial arts and working in the movies. In five years, I'll probably have retired from fighting.

Q: What makes you so successful at whatever you do?
Q: People tell me I'm very persistent. And I am. I k keep going, and I push myself hard while training and competing. Anyone who knows me will tell B you I don't give up easily.

Q: As a fighter, what's your trademark?

A: My persistence, and to a lesser extent my training. I try my best at everything I do, but I don't waste time doing things that don't get the results I want.

Q: Do follow a special strategy in the ring?

A: Always. However, it is not the same for each fight—it depends on my opponent. I approach every fight differently. For example, before I squared off with Laverne Clark, I trained to protect myself while standing. I also trained extra hard in takedowns. Laverne has long arms, so that's what I had to do to compete against him. When matched with other opponents who are built differently, I have various game plans and I adjust my strategy accordingly. Martial arts are about being flexible. You can't get dialed into one way of thinking, in fighting or in life.

Q: What do you fear in the ring?

A: Not getting paid after a fight—no seriously, I'd have to say nothing really frightens me. I know some guys are afraid to die in the ring but those are people who haven't done it very much. For the real pros I'd have to say that's one fear that never comes up. I actually think that mixed martial arts are one of the safest ring sports. In the ring, I think about more important things, such as fight strategy—my opponent's and my own.

Q: What's your edge in the ring?

A: I'm very focused when the bell rings. I expect to win every fight I enter. If you don't, you'll have a pretty poor fight record. The only thing that makes me nervous is when family, friends and fans pray for me and want me to succeed, because I don't want to let them down. I can deal with a loss but sometimes I think it is harder for my family and friends to deal with it that it is for me. So I like to get in there and do my best for them. Training hard for a fight, winning it, and knowing I've done a good job—that gives me a great deal of satisfaction. It is a validation of everything I work for. It doesn't get much better than that.

Loren Franck is a Los Angeles-based writer and researcher.

Jermaine Andre
Some Bash, Some Splash, and a Whole Lotta" Class

NHB and muay Thai fighter Jermaine Andre has used the ancient Budo warrior code of honor, respect, and courage to mold his life in a positive direction and serve as an example to those around him.

Todd Hester

Raised in the Gateway to the West, St. Louis, Missouri, Jermaine Andre knew from a early age that he was different. Acknowledging that he was "way to smart for my own good," Andre survived a childhood with an abusive stepfather by refusing to give in to personal negativity—even if physical abuse was the result. Supported by a mother who recognized his spiritual gifts, and taken care of by an older brother who taught him the basic precepts of the warrior's code, Andre followed the example of childhood hero Bruce Lee and formally pursued the martial arts at his earliest opportunity. Physically gifted, the under 6-foot-tall Andre could dunk a basketball by the time he was 15. But traditional sports did not compare to the deep personal values and philosophy he found in the martial arts. Soon, upon graduation from high school, he was testing himself on the modern-day battlefields of the no-holds-barred cage and the muay Thai ring.

With a gaudy 18-1-3 NHB record, and splashy good looks, Andre does not let his fighting expertise go to his head. In an age of poor sportsmanship, led by the examples of in-your-face multi-million-dollar professional football and basketball players, Andre doesn't despise his toughest adversaries but rather, in the true Budo tradition, respects them for their spirit and will. "A champion," according to Andre, "is someone who will fight their hardest and keep getting up. A champion is someone who can take a knockdown and bounce back up. Sometimes he's at the bottom of the pile and sometimes he's at the top; no matter, he's still a champion in his heart—not because of arrogance, but because of spirit and perseverance. He will always try even when he's losing and will take his losses in the same spirit that he takes his wins—humbly and respectfully."

Q: When did you get started in the martial arts?
A: I started the martial arts since before I can remember. All of my original training was in stand-up forms such as karate, jeet kune do, and kung-fu. Family life for me was back and forth. I was raised

Muay Thai Double-Kick
Facing an opponent (1), Jermaine Andre lifts the knee (2), kicks to the mid-section (3), switches legs (4), and than snaps a high roundhouse to the head (5).

Guard Pass to a Heel Hook
Trapped inside his opponent's guard (1), Jermaine Andre tucks his head to avoid blows (2), reaches back and traps the ankle (3), passes his leg over his opponent's body (4), and then falls back and applies the finishing heel hook (5).

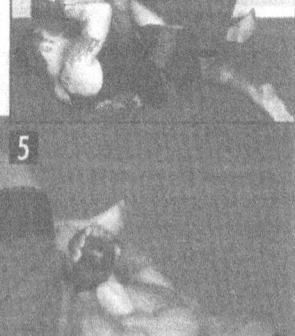

"I think muay Thai is the only stand-up art that works in NHB and I speak from experience. I have tried to use karate, kung-fu and other arts during NHB training and they all failed. The only thing that worked was muay Thai."

Master Ron Smith with Jermaine Andre.

by a loving mother and a stepfather who didn't like me much. My family was poor at times and wealthy at others. I spent time in crappy neighborhoods and nice neighborhoods. I was a very mischievous kid who was way too smart for his own good. I knew when grown-ups were full of it and I would pull their hole card at the drop of a dime. This led me to a lot of beatings from my stepfather but didn't change the fact that I would call an adult on his bull every chance I got.

I was raised with one older brother and two younger sisters. My brother and I were very close. We loved to spar and would do martial arts every chance we got. We were crazy—we even used real weapons on each other. My mother always loved me very much and supported me even when I was being difficult. My stepfather was very hard, but my little sisters were and are just the coolest. The oldest of them is in college now at Jackson University. The younger one is a model who just earned a full-ride scholarship to Arkansas. My older brother is my biggest fan and a hard-working father that I admire so much. Mom hangs out with me and keeps my warrior spirit strong and kicking. I also have a two-year-old daughter who looks and acts just like me, poor kid. She doesn't know it yet but she's going to be the deadliest female alive.

Q: Did you have interests other than martial arts growing up?
A: I wrestled, played football, and ran track in high school. I was also on the debate team, did a little acting and participated in YARC, the Youth Association For Retarded Citizens. I played basketball in my spare time and could slam dunk when I was fifteen. Believe it or not, just like Bruce Lee I also studied dance—jazz in my case.

Q: Did you admire Bruce Lee?

A: Bruce Lee had a big influence on me. I was always impressed not only by his movies but by his philosophies of life and fighting, which actually worked. The man was a genius with the guts to change tradition for the better. He looked cool, too.

Q: With such a traditional background in the martial arts, why did you enter the Octagon?

A: I decided to get into no-holds-barred because it is as close to real fighting as I can get. It allows me to test the effectiveness of my techniques without a bunch of padding and rules. We must all remember that "martial" means "war." The martial arts are the warrior arts. My record stands at about 18- 1-3. I also have many unrecorded pit fights and boxing matches. My wrestling record in high school was 17-1. I feel that martial arts were invented for the purpose of fighting so I use them for that. NHB gives me a chance to use just about everything I know. Inside the Octagon there is are no lies. You can't hide behind anyone else. It's as honest as a sport can get.

Q: What are some of the events you've fought in?

A: I am very proud to have fought in UFC 24, Rage In The Cage Hawaii, the Submission Fighting Championships, DangerZone under Bekki Levi and Dan Severn, the Japan Shootboxing Association, the United States Shootboxing Association, the Striker's Union Challenge, RINGS USA, and the Karate International Council of Kickboxing.

Q: Do you like muay Thai or NHB better?

A: It's hard to say which I like the most. I love the small gloves in NHB and the limited rules, but NHB can get sloppy in the striking area at times. Muay Thai stays beautiful and very technical, if you're watching real Thai boxers. The movements are always smooth and controlled. Sometimes NHB fighters tend to do whatever it takes to win. I have to say that I love them both.

Q: Which striking arts do you use in your NHB matches?

A: I think muay Thai is the only stand-up art that works in NHB and I speak from experience. I have tried to use karate, kung-fu and other arts during NHB training and they all failed. The only thing that worked was muay Thai. I think the main reason is because of the front stance, the footwork, and the power. The front stance allows you to sprawl when a grappler shoots in, the footwork allows you to move, and the power allows you to get a quick knockout because you usually only get one chance when you're battling a good wrestler. There are still adjustments that I make to my muay Thai when I fight NHB. I lower my stance for one thing, and I use a lot more hands. All of my NHB wins except for two have come by way of muay Thai knockout on the feet. The other two wins were by submission.

Q: Who were your submission teachers?

A: I was started in grappling by Bryan Madden who was one of the "Killer Bees" during an event called "Wrestling At The Chase." He and Joey Geromiller mesmerized me with the enlightenment of Brazilian jiu-jitsu and judo. Bryan Madden then brought in Coach Slava who taught me Russian combat sambo. I was then trained by Scott Ventimiglia, Kim Ventimiglia and Mark Ventimiglia in jiu-jitsu. I am now being trained by Dr. Darrin Pordash who is under Gokor Chivichyan. Joey Geromiller and Scott Ventimiglia are also training me in NHB. Our team is also joined by CJ. Fernandes who was a wrestling superstar. I like to think of myself as "The Product," because so many people have helped to make me what I am. My main trainer and master is Ron Smith of St. Louis. Missouri.

Q: Who were your toughest opponents?

A: My hardest fight had to be a shootboxing match against champion Bill Rosterfor—that fight is on my highlight video. I dominated the entire match with knockdowns, but Bill kept taking it and coming back for more. He showed true heart and spirit and took a beating like it was nothing. Fighting him was like beating a piece of iron. This impressed me totally even while in the ring because you tell how tough someone is by the beating they can take, not by the beating that they can give. He was definitely the toughest! Other tough battles I had were against Maurice Travis, who is a card-carrying, certifiable bad-ass, Adrian Serrano twice, and John Renken who is very, very slick.

My best win had to be against Adrian Serrano in RINGS USA in Moline on September 30, 2000. Adrian had beaten me in 1997 when I first started, in a fight I definitely shouldn't have taken at the time because my grappling sucked. I knew nothing about Adrian and was not in shape to battle a fighter of his caliber. In 1997 I hung strong, delivered a ton of leg kicks, and stayed on my feet until I finally got wind

ed. I then went to my guard and defended from there but was so tired that I could barely move. Adrian locked in a rear naked choke and I tapped out. I always wanted a rematch but knew I had better be prepared to deal with him next time. I trained hard with Master Ron Smith and Joey Geromiller for our battle in RINGS. My grappling was excellent and my striking superior. The cardio was highly impressive and my spirit soared because I knew I would win this time. I caught Adrian with a round kick to the head, taking back a win.

It was a good win because Adrian is a true warrior. I've watched him spank guys in my hometown who ran their mouths about him. He was undefeated in my hometown so I just had to get him. It was fun—two warriors battling it out again—and we smoked cigars together after the fight in RINGS just as we had done after the first fight.

Q: Do you consider yourself a grappler or a striker?

A: My fighting system is more stand-up. The reason is that I fight and train for the purposes of selfdefense. Even though NHB and muay Thai are sports to some, they are martial arts to me. It is my life and religion. Striking is more impressive in the NHB world than grappling. The fans would much rather see someone get knocked out than tapped out. I also use more stand-up because even though 90 percent of fights end up on the ground, 100 percent of them start on the feet. I don't plan to jump into the guard on the streets so someone's buddies can kick the side of my head in while I'm going for an arm bar. My training system involves, muay Thai, shootboxing, judo, sambo, jiu-jitsu, and wrestling. You have to be well-rounded to survive in NHB now. I also teach self-defense for men, women and seniors. My self-defense system differs from my NHB fighting system—it is far more brutal because there are no rules. I've written a book on women's self-defense which is going to be published soon.

Jermaine Andre Training Routine

"I train six days a week. I wake up with meditation, prayer, and incense offerings every morning and then I run 2 to 3 miles. On Monday, Tuesday, Wednesday, Thursday and Saturday evenings I do three hours of muay Thai, grappling, weights, and calisthenics. Friday is my heavy cardio day. On Sundays I always rest."

Jermaine Andre Fighting Strategy

"My fighting strategy is to read my opponent within the first 10 seconds of the fight. I look to see if he's afraid of me, overconfident, bored, excited, nervous, quick, slow, or strong. Usually I can sense where he's coming from and what he's planning to do. Reading a fighter with the eyes is not a good idea because deception is a part of the game. He may look mean but be as scared as hell. On the other hand he may look scared but be tough as nails. I feel for his energy and look for spiritual guidance. My main plan is to make sure that he doesn't read me."

Jermaine Andre Diet

"I used to be a vegetarian but I ended-up getting malnourished for a fight in Japan so I went back to red meat and chicken. I don't touch pork and I eat a lot of vegetables. I take vitamins daily but I don't use any other types of supplements or steroids. I am 100 percent natural."

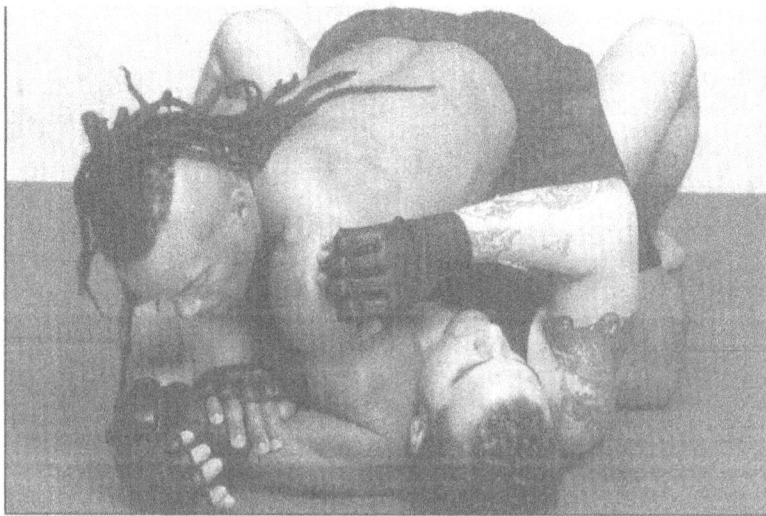

Q: What do you teach to your students?

A: I emphasize courage, loyalty, and respect. With courage you can learn and accomplish anything. Loyalty is a must or you can't be trusted. Respect is necessary for one to stay controlled and not become a rogue—an arrogant rebel who would use the knowledge that I am passing on to them for the wrong reasons. I believe deeply in the traditional, ancient ways and that's what I follow. I teach my students about selflessness, sacrifice and putting others before themselves. This causes me to lose about nine out of ten students because most people can't handle the thought of loyalty, respect and humbleness. A lot of people come to me not to truly learn, but just to see what they can get out of me and Master Smith for as little amount of money as possible. That is not the Way of martial arts and I will not corrupt it with incorrect values. This upsets a lot of people because they can't buy me or my knowledge of Bushido.

Q: What are your overall goals in life?

A: To make people realize what the martial arts are really about. People need to learn that the martial arts are not a business to exploit and see how much money you can make off of it. Don't get me wrong, one should get paid for services provided but not practice back stabbing, betrayal and lies just for the sake of making money. The martial arts are being treated like a business now and their true meaning is becoming lost. People think a martial artists talent and knowledge is measured by how big their school is. This allows businessmen who know nothing about the martial arts to open big schools and look as if they know the arts—it's corrupting the arts. Most "masters" don't even know what the martial arts are about and yet they have a black belt. There's more meaning to the martial arts than belts, money and arrogance. I'd like to teach that to the world.

I want people to understand that NHB is not barbaric or crazy. It is complicated and complex and the people who fight in it are geniuses not animals. We spend more time thinking during that 15 minutes of a fight than most people do all year—and we think under extreme pressure. That's what the martial arts are about: discipline, courage, loyalty, respect, and spirit. In general, NHB fighters are the friendliest athletes that you'll ever meet. I've never met an NHB fighter who was a complete jerk. I definitely can't say the same for the boxing world which is full of arrogance, disloyalty and attitude.

I would like to teach every woman in the world how to make a victim out of any loser that tries to attack her. It's easy and it can be done through my self-defense system. Women need to learn to defend themselves and quit counting on someone else to do it for them. They are more than capable. They only need the knowledge.

Most of all, I want to give guidance to knuckleheaded kids who are on the wrong track. I'd like to open a troubled kid's home which would center around the discipline of the martial arts. I don't believe a kid can be completely bad. Most troubled kids just see through an adult's insincerity and won't tolerate it. Phis pisses the adults off so they label him a troublemaker instead of admitting to their own faults. Then the kid rebels. All troubled kids need is a little guidance and something "real" to work towards. Nothing is more real to them than someone who can fight but yet who has respect and humbleness. It impresses them and when you impress a kid, they try to be like you.

Q: What is your definition of a champion?

A: A champion is someone who will fight their hardest and keep getting up. A champion is someone who can take a knockdown and bounce back up. Sometimes he's at the bottom of the pile and sometimes he's at the top. No matter, he's still a champion in his heart not because of arrogance, but because of spirit, and perseverance. He will always try even when he's losing and will take his losses like he takes his wins—humbly and respectfully. A champion knows that there are other champions around him—and just because they don't have a belt, it doesn't mean that they're not one.

One of the greatest champions that I ever met was Kevin Randelmann. The night before our fights in the UFC we hung out in his hotel room talking about discipline, respect, loyalty, and more. He knew and understood all about the traditional Budo Way and he's supposedly "just" a wrestler. I was totally impressed by his heart and spirit and I laugh at people who say that wrestling is not a martial art. He will always be a true champion and he is a true martial artist through his wrestling skills.

I also know champions who don't fight in the ring. My mother is a true champion who lived a life of bad breaks and screwed-up men but yet always kept a pure heart towards her children and her fellowmen. I know elderly men who train right next to me with hearts of gold regardless of their age. They are true champions unknown to the world. A title belt or a black belt doesn't make a champion. The way a person lives their life makes them a champion.

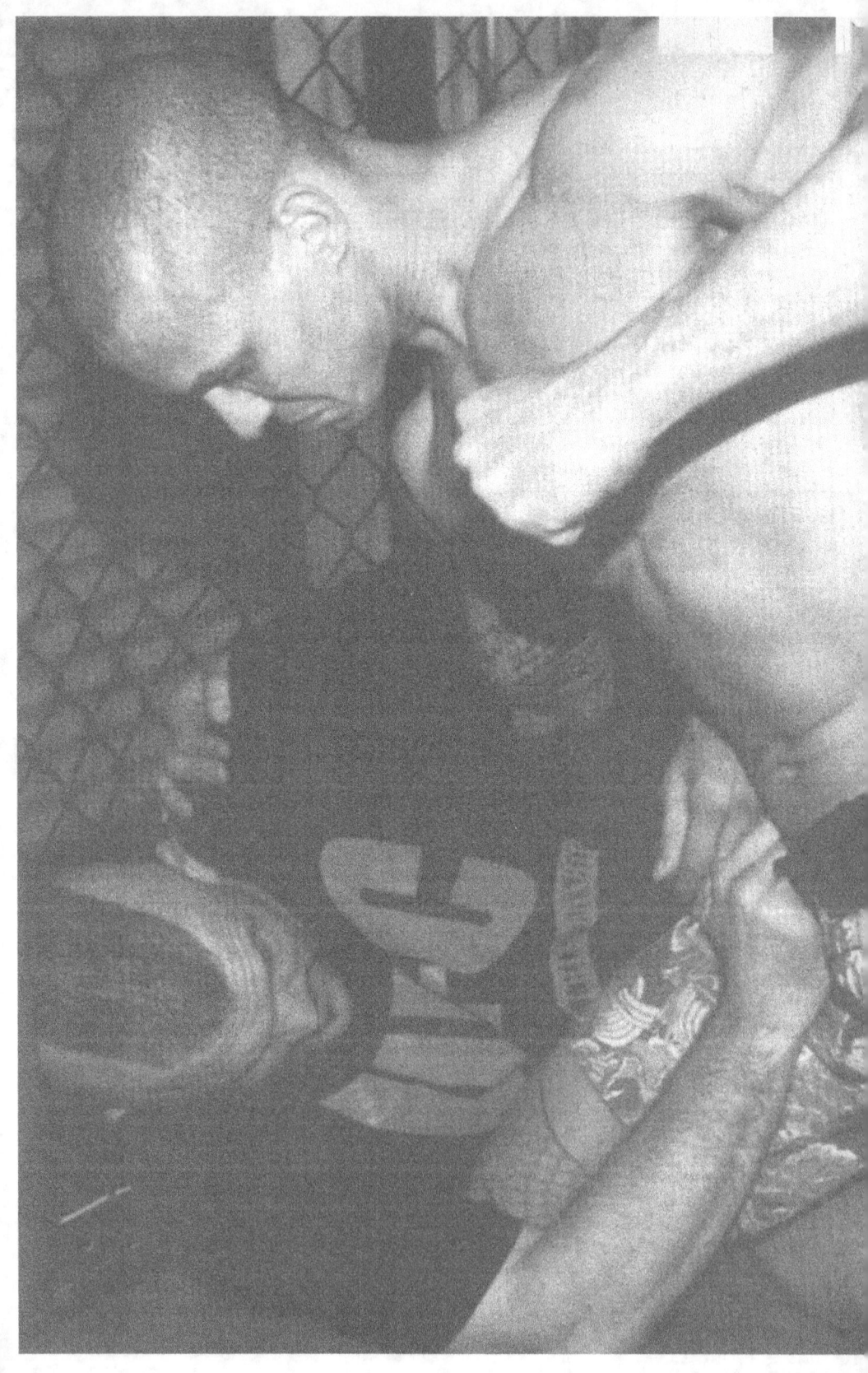

Cage Fighting Strategies

Well-rounded martial artists have to be ready to face opponents on any terrain and be ready to use that terrain to their advantage. This is true not only on the street but also when fighting in a cage.

John Lewis, photos by Todd Hester

One of the most recognizable features of no-holds-barred (NHB) fighting is the Ultimate Fighting Championship (UFC) Octagon. A fixture around the world since Hollywood director John Milius designed it for the first UFC in Denver, Colorado in 1993, it has become synonymous with *vale tudo,* or "anything goes" competition. While the actual eight-sided UFC Octagon is copyrighted, similar round cages that were derived from the Octagon have been used in many shows in the United States and also in some overseas events. While many no-holds-barred events still occur in boxing rings, including the majority held in Japan, a fighter cannot afford to assume that the two battlegrounds are equal. A martial artist with no experience fighting inside an actual cage will be at a definite disadvantage when facing a foe who has spent time inside the circle of steel. In fact, many modern mixed martial arts schools such as Tedd William's Combat Grappling school in Southern California's Inland Empire, and Brazilian jiu-jitsu star Fabiano Iha's Huntington Beach, California facility, have actually built cages into their academies in order to help their students and fighters become acclimated to proper strategies. I also have a full-sized cage in my Las Vegas school for the same reason.

Boxing Ring vs. Steel Cage

It is important to remember that while a boxing ring with its four ropes is used for NHB, it was not specifically designed for this type of eclectic combat. While sufficient for events where there is no grappling or throws, the standard ring is used because it is convenient, not because it is the best. One of the problems with the ring is that fighters can get thrown over the top rope by a judo throw, or can get shoved out of the ring by a hard-charging opponent. On the defensive end, a fighter who is being beaten on the ground in a ring can always perform the infamous "rope escape" which is such a problem in Japanese events such as Pancrase, where all you have to do to avoid a submission is to throw an arm over the nearest rope, causing the referee to restart from the feet. To keep this from happening the cage was invented.

The cage is important because a fighter cannot be thrown over it, pushed under it, or escape by grabbing onto the chain links. While this provides a measure of fairness to a fight by providing consistent and equal conditions for both combatants, it also creates certain problems. One of the main problems, and one that was obvious during the first years of the UFC was that opponent's would grab the chain links with their fingers and even their toes in order to keep an opponent pinned or to help the maneu-

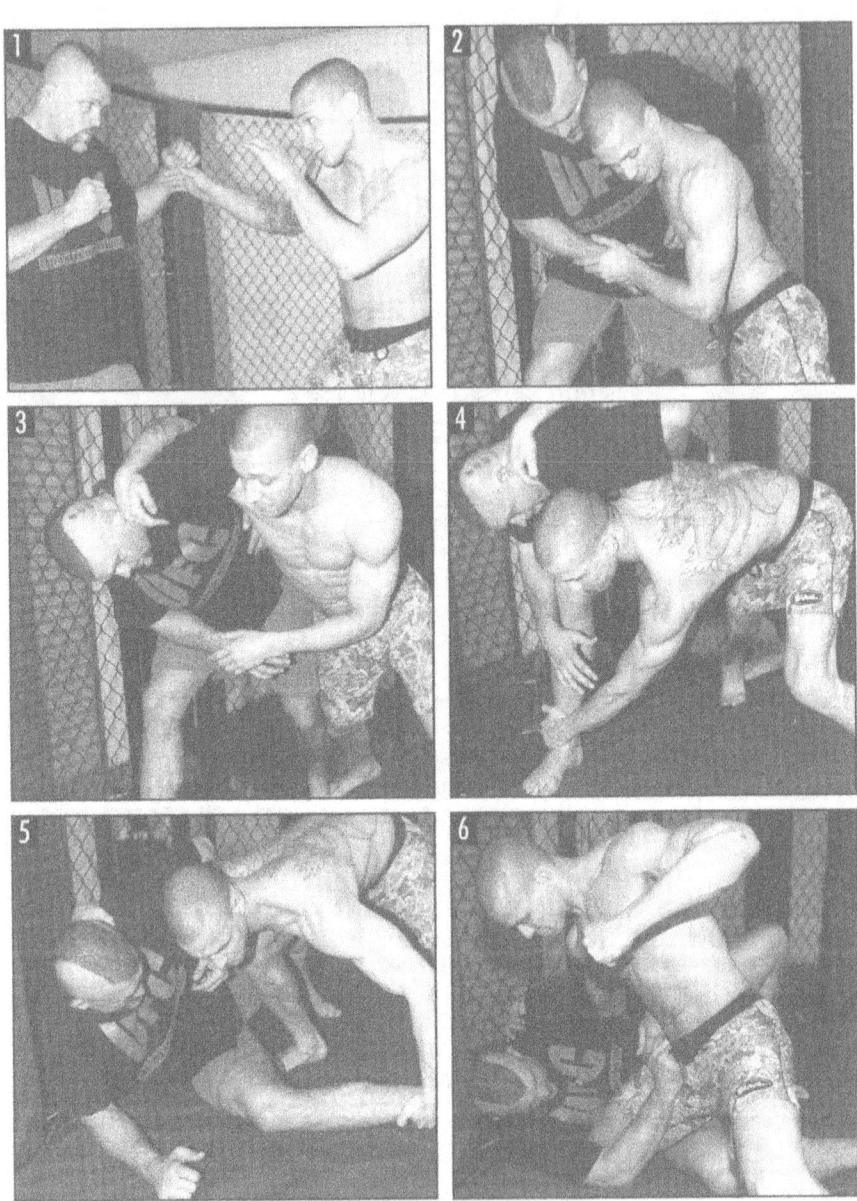

Successful Single-Leg Takedown With the Cage
Facing opponent Chuck Liddell (1), /ohn Lewis clinches (2), and forces Liddell back against the cage wall (3). With Liddell trapped, and unable to move away, Lewis then reaches down and grabs the leg (4), takes Liddell down (5), and then goes on top ready to punch (6).

  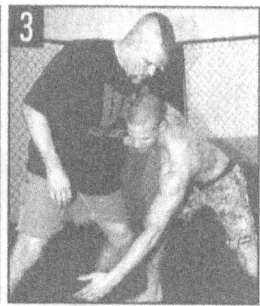

Failed Single-Leg Takedown Without the Cage
Facing opponent Chuck Liddell (1), John Lewis ties Liddell up (2). When he tries to take the leg, however, Liddell simply steps back from Lewis' grab to safety (3).

Failed Double-Leg Takedown Without the Cage
Facing opponent John Lewis, Chuck Liddell closes the distance and tries to take Lewis down (1), who sprawls and counters the attempt (2).

ver out of a difficult position. While the general consensus is that the safety benefits of the cage far outweigh any shortcomings it might have these problems are still factors that have to be dealt with.

Do's and Don'ts

Being pinned against the cage is one of the worst positions to be trapped in. If you are pinned against the chain links make sure that you are standing, and not on the ground. Conversely, however, one of the best positions to be in, where you can strike with impunity, is on the top position with your opponent crammed against the chain links. Many a top fighter has gotten himself in this position and lost to technically less-polished fighters, simply because they allowed themselves to get in this position.

Another very important way to use the cage is to maneuver your opponent into a position that limits his mobility and his chances of escaping when you shoot in. This is an especially important factor when a grappler is trying to take down a striker, or when an inexperienced fighter is facing a more polished foe.

Two matches that immediately come to mind that illustrate these points are the Jerry Bohlander vs. Fabio Gurgel match, which Bohlander won in an early UFC, and then the Jerry Bohlander vs. Romy Aram fight in a recent Gladiator Challenge, which Bohlander lost. In the first match against Gurgel, a world jiu-jitsu champion and a heavy favorite, Bohlander, in his first UFC bout, was able to pin Gurgel against the Octagon wall, keep him from escaping, and then take him down and land hard shots for the victory. In the match against Romie Aram, who was fighting only his third NHB match, Bohlander allowed Aram to push him to the side of the cage, take him down, and then land hard shots from the guard for the victory. Bohlander, trapped against the cage wall, lost because he was unable to move his hips to effect an escape due to Aram's effective positioning.

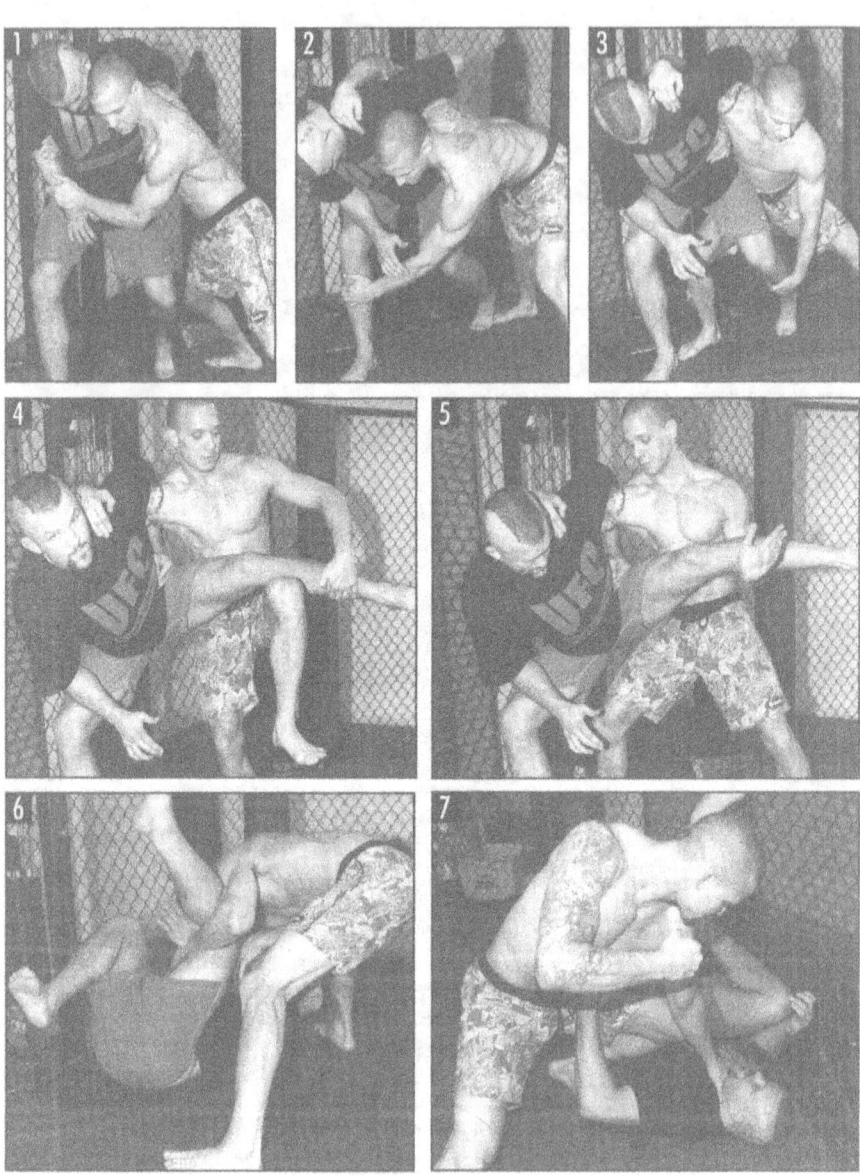

Successful Single-Leg Takedown Variation With the Cage
Facing opponent Chuck Liddell, John Lewis forces him against the cage (1), and then attempts an opposite grab, single-leg takedown (2). When Liddell blocks the takedown, Lewis then steps over Liddel's back leg and traps it (3). Lifting Liddell's leg up (4), Lewis underhooks It (5), then throws Liddell to the ground (6), and pushes him to the cage and prepares to punch (7).

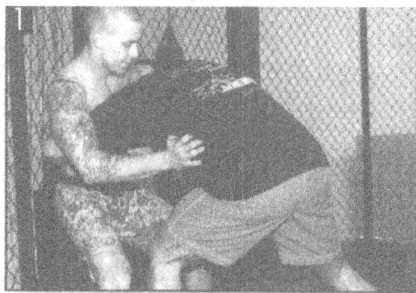
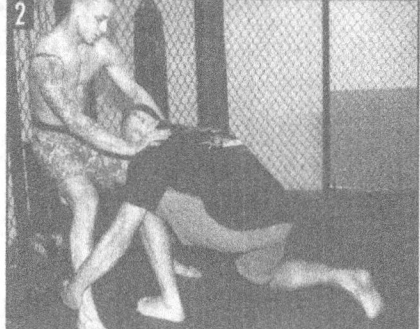

Successful Double-Leg Takedown With the Cage
Facing opponent John Lewis, Chuck Liddell clinches and forces Lewis against the cage where he cannot sprawl (1). Dropping down and grasping the legs (2), Liddell takes Lewis down (3), traps him against the cage, and delivers a knee (4).

When Life Gives You Lemons, Make Lemonade

Like anything else in life, when faced with adversity or with a difficult situation, you can either complain and accept the predicament or you can analyze, act, and overcome adversity. So rather than grumble about the cage's limitations, instead analyze its properties and devise certain fighting strategies to use its geometry to gain an advantage. I have seen many fighters, whether consciously or unconsciously, also devise effective techniques to use the cage to their advantage. When used properly, the cage can be an ally in the ring that can help you obtain and hold the ever-important superior ground position that is often the key to victory.

Royler Gracie
The Heart of a Champion

One of Brazilian jiu-jitsu's most enduring champions, Royler has never rested on the laurels of his famous family, but has let his fighting record and ring accomplishments speak for themselves.

Kid Peligro

Royler Gracie has been involved in martial arts his entire life and has been competing constantly since he was 7 years old. Having fought in more jiu-jitsu events than perhaps any other Brazilian jiu-jitsu (BJJ) fighter in history, Royler has attained the status of best in the world. His career has spanned over 28 years and three generations. During that stretch he has been a four-time BJJ world champion, a two-time Abu Dhabi Combat Club (ADCC) World Submission Wrestling champion, a Pan American Games champion, a Brazilian national champion, and Rio de Janeiro state champion. He also managed to fight in several memorable no-holds-barred (NHB) matches along the way, some against much bigger men. Undisputedly, one of the most scientific fighters in the world, Royler won the Most Technical award at both the 1997 BJJ World Championships and at ADCC 2000, making him the only man to have ever captured both prestigious awards.

The thing that strikes most people about Royler is his incredible desire to compete and his drive to succeed. In an era in which most fighters are worried about their records and won't fight outside their weight division, Royler has often taken on much heavier opponents. Royler's reasoning is simple and speaks volumes about the man himself: "I just want to see how the match will turn out and how I will do. More than anything else I want to learn more about jiu-jitsu, and in order to do that I have to challenge myself." Royler's competitive drive and his desire for success has made him a favorite of fighters and fans alike.

Q: Tell us a little bit about yourself.
A: I am 35 years old. I have been married for 13 years to my wife Vera and we have four daughters. They are Rayna 13, Rayssa 11, Rhauani 10, and Ratine 3. I started to train BJJ when I was 3. At the time I really didn't know what I was doing, I'd go to the academy to play soccer dressed in a gi. It was fun. Brazil is the land of soccer and you generally give your kids a soccer ball, but I was given a gi. So my father and my brother Rolls, in order to get me and the other kids interested in coming to class and to the academy, made us play soccer dressed in a gi. It was really fun then. All my brothers where at the academy also, so it was the gathering place. We practically ate, slept, and breathed jiu-jitsu then,

Using the open guard (1), Royler Gracie pulls his opponent down (2), grabs the belt (3), then throws (4). Rolling on top (5), Gracie puts the knee on the stomach (6), and then wraps the arm around the head (7), securing control.

so the sport took over my life very early on, but very naturally because all the other kids in the family did it too.

Q: When did you start to fight?
A: For my first competition I was only 7 years old. My dad came to me and said, "I want you to go there and have fun. If you win I am going to give you five dollars—but if you lose I am going to give you ten dollars." So I thought, "What a deal, if I win I make a little money and get the medal, and if I lose I get even more money." So I always looked forward to competitions because it was always a win-win situation. Now I see the wisdom of this, because no one enters a competition or a fight to lose; everyone wants to win. So in order to take away the pressure from me, he devised this reward. Because when you think about it, being that my family had many champions, the pressure for us to win was naturally stronger than for other kids. I believe it had a great effect on me and is why I still look forward to competing and why I thrive during pressure situations. In my mind I just need to do my best—before and after the competition. I mention before the competition because if, for some reason, I didn't prepare myself correctly, I would feel bad. But that's never happened before and I hope it never will.

Q: How many times did you fight?

A: I started at 7 years old, but I have lost count of how many times I have fought in tournaments. But just as a black belt I have approximately 300 fights recorded on video and film. But I didn't record all my fights as a lower belt so that number is much higher.

Q: Who where the big names when you started to compete?

A: I fought many people: Peixotinho, Marcio Simas, Marcio "Macarrao", Carlson Gracie Jr., Ricardo de La Riva, Amauri Bitteti, and so forth.

Q: So you have crossed several generations?

A: I believe that I have fought three generations of fighters.

Q: You also have fought several fights, including underground fights, like the time you fought Eugenio Tadeu. How old where you then?

A: I was 21.

Q: Was that your first vale tudo (anything goes) match?

A: Yes. That fight happened at our academy and it sort of happened without warning. I was teaching at the academy and my brother Rickson called and said, "Hey, Royler, tomorrow you have a vale tudo against a *luta livre* (free fighting) guy." At the time, jiu-jitsu and luta livre fighters had a real strong rivalry going so I accepted. Rickson called late in the afternoon and when I asked when, he answered, "Noon!" I then asked him if it was OK if I took the rest of the evening off and rested, and he agreed. So it was on the spur of the moment, at least for me, with no preperation.

So I showed up the next day to do a "fight-train" as Rickson called it, with Eugenio Tadeu, who at the time weighed about 25 lbs more than me. We fought for 46 minutes with kicks and punches, all done for free, because at that time there was no money in vale tudo fights—so we fought just to see who was the better fighter. There were six people from my team watching and six people from his team. I left the fight feeling great because I had never done a vale tudo before and it was a new experience in my life.

Q: Tadeu already had a few matches prior to that, right?

A: He had a few fights, was used to street fighting, and he really liked fighting. I believe he is still active in vale tudo.

Q: Then after that you had a series of vale tudo matches?

A: Over a period of time. I fought one in Brazil, then I fought in Japan Vale Tudo 1996 against Noburo Asahi who was ranked number one in the Shooto organization at the time. Then I fought in Pride 2 against Yuhi Sano in 1998. After that I did the fight with Sakuraba in October 1999 and just recently in Deep 2001 against Japanese fighter Murahama. During that same time I was also fighting the world BJJ tournaments. I was the champion four years running in 1996 through 1999. I also fought in the ADCC championships and won both in 1999 and 2900. I fought in a few Brasileiro's (Brazilian national tournaments). I also did a few special events like the Copa Pele. The Copa Pele had special jiu-jitsu matches in an outdoor arena that was set up every summer on the beach in Rio. I also fought in the 2000 International Pro-Am. So I have stayed busy the last few years.

Grabbed from behind (1), Royler Grade holds the arm to protect his neck (2), steps to the side (3), throws his opponent over his back (4), traps the arm (5), and applies a wristlock/choke combination (6).

Q: Describe the Deep 2001 match.

A: During the first round I was able to get Murahama's back right away, I believe by the third minute I was on his back. He was, however, an experienced fighter with many professional stand-up matches and he knew how to protect himself. The fact that he was only 5'2" made it easier for him to protect his neck. I spent about six minutes of the first round on his back trying to submit him. Around the ninth minute I decided to try an arm attack but we ended up too close to the ropes and his arm was wrapped around the ropes and the more I tried the harder it got.

In the second round he was feeling more confident and we exchanged some punches while standing up. I got a little tired and I started to have a harder time taking him down. I finally took him down and attempted a foot lock but it was quickly defended by him. I believe that the fight was pretty even—he is a good striker and only needs to connect with one good shot to end the fight. Because the fight is never over until it's over, one mistake with a good striker can be fatal. A grappler, however, has to work a lot harder to get the precise moment to sink in the submission. The draw was a fair result. I have no complaints. I think that we both deserved the draw, but I also believe that the rules favored a draw.

Q: Why was your fight two rounds of 10 minutes each?
A: Well, my fight was the main event so I believe that the promoters decided to make it longer. I think this would have been better for the other fights also, because it gives the fighters more time to develop a strategy and positioning. The person with the least amount of endurance would prefer a shorter fight, and the person who is more technical prefers a longer match. I am not talking about a three-hour fight, but two ten-minute rounds or even three rounds of that length. I believe anything longer than one hour makes for a boring fight. To my way of thinking, if a fighter who is my size draws with me after 20 or 30 minutes, then it is fair to say that we are even. Of course, if you go another round then anything can happen, but they can happen just as much to me as to him, so it goes both ways. I do not believe in saying that if a fight had gone longer I would have won. I believe that from a promotion and entertainment standpoint you have to limit the matches to under one hour—and my preference is 30 minutes.

Q: It seems that the Gracie family is always accused of going to an event and changing the rules at the last minute. Is there any truth to this?
A: I really don't understand that criticism. I always leave for an event with the rules already agreed to by both parties far in advance. As a matter of fact, when I arrived in Japan for Deep 2001 a reporter asked me that same question and I turned around to him and said that I didn't know of any changes and asked him to tell me what had changed. He couldn't answer. I remember the time I fought with Sakuraba, who was 40 pounds heavier than me, and all that I asked was for longer rounds—two rounds of 15 minutes instead of 10 minutes. I don't think that that was an unreasonable request. I have never had the chance to fight someone who was 40 pounds lighter than me. But if that ever happens and he asks for three rounds of 20 minutes each, I am going to agree. If he asks for 20 rounds of three minutes each I'll also agree! The fact of the matter is that the contracts are drawn way in advance and the rules are set before anyone signs a contract; so I don't know where these stories about last-minute changes come from.

Q: What are your fighting plans for the immediate future?
A: Right now, my focus is on ADCC 2001. I am going to start my training a month and a half prior to the event as I usually do, and then after ADCC I'll think about NHB. There is a possibility of an event for Rickson this year that I would train with him for, and there are other offers for me to fight in Japan again.

Q: What motivates you to keep fighting?
A: I have always loved fighting. After a while it becomes a natural part of your life. I live exclusively from fighting and teaching jiu-jitsu, grappling, and NHB. So I eat, sleep and breathe it. I look at it

as a way to measure myself and to make a living at the same time. I focus on my work which involves teaching at academies that I have in Rio, doing seminars that I conduct everywhere in the world, and then fighting. The fights give me an extra income. So today I see NHB as a way to broaden my career, while at the same time making extra income. I don't believe that anyone will tell you that they love to fight NHB. People may love the attention and the exposure and the perks, but no one in his right mind likes to hit someone or to get hit in a fight. You may love the challenge that is fighting but I don't believe that you can love to fight NHB. Fighting is something that traumatizes the body and it not something that I believe anyone would realistically do just for the pleasure of it.

Q: Did you ever think when you fought Eugenio Tadeu for free, that NHB would become so well-established and popular?
A: Vale tudo has become a money-making machine for an elite few. However, there are many athletes that are fighting for very little. There are many people that are not getting what they deserve. Fighters need to be able to get a fair payment; but for various reasons, some of which are the fighters' own fault, they will fight for any amount. I believe that anyone that fights deserves to get more than they are getting now. Luckily, the events are getting more popular and the new promoters are people who love the sport and who are visionaries. They are making big strides to fairly compensate the fighters. I am very excited about the new owners of the UFC, Frank and Lorenzo Fertitta, for example. From what I have been told about them, they will be very good for the sport.

Q: You are known for your ability to think and adjust your strategy during a fight. How did you develop that mental skill?
A: I have read the book, *The Art of War,* at least 50 times. It has influenced me a lot. One of the things that it says is, "If you know yourself but don't know your enemy, for each victory you will have a defeat. If you don't know your enemy and you don't know yourself then you will lose every battle. If you know yourself and your enemy then you don't have to fear the result of 100 battles." I was also lucky to have been born into a family of fighters and was fortunate enough to have grown-up around fighting. So I learned from watching and absorbing the experience of many champions—and not just those from my own family.

Q: What do you think of the evolution of submission grappling? Since the early days of Brazilian jiu-jitsu, when you taught out a garage in L.A., it has become an established sport with a huge number of followers. Are you surprised?
A: Not really. Think about it. Years ago there wasn't a magazine dedicated to grappling alone; nowadays you have *Grappling Magazine* in the U.S., *Gracie Magazine* in Brazil, and many other magazines totally dedicated to the sport. I think this whole thing has been because of the success that BJJ had in NHB. I believe that BJJ had a tremendous influence in the media in turning public attention to the idea of wrestling and submission styles being a legitimate combat art. All of a sudden, out of nowhere, there was something very different and fresh and very effective that changed the way people viewed fighting. There is not a top-level fighter today who doesn't have BJJ knowledge. Likewise the world of stand-up fighting has made BJJ practitioners look to develop skills that complement their style as well. But when BJJ came into the scene it really created a revolution. Judo is very important, luta livre is very important, wrestling is very important, and sambo is very important—but it was BJJ that initially showed that ground fighting is at least as important as stand-up striking in a fight.

Fitness Training

Training for me is part of my life, the thing that I try to do is to adapt my lifestyle depending on what I am training for. I strongly believe that you have to be extremely fit to be ready for battle. So I have different routines depending if I am going to fight a BJJ tournament, a no-gi grappling event like ADCC, or an NHB match. The only common ground in my training is the aerobic part. I believe that you have to have strong endurance in order to perform at high level. For that I do a lot of running and biking. I like biking a lot because you get to see a lot of things and the exercise is more fun. If I am going to be in an NHB match, then I will lift weights according to a specific routine set up for me by my trainer Jayme Rousso and also take supplements according to the advice of my orthomolecular nutrition advisor Dr. Osvino Pena. I also train boxing with Professor Claudio Coelho.

Brazilian Jiu-Jitsu Training

If I am going to compete in BJJ, which means fighting with a gi, then I will do a lot of judo and do a different series of weight training than I do for NHB. The emphasis is more on endurance rather than strength, so I will focus more on repetitions with lighter weights rather than fewer reps with heavier weights. Also I will train more the auxiliary muscle groups rather than just the main muscle groups of the chest, arts, legs, et cetera. I find that combination strength, where you are working several muscle group together at the same time, is more realistic to how the body will work during a right. This is especially true with the gi, because of the unlimited positions that can result from the grabbing of the gi. I also believe in focusing mentally in order to truly achieve peak performance. The mental aspect is at least as important as the mental. I sometimes focus so hard that I get cranky and irritable. So after the training is done and the event is over I sometimes had to apologize to a lot of people! In the past I have rented an apartment and left my house so that I could concentrate 100 percent on training for events. That of course is really hard because I love my family and I miss them. But becoming a champion requires personal sacrifice. I am very lucky to have a very understanding and supportive wife who has made my life easier rather than make it harder.

No-Gi Grappling Training

If I am training for a grappling event then the training is similar to what I would do for a BJJ tournament but the emphasis is once again different. Grappling is a much more slippery fight than BJJ, because of the fact you don't wear a gi, and the need is for quick explosive motion rather than slow and methodical techniques. Because of this, I adjust my weight training and my cardio exercise accordingly. I do explosive repetitions with heavier weights and other things like that. As far as techniques go I concentrate more on takedowns and on getting

Rodrigo "Comprido" Medeiros
The Tao o f Hard Work

Rio de Janeiro native Rodrigo Medeiros could be the poster boy for the overachievers of the world.

Kid Peligro, photos by Todd Hester

Tall, gangly, and awkward in his youth, Medeiros' first experience with martial arts was in judo, taekwondo, kickboxing, and just a few months of Brazilian jiu-jitsu. Giving them all up by the age of 12, "because I was no good," he stayed away from martial arts until the age of 16. With the academy of world-famous jiu-jitsu instructor Romero "Jacare," Cavalcante, just down the street from his house, though, he used to stop in "just to hang out." Soon, he was befriended by jiu-jitsu phenom Leo "Leozinho" Viera, who eventually talked him back onto the mat at the age of 16.

During his first year he struggled, but despite his lack of success he continued to train hard, spending long hours on the mat when all others had gone home. During his second year, though, his hard work and refusal to quit paid off. He won a succession of state and national weight class and open championships and gained a reputation for his technical, never-say-die attitude of fighting.

When he earned his black belt in 1999, he fought his way to the finals of the Mondials, where he faced the great Mario Sperry. Not given much of a chance, Meideiros shocked the jiu-jitsu world, and himself, by dethroning Sperry. The next year he beat Sperry again and also walked away with the world title. If there was any doubt that he might not be for real, he staked his own claim to greatness when, after losing to Saulo Ribeiro in the 1999 Rio State Championships, he met him at the International Pro Am in North Carolina, and came away with a victory.

Rodrigo Medeiros is an example to all who feel that they lack the talent to succeed. Refusing to be bound by a perceived lack of natural physical ability, Medeiros made up for it with hard work, dedication, and mental toughness. He is a champion in the truest sense of the word.

Q. How did you get started in martial arts?
A: I started with judo when I was 6 years old, I trained judo for two months, then stopped. At 12 years old I did two months of jiu-jitsu but stopped also. Then I did taekwondo and then kickboxing. Then at 16, I started to train jiu-jitsu again.

Q: How did you start training with Romero "Jacare" Cavalcante?
A: My cousin was already training there and the school was really close to my house—right next door, almost. I was a student of Jacare and Leozinho. I already knew Jacare from the area and had been to

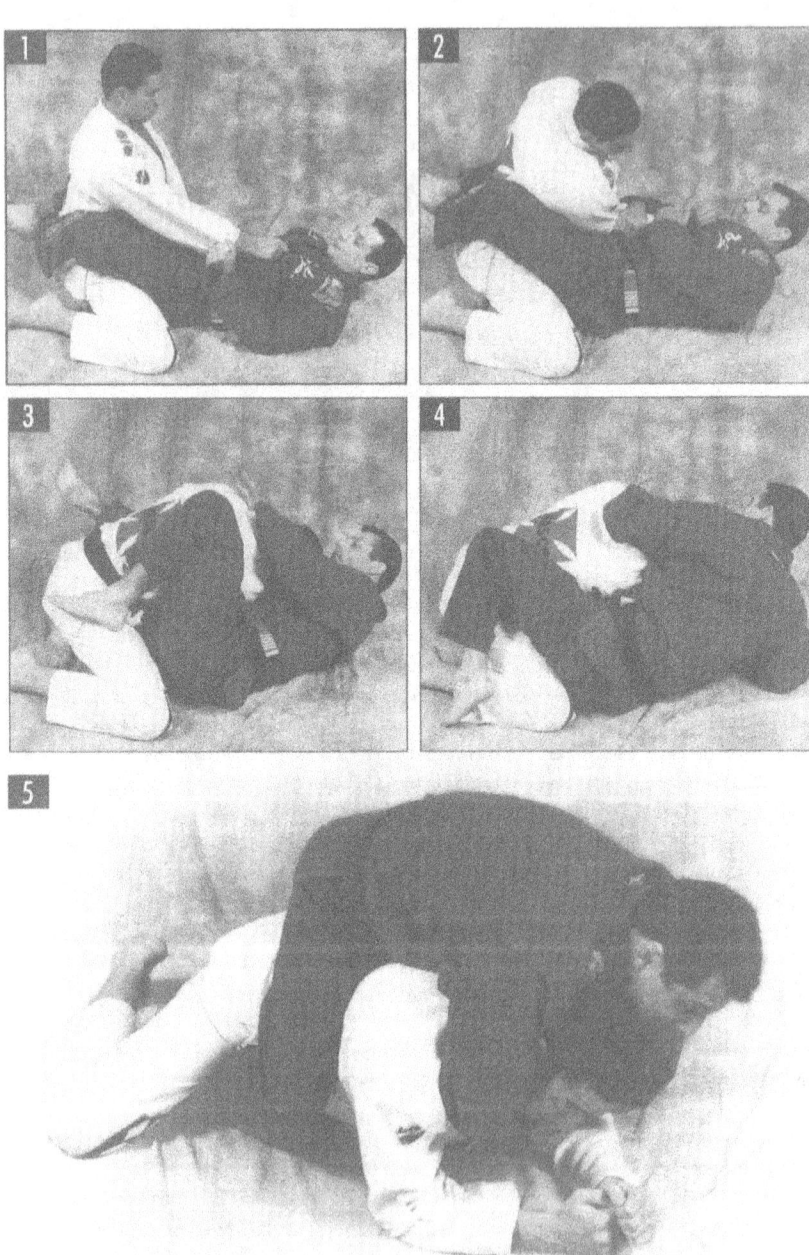

Rodrigo "Comprido" Medeiros is in the guard of instructor Jacare (1). Jacare traps the arm (2), releases his feet into an open guard (3), slides to the back (4), and applies the rear choke (5).

the school when I was 9, and I stopped by the academy many times to hang out because it was so close to my house.

Q: So Leozinho was ahead of you?
A: Yes, he was a purple belt. He was an instructor at the academy and I knew him from my street. We were friends already because he lived next door to me. That was seven years ago, when I really started to take the sport seriously.

Q: Do you practice other sports?
A: I do some judo, and I rock climb, and I boogie board. But jiu-jitsu is not a sport for me—it is my life!

Q: When you started to train, were you great at it right away?
A: No, quite the opposite. I feel that I am still not that natural at it. I feel I am very awkward. The first year I could only do closed-guard; if I ended up in a tournament and happened to get to the open guard, then all hell would break loose—it was desperation time for me. And I couldn't fight from the top at all. My first year of competition was a succession of disasters and I got beat all the time. That happened until almost the last tournament of the year, the 9th Copa Atlantico Sul. I entered that and won not only my weight class in the Juniors 17, but also the Juniors 17 open division. Then the very next week I went to Sao Paulo and won my weight class again. Then next year in the Brazilian Team Championships, I was a new kid, having just got my blue belt, and I beat Ricardo "Cachorrao" Almeida, who was the favorite at the time and almost a purple belt. From then on I started to get on track and do well consistently. I won a few other tournaments that year but the first national title I won was as a brown belt.

Q: What turned you around so suddenly? What was the difference?
A: I always trained very hard. From the moment I got back into jiu-jitsu, I trained twice a day. Leozinho was always there helping me out and taking a personal interest in me. I would always go to the tournaments with Jacare and he would always dissect everything—why I had won, why I had lost, everything about the match—and that helped me to keep on learning. In the beginning I just trained and got better. I don't have a natural gift but because of my hard work I have been successful. I am not like Leozinho, who pulls things out of a hat from nowhere—everything came to me because of extreme hard work and dedication. For example, I would always spend my summer vacation training, while everyone else would stop and just have fun. In my mind, I thought that if others took the time off and I didn't, I'd come out ahead of them at the end of the vacation. I think that gave me a mental edge also.

Q: When you fought Mario Sperry in the 1999 World Jiu-Jitsu Tournament, were you expecting to win?
A: I always enter every match and every tournament with winning on my mind. I knew that it was going to be very difficult because he is a difficult guy to beat. But I had a plan and a strategy to defeat him. I believe that everyone can be beaten. Depending on how you fight you can beat anyone.

Q: So you weren't that surprised when you won?
A: No, that is not it, it was one of the biggest wins of my career. He is a person whom I admire a lot. He has been around for a while and has conquered many things that I haven't. He was the Abu Dhabi

champion and has won several vale tudo matches. But me, my instructors, and all my friends knew that I was capable of beating him. That gave me a lot of strength. So when I entered the absolute division I entered ready to win. I told my instructors, "Put me in because I am going to win." The confidence that I had in myself permeated to my friends and staff and they also started to believe. And in turn their belief in me gave me a lot of power. There were a lot of people with the same objective and the same belief.

Q: You fought Saulo Ribeiro in the Rio State Championships in 1999 and lost. Then you recently came back and beat him in the 2000 International Pro-Am in the United States. Where you surprised to have beaten him?
A: Saulo is a competitor who has many similar traits to me. He is superior to me in that respect—he knows exactly what he needs to do at every point of the match. He dominates the fight all the time, and I knew that he had a strategy to use against me. I am sure he had conceived a plan to beat me: two minutes into the fight he was going to do something, five minutes into the fight if that didn't work he'd do another thing and with eight minutes gone something else. But I, too, had my plans for the fight. I had talked to Jacare and to Leozinho and we determined some things that I should do in the match. And this time my strategy won over him, and I was able to succeed.

Q: Who did you admire in jiu-jitsu when you were growing up?
A: I always admired Fabio Gurgel and Roberto Traven—those where two of the people whom I admired the most. I always admired the way that Jacare conducted himself as a teacher and as a person. Someone else that I admired in a different way, because we were friends even before I started jiu-jitsu, is Leozinho—he is practically my brother. He has always helped me tremendously, and I am sure I would have never had the success that I have had without his help. He has always invested a lot of himself in me. He has always been a spectacular person and fighter. I have been fortunate enough to have seen him training and competing more than most people, and the things that I have seen him pull off are just indescribable. Nowadays another guy that really impresses me is Leo's brother, Ricardo, who is my partner in the school here. Watch out for him—he is going to do some pretty incredible things in the very near future.

Q: Who do you admire today as vale tudo fighters?
A: As fighters, aside from the ones that I have already mentioned, I admire Murilo Bustamante and Ze Mario Sperry, who are great competitors. Also I greatly look up to Royler Gracie, who has been competing forever and always with tremendous success. Many years before I even started to train he was already a black belt and he was fighting all the tournaments never backing down from anyone. I also admire Saulo Ribeiro, Nino and many others. There are too many people I admire to list them all.

Q: Why are you so successful in sport jiu-jitsu?
A: I believe that an athlete cannot allow himself the luxury of being lazy. There are many times that I get home, exhausted from the workout, and I don't feel like training or doing something that is beneficial to my improvement. But I say to myself, "The others that I am going to compete against are training, so I better train." And that motivates me. I am not physically strong, so in order to compensate for that I have to have more endurance and be more technical than the other guys. So I need to train harder than the rest. Nowadays I have a fair amount of tournament experience and that helps a lot. There is no substitute for experience. You just have to get on the mat and compete.

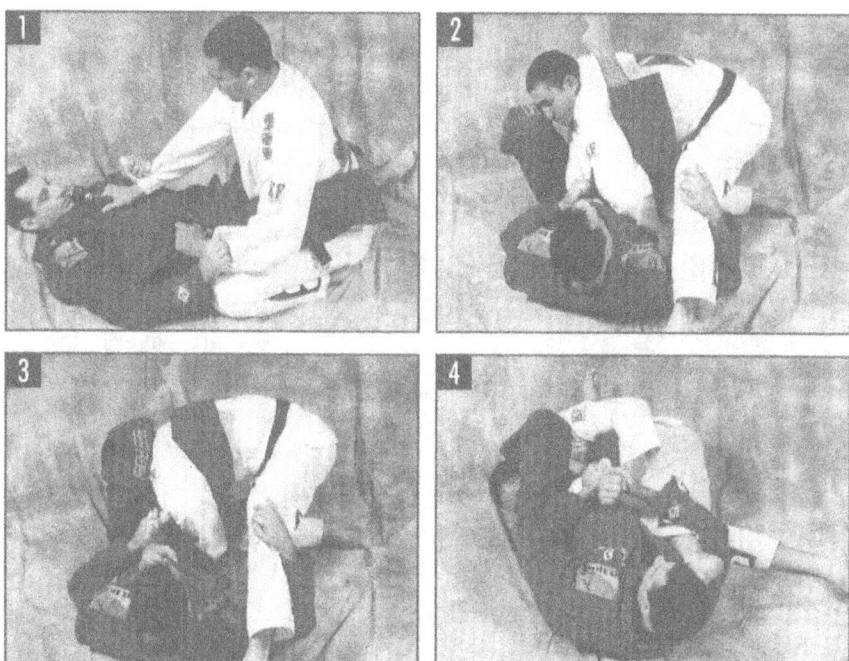

Jacare holds Rodrigo "Comprido" Medeiros in the closed guard (1). Opening his feet, he slides to the outside (2), passes his outside leg over Comprido's head (3), and applies the opposite-side arm bar for the submission (4).

Q: What is your training routine like?

A: My typical day starts by going to college. After that I go to the Vasco da Gama Athletic Club to participate in the physical training of their judo team, under the supervision of Professor Marcus de Albuquerque, who also trains Pedro Rizzo. I train there for 2 1/2 hours. I never leave there extremely tired; it is a specialized training with an objective. He is not there to kill me so that I can't train jiu-jitsu later, that is not the idea. I work specific aspects of movement and balance. Then I teach jiu-jitsu in the afternoon, and when I teach I also practice with my students. Night is the hardest part of the training unless it is near a competition, then I may incorporate a strong training session in the early afternoon also. But I learn a lot from teaching. I believe that when my students ask me questions, I learn a lot from their difficulties, because their questions make me stop and think and improve. I have to figure things out that perhaps I never thought of before. So by teaching you also learn because it forces you to understand the why and what of every position. I also have some questions myself and when I do, I go to Ricardo Vieira or Roberto Traven or Magrao Gurgel, Fabio's brother. I like specific training like side attacks or interval training or stand-up or guard passing. Then we do regular sparring.

Q: Have you ever fought vale tudo?

A: No, I have done some grappling where open hand strikes are allowed but no NHB yet.

Comprido (right) with Jacare.

"In the beginning I just trained and got better. I don't have a natural gift but because of my hard work I have been successful. I am not like Leozinho, who pulls things out of a hat from nowhere—everything came to me because of extreme hard work and dedication."

Q: Are you interested in NHB?

A: Of course I am because it is a very profitable part of the sport. But I am not ready to fight for nothing. If the right sponsor comes along and offers me the right package then I will fight. But I am not in any hurry. I need the right conditions to be able to train for NHB, because the preparation for NHB is quite different that the preparation for a jiu-jitsu match.

Q: What do you think of the jiu-jitsu movement in the U.S.?

A: I believe that jiu-jitsu in the U.S. is growing incredibly well. There are already great fighters such as BJ. Penn who won the worlds as a black belt. Then there is Matt Serra and Bob Bass and others. There are quite a few guys that are starting to make an impact in the international scene. The thing that I believe can harm the development of jiu-jitsu in America is submission fighting. Submission fighting, in my opinion, brings down the technical standards. Because when you take away the gi, you take away a lot of the technical aspects that helps fighters to improve. In submission, strength is worth more than technique, so sometimes you get a purple belt with reasonable skills but a lot of strength going against a black belt. The purple belt may win and that confuses people. Then they go and ask, "Who is the top in jiu-jitsu?" Well, I answer that the top guy is obviously Saulo Ribeiro, because he has won five world titles. But then they go, "Yeah, but who is the best at submission?" My answer to that is also Saulo Ribeiro, because he has also won Abu Dhabi. So these people may decide just to train submission fighting without the gi, because it is more available in the U.S. They lose sight of the fact that the reason he is winning the submission tournaments is because he is so good at jiu-jitsu. So the growth of submission tournaments may affect the growth of jiu-jitsu in America.

Q: What do you think are the Americans greatest strengths and greatest weaknesses? What should they work on to improve?
A: The greatest strength the Americans have is their stand-up skills. Also, because of the background and educational structure they have in wrestling, they have a great advantage there. Their weakness is generally in submissions. I believe that nowadays, just as much as we in Brazil are trying to improve our takedowns and stand-up, the Americans are seeking out good jiu-jitsu instructors to develop their submission skills.

Q: Do you have any plans to conduct seminars in the U.S.?
A: I do. I have made arrangements with Jacare to become the person in charge of coordinating these for the U.S. market. He can be contacted at (404) 843-0606 for that. He is going to be the person in charge of all the seminars for me here, and I want to make regular trips here to share my knowledge with those who want to learn it.

Q: How did you feel about your performances in Abu Dhabi, and what are your plans for it?
A: Abu Dhabi is a great experience, but I never go to a tournament just for experience—I always enter a tournament to win. I haven't been that fortunate there, so I have to gain knowledge from fighting there to do better. I believe that I need a much better understanding of the rules and the style. In retrospect, I certainly would do a few things differently in some of my fights. As far as my performance, I believe that I fought some very good fights from the spectator point of view, with a lot of movement and excitement, but it wasn't enough to win. Eventually, I believe that I can make a big push to be in the finals both in my weight and the absolute division.

Q: What are your plans for the future?
A: There are many avenues that I might choose. There is jiu-jitsu, of course, and also submission grappling and NHB. Right now my objective is the next Abu Dhabi. But I cannot forget about the jiu-jitsu worlds, and I cannot refuse a good offer to fight NHB for the right amount. I am going to take things as they come and strive to improve everyday. I believe that things will sort themselves out and that I will be able to make the right choices given right the opportunity.

Rodrigo "Comprido" Medeiros is available for seminars in the United States by calling Romero "Jacare" Cavalcante at (404) 843-0606. He also has a video tape instructional series available through Unique Publications by calling 800-332-3330.

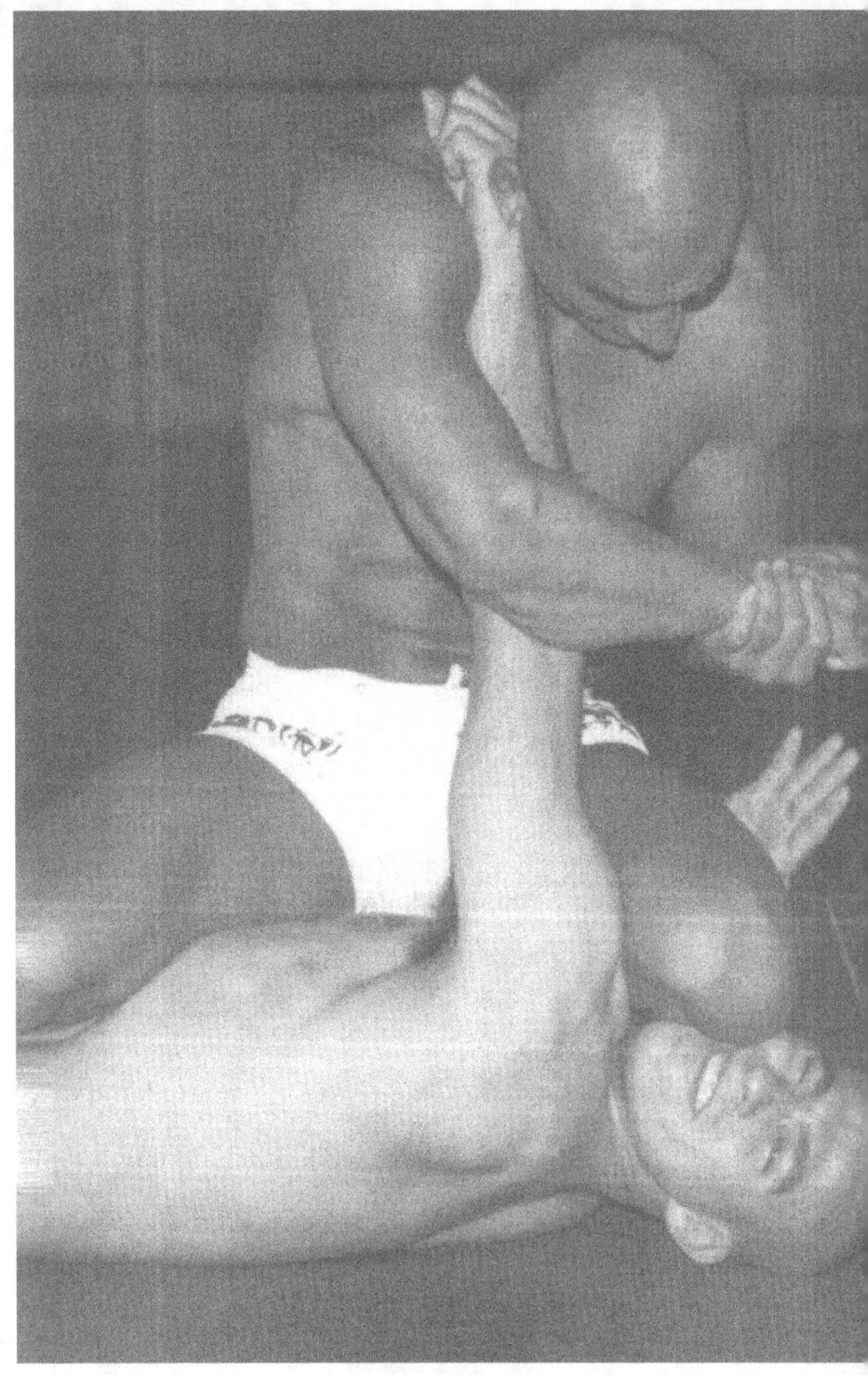

Fabiano Iha's Winning Fight Strategies

Like a calculating chess master, Fabiano Iha checkmates his opponents by anticipating their plans several moves in advance and then leaving them with no way out.

Loren Franck, story and photos

Fabiano Iha looked like a predator as he stared Phil Johns down seconds before their Ultimate Fighting Championship bout last February 23. The semi-main event, scheduled for three five-minute rounds at the Trump Taj Mahal Hotel and Casino in Atlantic City, New Jersey, lasted just 100 seconds. Before his unwary opponent could defend himself, Iha slapped a torturous arm bar on him, forcing Johns to tap out feverishly.

The 30-year-old Iha is proud of his professional fighting record of 12 wins and three losses. Standing only 5'8" and weighing a rock-hard 170 pounds, the native of Florianopolis, Brazil, appears anything but threatening. And though he competes as a lightweight in no-holds-barred and in the UFC, he's clearly a heavyweight in fighting strategy. In Atlantic City, Iha outsmarted Johns more than he overpowered him.

"Johns' level to the ground is different than mine," Iha explains, "which is one reason I could lock my arm bar on him so quickly. I always try to stay a step ahead of my opponents mentally. Fortunately, Johns didn't know what to expect from me, so he was helpless."

Strength, Size And Smarts

A smart grappler will usually defeat an opponent who relies on size or strength alone. In other words, technique is more crucial than strength in the ring. "It is important to use the strength you have," Iha admits, "but you shouldn't rely only on it exclusively. In Brazilian jiu-jitsu, a small fighter can do well against a big one. Big guys who don't train in jiu-jitsu usually don't know how to conserve their energy, so they tire easily during a fight. And once they start to wear out, they become like babies, lacking strength and ability to move quickly."

While fatigued, it's even hard for big, strong and highly skilled grapplers to make an opponent submit. Iha has mastered special techniques that fatigue opponents rapidly and make them extremely vulnerable to his advanced submission holds.

These sophisticated skills are included in the curriculum at the Fabiano Iha Academy in Huntington Beach, California, where the 1994 and 1995 national jiu-jitsu champion of Brazil eagerly

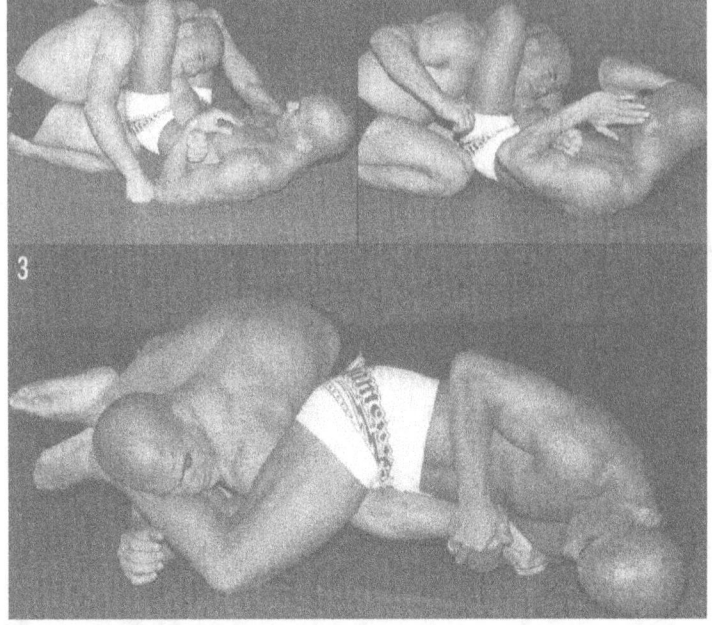

Triangle Arm-Bar
Fabiano Iha holds an opponent in triangle (1). When he refuses to top from the choke (2), Iha releases the triangle and spins over for the arm lock (3).

trains upcoming grapplers. In fact, the school is one of Southern California's most hard-core stables for students of the grappling arts.

But every student at Iha's bustling and spacious training center isn't planning to become a professional grappler. Fewer than 20 percent intend to enter the ring competitively. Most under Iha simply train to improve their confidence and self-defense skills, which is fine with Iha. His classes get great results no matter what his students' goals are.

The Complete Package

Whether in the ring or on the street, no single ingredient makes a good grappler. Rather, it takes "the whole package," Iha claims. "A combination of mental and physical ability can subdue even the toughest mat men."

But don't be fooled. You won't become a champion grappler by perfecting just your submission holds, Iha warns. And you can't depend on only takedowns or escapes. "My fight plan relies on a complex series of strategies rather than a few techniques," Iha elaborates. For example, in an ideal fight scenario, he'll take an opponent to the ground and quickly make him submit using a Brazilian jiu-jitsu finishing hold. It's an excellent fight strategy when he can pull it off—and he usually does.

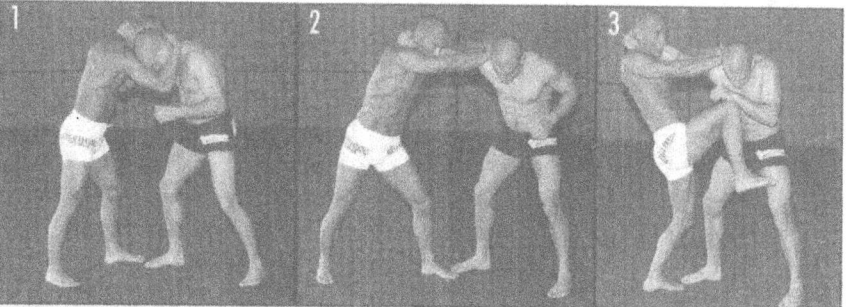

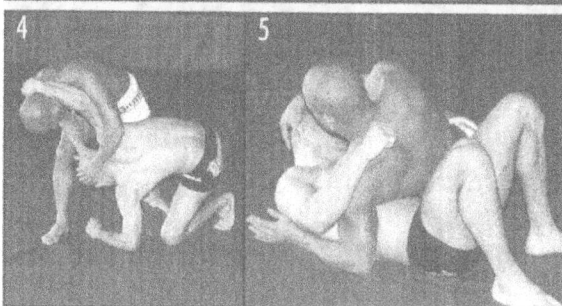

Knee Strike to Side Control
Fabiano Iha is tied up with an opponent (1). Stepping back to create space (2), Iha knees to the chest (3), over-rotates the arm to down his opponent (4), and then follows him to the ground where he establishes side control (5).

"Nevertheless, a champion fighter needs all possible tools," Iha declares, "and he must use them skillfully and with speed." For Iha, there's a sequence to winning a fight. First, he needs his opponent on the ground in a defensive position, so Iha gets close to him at the very beginning of round one. If Iha's opponent excels at kicks or hand strikes, Iha repositions himself frequently. Why? To close the distance without being hit or taken down.

Once he's positioned his opponent in close, he takes him down. "I control him on the ground right after that," Iha explains. "If you can't control him down there, he'll stand up again and try to strike or control you."

As soon as Iha controls his adversary on the ground, he attempts a submission hold or a strike that, in turn, will set up a submission hold. Generally, no matter whom he's facing, Iha's strategy is to close the distance between himself and his opponent, take him down, control him, and end the fight with a submission hold.

Practice Makes Perfect

If you think Iha bases his phenomenal success on new techniques, think again. Although he always seeks better ways to dominate the competition, he's already mastered many fundamental match-winning moves. Repetition of these techniques, he insists, is a main ingredient of mastery in the ring.

"I learn new techniques throughout my training and, of course, share them with my students," Iha concedes. "But I also constantly review old moves. For example, like other grapplers, I use the basic positions to protect myself on the floor, and I implement fundamentals in countless other ways. They're very important."

And because he's deeply rooted in fundamentals, Iha has been able to progress to exceptionally advanced techniques. Most grapplers take years to master these moves. Yet, despite all of the fighting

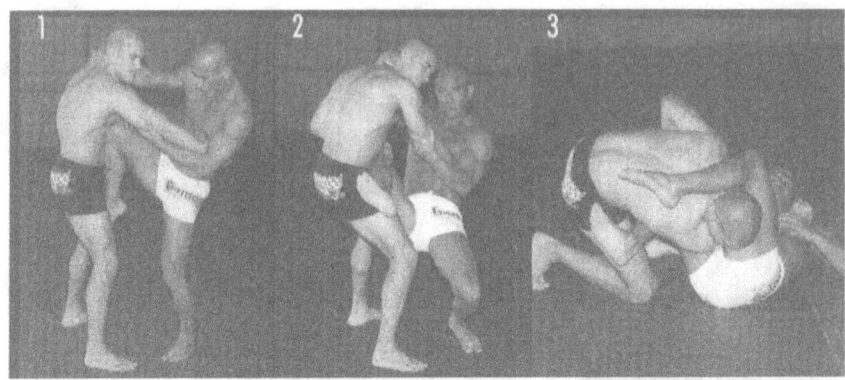

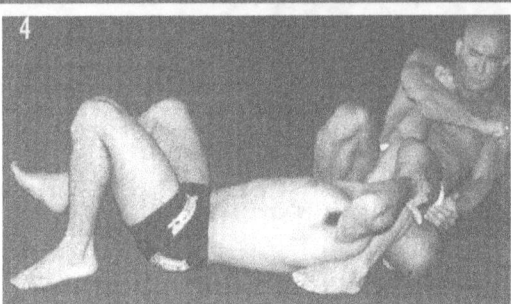

Flying Takedown to Straight Arm-Bar

Tied up with an opponent, Fabiano Iha places his knee in the chest (1), then leans back and puts his shin on the stomach (2), and falls to the ground, bringing his opponent with him while hooking his outside leg over the head (3). Pulling on the arm and extending the hips, Iba applies the straight arm-bar (4).

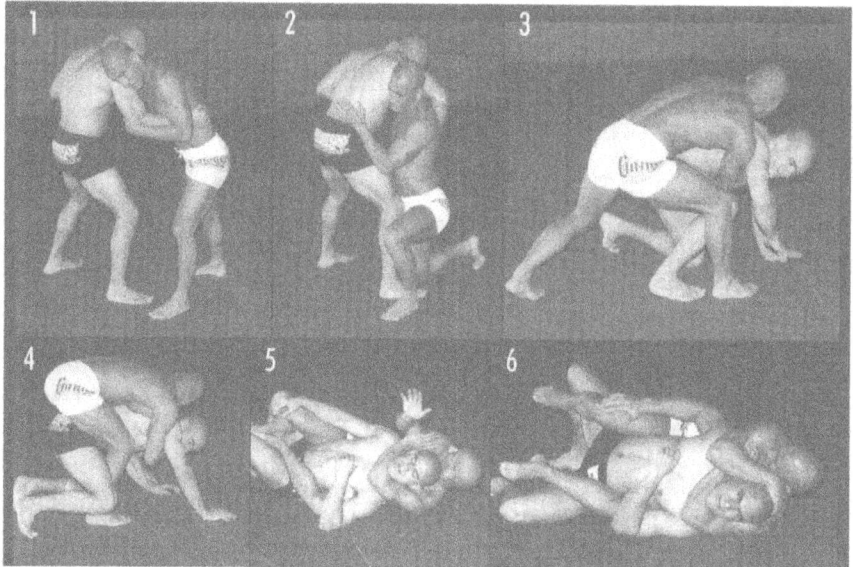

Duck-Under Takedown to Back Choke
Clinched with an opponent (1), Fabiano Iha ducks under his opponent's arm (2), circles to the back (3), puts the hooks in (4), rolls to the ground (5), and applies the naked rear choke for the submission (6).

skills he's perfected throughout his training, Iha drills continuously in the basics and in advanced techniques so they'll remain second nature to him. "When you can do counter moves, escapes, takedowns and submissions without thinking," Iha reflects, "you'll rarely get caught repeatedly in one position. You simply won't let it happen. That's the advantage of constant practice."

Star Power

Submission holds are crucial skills that quickly end fights. Iha learned this lesson when he began his martial arts training more than 15 years ago in Brazil. He knows that the time invested in perfecting submission holds is well spent. But Iha believes that many grapplers need more extensive escape training. That's unfortunate for these fighters because escapes often mean the difference between winning and losing—between a stellar grappling career and one that dies soon after it's born.

Through years of diligent training and experience inside the ring, Iha has discovered that there's an escape for every submission hold. "Timing is very important in escapes," he points out. "As you can imagine, I have to escape before my opponents lock their submission holds on me. Otherwise, it's usually too late."

At his academy, Iha drills students in standard escapes, but he also reveals plenty of more sophisticated fight stoppers. "Everyone can naturally protect himself, even if he doesn't train in the martial arts," Iha says. "This instinctive skill doesn't protect you 100 percent, but you can still look after yourself to some degree." In his workout regimen, however, Iha has gone far beyond instinctive basics.

There are two parts to his escape training. First, Iha gains rudimentary information about each escape. And second, he trains in each technique thoroughly, experiencing how the movements work. He then practices them until he can perform them perfectly. "I've found that the more I train, the better I can escape," Iha reflects. "And once I escape, I can try to control my opponent and make him submit." Prevention and self-protection are also important to Iha's escapes. Essentially, he tries to prevent those he faces in the ring from locking or striking him. "Only after I've protected myself and prevented my opponent from striking or controlling do I try a submission hold on him," Iha says.

Anyone For Chess?
Grappling is like chess, Iha claims. In both pursuits, for instance, participants must know the game and their opponents well enough to anticipate future moves and then take advantage of them. How does Iha know which submission hold his opponent will attempt? And how should he respond to it? This is where Iha's training really pays off. It's given him tremendous insight into every possible situation he could face in the ring.

"The more you train, the more you'll see what submission hold your opponent will try," observes Iha, who routinely takes all information opponents give him and uses it against them. "That's why, when attempting a submission hold, I work two or three submissions in advance. That way, if my opponent escapes from one, I can apply another."

As in chess, this give-and-take is part of the game. When Iha faces an opponent in the ring, he wants a checkmate, so to speak. But sometimes, he must relinquish a short-term objective, such as an advantageous ground position, for the long-term result of winning the fight.

Experience teaches Iha that techniques usually work best in rapid succession. Likewise, it didn't take him long to realize that winning a grappling match can be a numbers game. The more takedowns, controls and submissions you attempt, the more you'll successfully execute, and the more likely it is you'll win.

"It's all very quick, one move right after another," Iha explains. "That's why my submission holds are most effective when my opponent gets tired during a fight. He can't think as fast or move as quickly as when he's fresh, so it's hard for him to escape."

Like A Snake
One of Iha's imperative fight strategies is to maintain control throughout a match. An excellent way he does this is by keeping his opponent's back flat on the ground and by making sure his hips remain close to Iha's body. Iha knows that an adversary in any other position can be dangerous.

Accordingly, he keeps each opponent's body straight and close to the ground during a match. "I handle them as I would a snake," he says with the self-assurance of a reptile expert. "Typically, snakes are weakest when flat on the ground. It's hard for them in that position to bite their victims or wrap themselves around them. So, I don't let my opponents coil and strike. With his back flat on the ground, it's easy to control him."

Iha also endeavors to keep opponents off their feet and out of ground positions where they can take advantage of him. The last thing he wants them to do is gain control of the match and make him submit. "Do your best never to lose control in a fight," Iha admonishes, "because, too often, it's hard to get it back."

The Big Secret
What's Iha's deepest, darkest secret of success? Is it hard training? A special diet? Groundbreaking techniques? Hardly. While hard training, sound nutrition and cutting-edge fighting ability help explain why Iha is such a powerful force in grappling, he maintains it's even more vital to go all-out in body, mind and spirit.

"What will make you a champion?" Iha asks. "Putting your heart into what you do. That's not

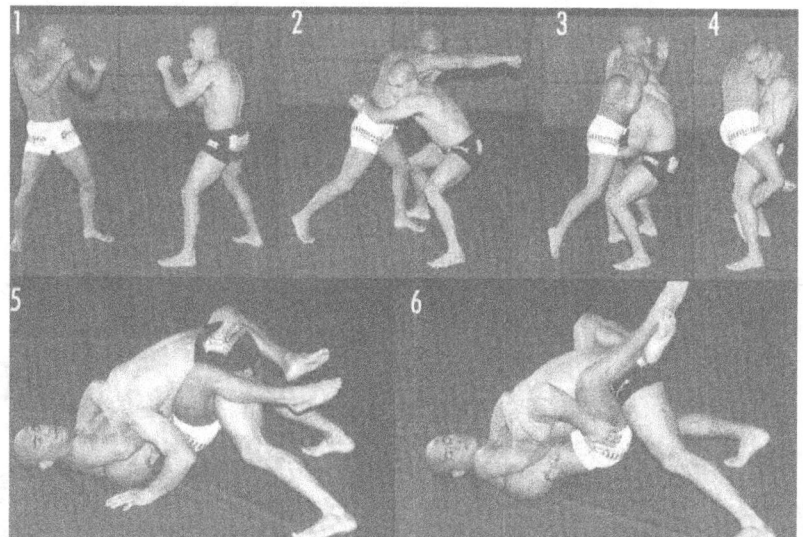

Takedown Counter to Front Choke
Facing an opponent (1), Fabiano Iha throws a straight right which his opponent ducks under and then applies a body lock (2). When his opponent lifts him off the ground (3), Iha hooks the neck (4), falls backwards into the open guard (5), then closes the guard and extends his hips for the front choke submission (6).

only true in NHB and in the UFC, but it's true in any sport." The lust for money and fame never made anyone a true champion, Iha asserts. What counts is the unbridled investment of the heart. "It makes the difference between a champion and a mere contender," Iha concludes. "People who put their heart into grappling learn much faster than those who don't."

So, why is a tough guy like Iha singing the praises of the heart? It all boils down to results. When he speaks about putting his whole heart into grappling, he knows what he's talking about. The rewards keep coming. And he wouldn't have it any other way.

Loren Franck is a Los Angeles-based writer, researcher, martial artist and a frequent contributor to Grappling.

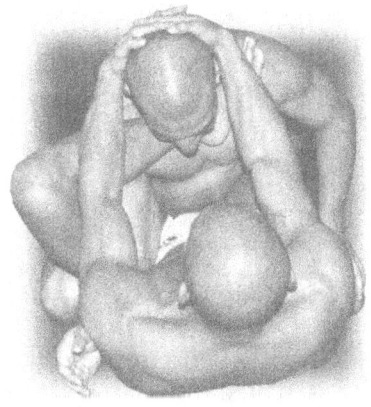

"Big guys who don't train in jiu-jitsu usually don't know how to conserve their energy, so they tire easily during a fight. And once they start to wear out, they become like babies, lacking strength and ability to move quickly."

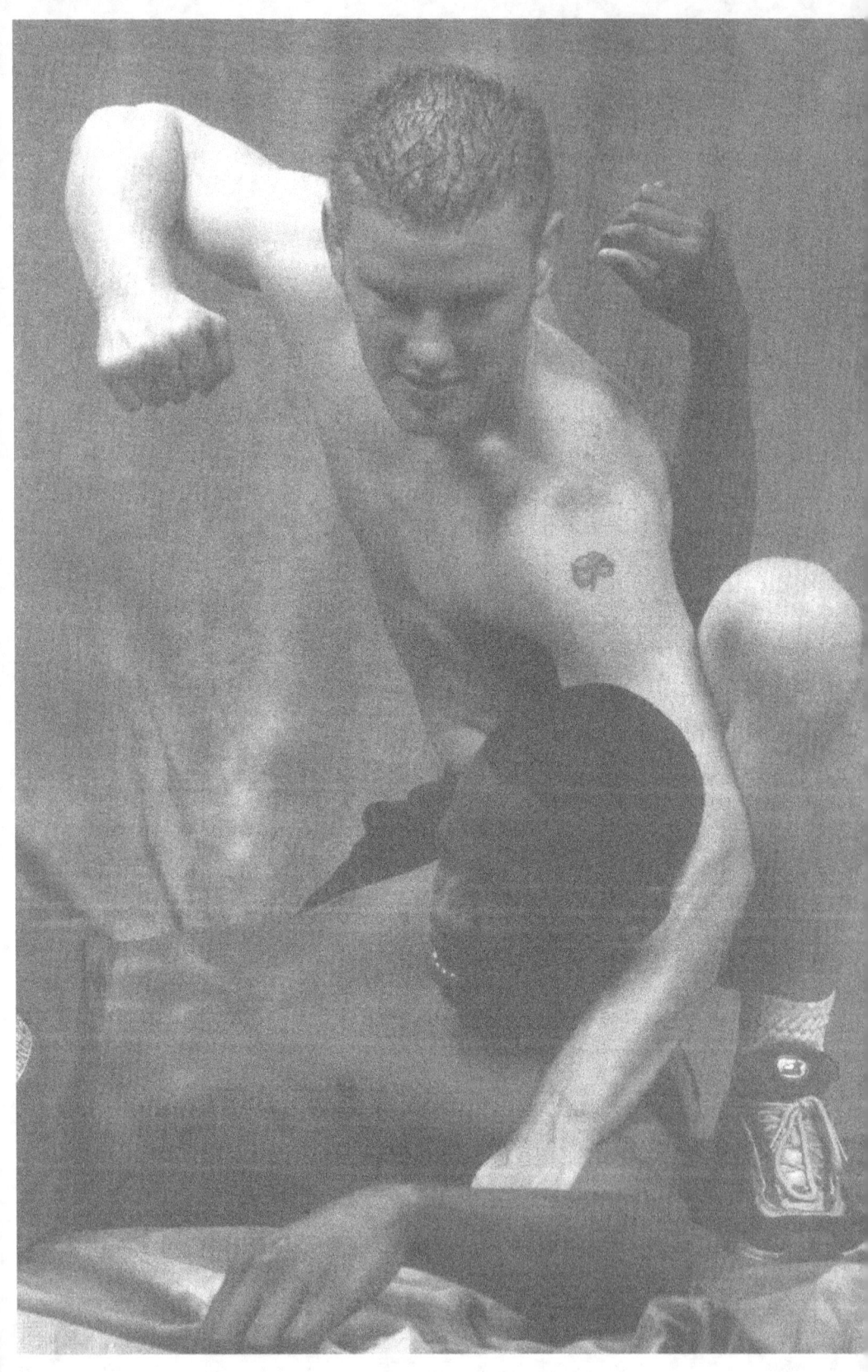

Joe Hurley
They Call Him The Rapper

Joe Hurley has a simple pound-'em-to-the-ground strategy for winning fights—and it works.

Loren Franck

No-holds-barred fighting has never been easy for Joe Hurley. You probably wouldn't call him a natural fighter, and other ring warriors are more highly trained. But that doesn't stop him from winning fights one single bit. Although only 5'8" and a lean 163 pounds, Hurley isn't a lightweight in fighting ability. His career blasted off when, at age 18, he sought out the legendary Ken Shamrock, who quickly recruited him to the Lion's Den stable. After initial training, it didn't take the young, ambitious scrapper long to discover what works best for him in the ring. "I pound my opponents right from the start," explains Hurley, who turned 23 years old in June. "I usually hit them non-stop in the head, even if I just slap them there. Nobody likes it, and after 15 minutes of being rapped in the head, most of my opponents are worn out." A sophisticated fighting strategy? Hardly. Simple-minded? Perhaps. But the soft-spoken, self-effacing Hurley doesn't plan to change. After all, he reasons, why argue with success?

True Knockout Power

Although a growing number of mixed-fighting competitors rely on Brazilian jiu-jitsu and other grappling arts, Hurley would rather invoke pure punching power inside the ring. There's nothing fancy about his blows, however, so he doesn't consider himself a boxer. But he's skilled enough to teach the art along with kickboxing and submission fighting at the Lion's Den in Napa, California, his training headquarters. "I am a puncher," Hurley makes clear. "I use my boxing skills more than anything else during my fights. And when I start pounding an opponent, boom-boom-boom, it's all boxing." Clearly, then, a knockout punch is Hurley's favorite way to win a fight. But if he can't pummel an opponent into submission, he'll use a heel hook, an arm bar, a hammerlock or a choke—anything to make the other guy give up.

Lessons Learned

Not satisfied dispensing cuts, bruises and pain with his fists, Hurley also loves to pummel opponents mentally. Because he's small, he can rarely take other fighters to the mat and overpower them, so he intimidates them with a barrage of hand strikes. "When you watch my fights," Hurley enthusiastically explains, "you'll see that I let the other guy have it with all I've got." That's Hurley's plan for

Takedown Sprawl to a Guillotine Choke
An opponent shoots a takedown on Joe Hurley (1). Sprawling backwards Hurley wraps his arm around his opponent's neck (2). Straightening his back to gain leverage (3), Hurley pushes his opponent's neck into the choke for the submission (4).

every fight. The bare-handed blitzkrieg usually destroys his opponent's psyche as it takes its toll physically. If an opponent takes him down, Hurley quickly tries to stand him up again and punch him into submission, or better yet, knock him out. It's a bizarre tactic, but given Hurley's impressive 11-1 fight record, it works—most of the time.

Following the first loss of his career to Gil Castillo last April 29 in Calusa, California, Hurley was forced to reevaluate his fighting strategy. "When I fought Gil, I went out there and tried to pop him the same way I pop all my opponents," Hurley remembers. "And I did pop him a couple times. But then he took me down, passed my guard, and got on top of me. I couldn't do much. He didn't hurt me, and the fight went the full three five-minute rounds. But he's a big guy and just sat on me." Unfortunately, bodyweight sometimes challenges Hurley, who usually competes at the bottom of the lightweight class, where an opponent can outweigh him by 12 pounds. And when he fights in King of the Cage events as a middleweight, he could face someone 17 pounds heavier than he is. "I don't mind fighting guys who weigh more than I do," Hurley hastens to add, "but when you're in the ring with someone almost 20 pounds heavier than you are, he's going to hit harder because of his extra body weight." Whether the loss to Castillo was a fluke or a simple blunder, Hurley is adamant he won't lose again. And despite the mishap, he'll continue to use his pound-'em-to-the-ground fight-stopping strategy. "Oh, I definitely learned my lesson when Gil beat me," Hurley says, still unnerved by the experience. "No one's ever passed my guard before, and he did it five times. I'll have to figure out how and make sure nobody does it again."

A Versatile Fighter

Although Hurley prefers to punch his opponents into short-lived oblivion, he has additional finishing techniques if necessary, that he has adapted from Thai boxing. To defeat today's fierce and highly skilled mixed-fighting competitors, you can no longer rely on a single technique. You must master various moves that will do the job with equal effectiveness. Hurley learned this early in his career and admits he needs more than punches and elbow smashes to make it big, which is why he trains feverishly in muay Thai kicks and knee strikes. While Brazilian jiu-jitsu is extremely popular in mixed fighting, Hurley uses Thai boxing to supplement his punching skills. When he began training, he learned basic muay Thai from Shamrock and Maurice Smith, a legendary fighter in his own right. And once Hurley became seriously interested in Thai boxing, he found a gym where he could perfect his skills in the lethal art. Further demonstrating his versatility in the ring, Hurley can also sweep an opponent before his adversary knows what hit him. He uses muay Thai takedowns mainly to prepare opponents for his punches. "I'm not a master of anything yet," Hurley maintains, "but I'm pretty good at everything." And what if Hurley takes someone to the mat but can't pound him into submission? He'll pummel him while they both stand.

> "I usually hit them nonstop in the head, even if I just slap them there. Nobody likes it, and after 15 minutes of being rapped in the head, most of my opponents are worn out."

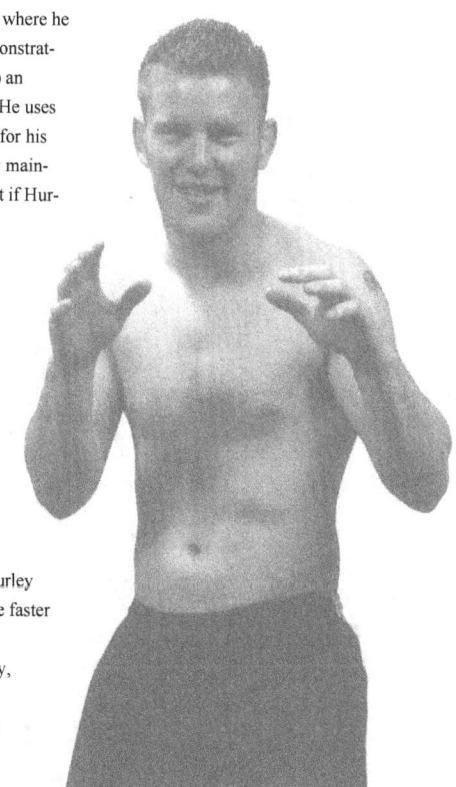

Hurley depends on speed in the ring. In fact, it's one of his specialties. His quick boxing punches frequently catch opponents off guard and send them flying to the canvas. "Speed has always been one of my best assets," he insists. "And when there's a scramble on the mat, I can usually get to my feet more quickly than the other guy can. I'll start to pound him again as soon as I stand back up. "I'm proud to be the squirmy little scrawny guy everyone outweighs," Hurley gloats. "And because I'm small, I'm probably a little faster than most of my opponents."

Never too proud to win a fight quickly and easily, Hurley strikes with other parts of his upper body besides his fists. Muay Thai supplies him with a full range of hand strikes and kicks. Besides punches, powerful, instantaneous elbow strikes are perhaps his favorite moves. "People tell me I'm notorious for my elbow strikes," Hurley admits, flashing a mischievous a grin. Notorious may be the wrong word, however. Hurley cut Charlie Kohler to shreds with elbow strikes in a recent bout, and he KO'd another opponent with one. Other recipients have seen stars after being belted with a Hurley elbow strike.

Wear And Tear

The punches, kicks and elbow strikes Hurley delivers in the ring are deceptively powerful. As a result, most of Hurley's opponents try to extend their distance or close the gap when

Inside Guard-Pass to a Straight Knee-Bar
foe Hurely fights for position inside his opponent's open guard (1). Stepping inside, Hurley spins to the outside (2), secures the ankle (3), leans to his side (4), then extends his body and applies pressure to the knee and ankle for the submission (5).

Best of Grappling, 2001

they square off with him. Unfortunately, during a recent fight, one of Hurley's opponents didn't get the message soon enough. "I broke the guy's eye socket," the now penitent Hurley recalls. "He ate 25 knees to the head, and officials still wouldn't stop the fight. He looked really bad afterward." If Hurley can't submit an opponent or knock him out, he'll wear him down and eventually wear him out. His daily six-hour workout regimen—cardio, weight training, boxing and muay Thai—keeps him in terrific shape, imbued with noticeably more muscle tone and endurance than many of his opponents. "I'm pretty good at wearing people out," Hurley concedes. "For instance, when I'm on my back and lock my opponent between my legs, I can hold him there while I beat the hell out of him. He'll be too tired to fight back because I've worn him down."

An Eye On The Future

Most mixed-fighting competitors claim to love their sport. Such sentiment is common among professional athletics, and mixed-fighting competitors are no exception. Many retire only when their bodies finally can't take the abuse suffered in the ring. Yet Hurley takes his dedication to the sport one step further. He's obsessed with submission fighting. "HI do it until the day I die," he swears. Before he stops fighting, however, Hurley plans to cash in on the big money he predicts will soon permeate the sport. Far from being the mixed fighting's highest-paid competitor, he hopes that will change. "I'm waiting for the money to hit the sport," he says with relish. "It already has to some degree. A few of my buddies are making more money in it than ever, so I'm waiting for my turn." Meanwhile, Hurley continues to train hard, plan his career carefully and expect the best. Still waiting for his next fight to be scheduled, he claims, in classic mixed-fighting bravado, that he'll take on anyone who's close to him in body weight. "Actually, I don't think anyone really wants to fight me," Hurley says. "Even if someone defeats me, I will have abused him quite a bit in the process. People know I'm a pounder, so they know it's coming. They just don't know how badly. And what they don't know will hurt them."

Loren Franck, a frequent contributor to Grappling, *is a Los Angeles-based writer, researcher and martial artist.*

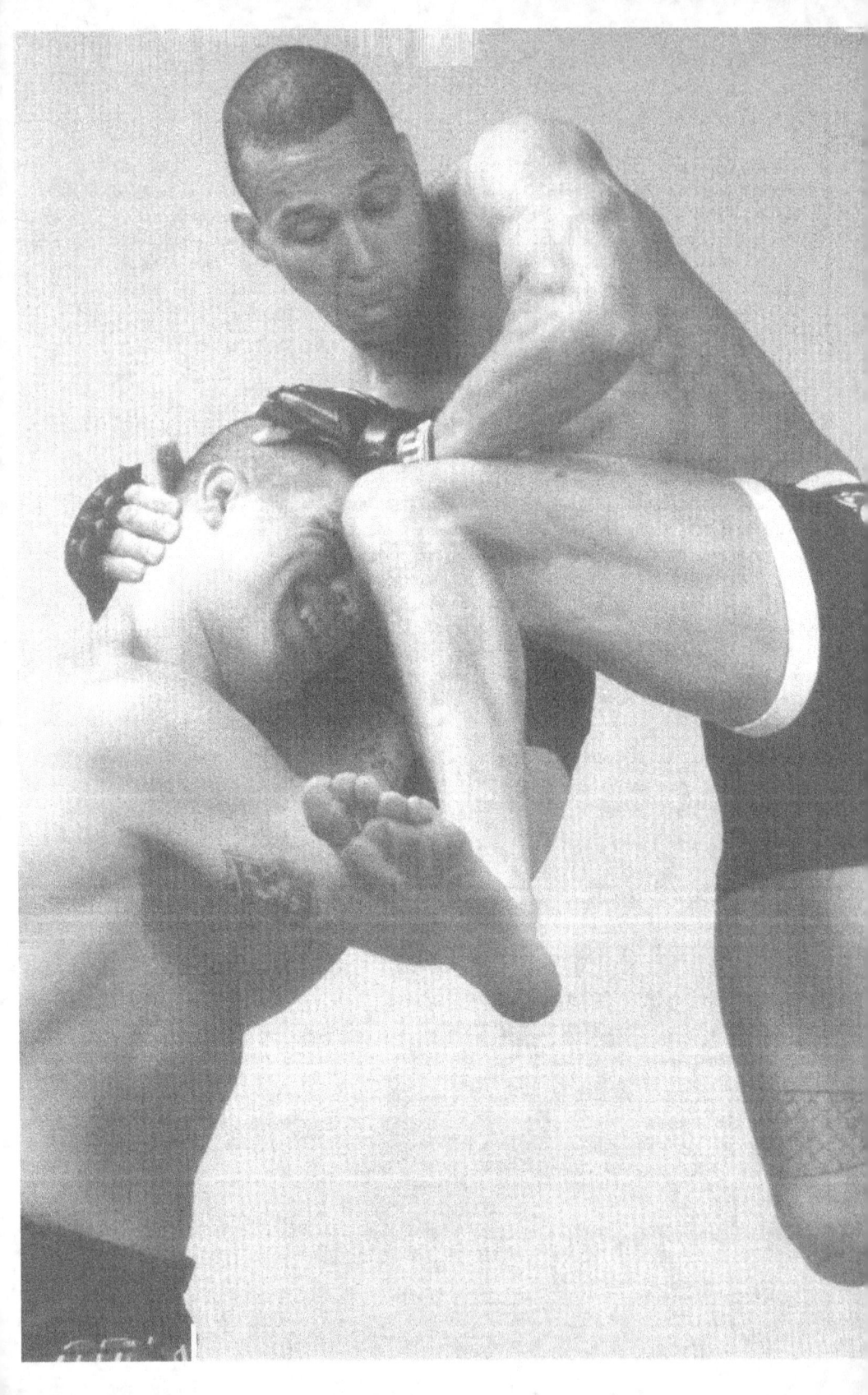

John Lewis
Warlord of the New Millennium

*Multi-cultural, multi-talented, and multi-faceted,
John Lewis is the physical, spiritual, and mental embodiment
of the term "mixed martial artist."*

Todd Hester

John Lewis is on a roll. No matter what mixed-martial-arts (MMA) show you attend, whether in the U.S. or Japan, it is hard to find one that doesn't feature a competitor who has either trained with or under, the Las Vegas-based fight guru. From Tito Ortiz, to Fabiano Iha, to Chuck Liddell, to Maurice Smith, to Marvin Eastman, to Tony Desouza, to Egan and Enson Inoue, to Eric Pele, to BJ. Penn, to Marc Laimon, and more—Lewis-influenced fighters populate the upper stratosphere of the no-holds-barred world. As impressive as his teaching credentials are, however, what sets Lewis apart is his uncanny ability to relate to and understand, people from all races, cultures, and backgrounds. Lewis recently added another feather to his cap when he became one of the first two people ever granted a mixed-martial-art promoter's license in the State of Nevada. But Lewis is not one to stay in one place. "If you're not moving forward," Lewis says, "then you're going backwards. I always try to challenge myself with new ideas and new projects." True to his words, Lewis recently formed the World Fighting Alliance (WFA), and plans to hold MMA shows in Las Vegas later this year. If Lewis meets with the same success that has become the trademark of whatever he does, expect to hear big things from the WFA in the very near future.

Q: What is your family background?
A: My mother is originally from New York and my father from Gainesville, Florida. I was born in Hawaii on February 8, 1968. My father is an executive chef and he moved to Hawaii for a job. I think a big part of the reason they moved there, though, was for me and my sister Terri. My father is black and mother is white and there was no real racism in Hawaii. In Florida, though, during the late '60s, that wasn't the case. After 4 or 5 years in Hawaii we moved back to Daytona Beach, Florida for 3 or 4 years. I was older then and racism was very obvious. In elementary school I got into a lot of fights because of the racism and so we moved back to Hawaii after I got out of the fifth grade. I've always been a calm person at all ages. I wasn't a punk or a rabble rouser. I tried to be as friendly as I could in school. But if someone was unfair to me or to my sister, who is two years younger, I had no qualms about standing up for myself.

In Hawaii it was different. There is no real racism there because the society is so multi-cultural, but if you weren't a local you got a lot of attitude. I was constantly called *haole* (outsider). In Hawaii, the testosterone level is very high, and the people are very fast to fight. People will fight at the drop of the hat, and if you don't stand up for yourself and fight then you'll get a reputation as a punk and will get picked on more. So I got into a lot of fights because I never backed down. Being of mixed race, though, I grew up with a lot of tolerance for everybody. I never viewed myself as black or white—just as myself. My friends were just my friends and I always treated people based on how they were as human beings, not on the color of their skin or their ethnic origin.

Q: Did you take any martial arts as a kid?
A: No, but I was always really athletic and I could naturally fight well—I remember the only streetfight I lost was in the sixth grade. I didn't really know anything formal, but I always had a strategy of how I'd fight. I just wouldn't put my head down and fight—even if it probably looked like that. But even though I never picked fights, I saw that the more fights I won the more accepted and popular I became. Looking back, it certainly isn't something I'm proud of—but at the time it was all I knew and so that gave me reinforcement in the fighting mindset. In the eighth grade I got into "popping" or street dancing- which is like stand-up break dancing—it was very popular at the time. Because I was very athletic I was good at it.

Q: So did you stop fighting?
A: No. In the ninth grade we had our own high school version of fight club. We would meet below a bridge near the school and a bunch of guys from all the local schools would just meet and fight one- on-one. There were no weapons or anything—and no one ever got hurt beyond a black eye or a bloody nose. But I never lost one of those fights and it made me start analyzing how I was fighting and what worked and didn't work. So that is when I started to get a formal interest in martial artists. A lot of guys that I fought did take martial arts—I still beat them but it did make me think that I should get more formal training. So I started taking kickboxing and I got better and better. Probably my dancing helped me to progress fast. During my time in high school I was dancing professionally all the time. I opened for Menudo three times at the Blaisdell Arena and many other shows.

At the end of my senior year a friend of mine named Steve Silva called me from the mainland and had me come out to audition for a show in Las Vegas. This was big step for me because I had just turned 17. Because my parents always supported me in what I wanted to do, they let me go. I got accepted for a show at the Riviera called "Splash," which was the number one show in Vegas at the time. During this time I was still training kickboxing. It was definitely second to my dancing—but I still did because I liked it. After two years of doing the show, I decided that I wanted to get into writing and singing music so I moved to Los Angeles where the music business was.

Q: So with whom did you train there?
A: When I came to L.A. I met a man who would change my life—Dan Koji. He was from Japan and had his own system that I can best describe as muay Thai for the street. He called it "Shokondo." It was the first intense, philosophical, real martial art that I had respect for. As good as I thought I was at fighting, Dan could take me out at will. To me, he was every bit as good as Bruce Lee. He's back in Japan now, but he is still phenomenal. He liked my talent immediately and started teaching me privates. Within two years I had earned a black belt in his system—the first black belt he ever awarded. I was living in Culver City at the time, and my backyard was set up like a training center with

Training Tips For A No-Holds-Barred Fight

Assuming that you're always in shape, start training two months in advance. The first two weeks of the 8-week training regimen is pure conditioning to prepare you for the 6 weeks to follow. The routine varies according to the fighter, but the basic concept is to start with one hour of cardio every morning which can consist of various gym machines such as treadmills, stairmasters, and climbers. I also advocate swimming, jogging and sprinting. After a small breakposition drills until 1:00 pm. We then have lunch and meet at 3:00 pm at the UNLV boxing gym and train with Skipper Kelt. We box for two hours and also run hills.

Lewis drills Fabiano Iha

The intensity of each day may vary, but the training is always hard. We follow this routine five days a week and take the weekends completely off.

Lewis training Tito Ortiz (standing) and Marc Laimon while Egan Inoue looks on.

heavy bags, double-ended bags, a mat area, a wing chun dummy, and sticks for Filipino martial arts. I was exposing myself to as many arts as possible because I felt that no one art was complete and that they all had important aspects. I would go to a lot of different schools for several months as a time until I felt that I had the essence of what they were teaching. Then I would incorporate what I liked and move on to something else.

I was influenced a lot by *The Tao ofjeet Kune Do* by Bruce Lee. He was the first guy who realized you had to know different things. I felt the same way before I ever

Open-Guard Pass To Side Control *John Lewis faces an opponent in an Abu Dhabi no-gi submission match (1). Lewis splits the open guard (2), leaps over his opponent's knees (3), lands on his shoulder, trapping the stomach (4), then turns inside, blocking the head and leg, to establish side control (5).*

read his book, but when I did it made me think even more that way. I wasn't necessarily trying to become a JKD artist, because from reading Bruces book and notes I felt that even that would be too limiting.

Q: Were you influenced by anyone else?

A: Oh, yeah. While I was doing all this experimenting, a friend of mine wanted me to meet his teacher from New York who was a wing chun instructor and a former kickboxing champion. So he came out from New York and we sparred together—his name was John Peretti. He told me about Gene Lebell and introduced me to him in his cabin in the mountains. Gene is great guy and he would have a select group of students to come up to train at the cabin. A lot of the best martial artists in the »«««MSM®si«mmm^ world have learned and trained at Gene's cabin. So I started grappling with Gene and it soon became a real passion. I ended up training consistently with him for 5 or 6 years—I still consider myself to be his student and I go back and train with him when my schedule permits. While I was training with Gene, a friend of mine told me about the Gracie family who were great at the ground game and he took me to Rickson Gracie's school in Los Angeles. So I started training jiu-jitsu with Rickson.

> "There are certain things that you can only learn from stepping into the cage. My biggest lesson was that no single technique or strategy works best in cage fighting. You have to be flexible and adaptable."

Q: Was Brazilian jiu-jitsu different from Gene Lebell's style?

A: Gene knows a tremendous amount so none of the techniques were new to me. What jiu-jitsu mainly taught me was the smooth transition between positions and submissions. In jiu-jitsu, the smooth transition between positions is unique to the art. So I started accelerating at a fast rate in jiu-jitsu because I already understood so much from Gene and had the basics down. I became the first person to go from white belt all the way to black belt with Gene—that was a great honor for me. Gokor was there before me, of course, but he was already a master grappler and Gene just fine-tuned him. So it was special that I was given that rank.

Q: When did you start fighting?

A: I began my fight career in an Hawaiian show called UFCF, put on by Matt Hume. I fought a Pancrase fighter who was one of Karl Gotch's top students and I won in 1:42 via an arm-bar. John Peretti and Gene LeBell were both in my corner for that. When I got back from the states I got a call from John Peretti saying that if I really wanted to test myself that he was starting a show called Extreme Fighting—and he needed someone to fight Carlson Gracie Jr. At the time, I was training with the Gracies and I was a big fan of theirs. I was only a blue belt and everyone was telling me not to take the fight because they were sure there was no way I could beat Carlson. But I knew that I had a lot more than just jiu-jitsu to bring to the

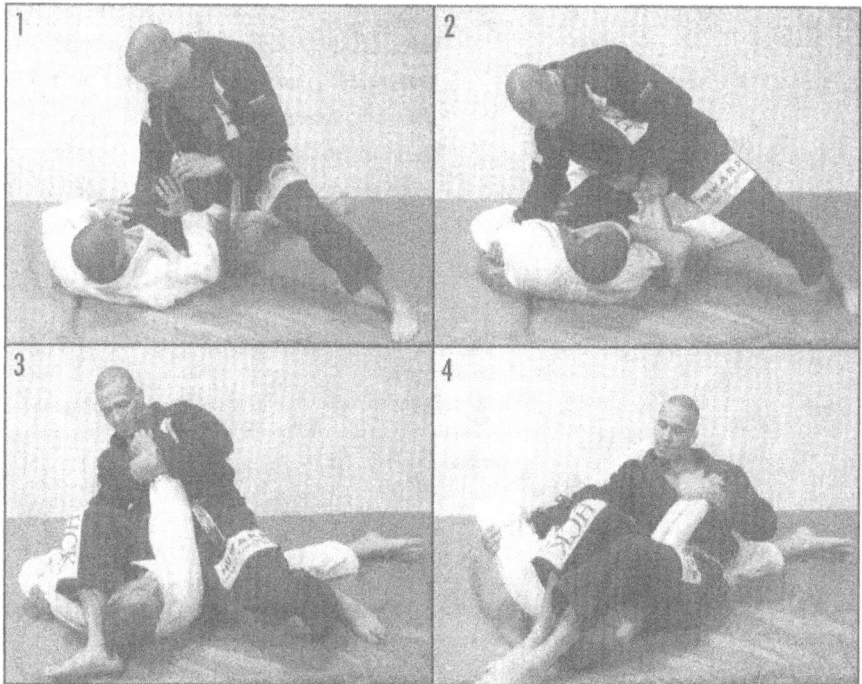

Knee-On-Stomach Arm Bar
Controlling his opponent in a jiu-jitsu match (1), John Lewis under-hooks the arm pit and secures the near arm by grabbing the lapel (2). Passing his leg to the far side of his opponent's neck (3), Lewis straightens the arm and applies the elbow-joint submission (4).

table because of my stand-up experience and my years with Gene. I think I might have been a little tentative for that fight, but even then I controlled the fight and fought Carlson to a draw. And this was when everyone was being dominated by the Gracies, so I felt very good about it.

Q: What did the jiu-jitsu community feel about you fighting a Gracie?
A: Well, before the fight everyone said how great Carlson Jr. was and that I didn't stand a chance against him—but afterwards those same guys told me he wasn't one of the top jiu-jitsu men. So I have to laugh about that. It isn't that Carlson Gracie Jr. is not a good fighter—that's not true at all—he's very, very good. I just think that he was expecting someone who was a jiu-jitsu blue belt, and I was actually a black belt under Gene Lebell and had also been training Brazilian jiu-jitsu for two years. So I had 8 years of grappling and even more years of kickboxing. I think I took him by surprise.

Q: So did you continue to train BJJ?
A: Of course! After that fight I was introduced to who I consider to be one of the top jiu-jitsu instructors in the world—Andre Pederneiras. Andre is a black belt under Carlson Gracie Sr., and is also the founder of top jiu-jitsu team in the world, *Nova Uniao* (New Union). I trained with Andre in the

> "Hopefully you can learn to attack like a professional—but if not you have to learn to defend like one. Most importantly, if you ever want to be great you have to have a strong sense of strategy."

U.S. and I was so impressed that I eventually went to Brazil and trained with him there. I'm now a second degree black belt under him and I give him 100 percent credit for my rapid progression in jiu-jitsu and my current technical level.

Q: Did the Carlson Jr. fight lead to more offers?
A: Quite a few. I took every fight that I was offered against any opponent. I went even further and always asked the promoters for the best opponents. I fought Rumina Sato, Johil De Olvira, Kenny Monday, Lowell Andersen, and many others. I learned from every fight. Each time I fought it seemed like I had someone with different skills and different strengths. I would always concentrate on the skills I needed to compete successfully with them. There are certain things that you can only learn from stepping into the cage. My biggest lesson was that no single technique or strategy works best in cage fighting. You have to be flexible and adaptable. In the cage, you can never be at a loss in a ground position—you have to know how to attack and defend wrestling takedowns, and you have to understand kicking and punching, Hopefully you can learn to attack like a professional—but if not you have to learn to defend like one. Most importantly, if you ever want to be great you have to have a strong sense of strategy. A lot of my current stand-up strategies come from my current mentor and trainer, former pro-boxer "Saigon" Skipper Kelt. Skipper was a top-level boxer who fought for the welterweight title many times. Even now he is just a stud in the ring. He's the current boxing coach at UNLY and the Lewis/Pederneiras Vale Tudo Team boxing coach.

Q: What led you to open a martial arts school in Las Vegas?
A: I love martial arts so it was only natural for me to come to Las Vegas to open it because of my connections from the time I was a dancer. As soon as I opened the school, students enrolled and it started moving forward. I was a little nervous when I opened it, of course, but I felt that I had something important to teach. I was very gratified when it went so well. I met Chuck Liddell a couple of years after I opened the school. He told Tito Ortiz about me and Tito joined the training group also. We got along so well that Tito asked me to be his trainer and cornerman for his title fight against Van- derlei Silva.

Q: How did you help Tito prepare for Vanderlei?

A: Well, Tito and I both knew that Vanderlei would be a tough match, so we devised a strategy that we felt would give Tito a 90 percent chance of winning. We planned on using Tito's wrestling skills to neutralize Vandelei's striking power. Vanderlei always comes forward aggressively with very bad intentions. So knowing that, we decided that Tito would stand straight-up like he was going to punch, then drop under Vanderlei's punches at the last second and shoot for the takedown. That didn't give Vanderlei a chance to sprawl and counter the takedown because he was coming forward to punch. This worked the entire night. In our ground training, we attacked Tito from our guard constantly, doing sweeps and trying to get to our feet—just as we thought Vanderlei would do. We did this over and over. With this strategy, we felt that Tito could take him down at will at the beginning of each round, then ground and pound and work from there. So in my mind there was no way Tito was going to lose except to a lucky punch. That didn't happen and Tito dominated for the decision victory.

Q: Did this victory attract more students?

A: After Vanderlei, a lot of guys wanted to train with me and start fighting—I now have hundreds of students. I don't let anyone even think about fighting, though, until they're at least a purple belt in jiu-jitsu. They also have to have a high intellectual and athletic ability. Nowadays, I have people moving to Las Vegas from all over the world to train with me. To qualify for the Lewis/Pederneiras Vale Tudo Team they first have to be very strong in one area—meaning they have to be a strong kickboxer, or a jiu-jitsu man, or wrestler, or whatever. They have to have a special skill I can build on. The success of our team doesn't come from making a generic mold that I try to fit all my students into. It comes from my ability to recognize and build on people's individual talents.

If you're a strong kickboxer, for example, I'm not going to try to turn you into a jiu-jitsu fighter, I'm going to teach you how to avoid being taken down. If you are taken down, I'll work on how to fight from your back so you can get to your feet and attack with your strength again. If you're a strong submission artist, then I'm going to teach you superior takedown abilities so you can take your opponent down and implement your submission skills on the ground. I also work to develop everyone's stand-up game, because everyone in vale tudo needs striking skills. I try to make people great at whatever they're good at.

Q: You are one of martial arts most popular figures. Why?

A: I think part of what makes fighters feel comfortable with me and contributes to the team's success, is that I'm not so egotistical to think I am a god-like instructor. I exploit the strengths of the best guys on the team to teach the other guys. For example, Maurice Smith teaches leg kicks, Tony DeSouza teaches takedowns, Marvin Eastman teaches muay Thai, et cetera. I let the experts be the experts and I learn from them also. The end result is that there is no situation in the mixed martial arts game that we don't have an answer to as a team.

For information about training with John Lewis and the Lewis/Pederneiras Vale Tudo Team visit www.lewisjiujitsu.com or call 702-248-3432.

5 Spinning Killer Knee-Bar Attacks

Erik Paulson

Many people feel that knee-bars are advanced moves which are difficult to set-up and to lock in. This is not true. If you can use the arm lock then you can also use a variety of leg and knee bars with equal success.

The knee bar or knee lock is a submission that can be approached from every ground position. The options on the attack can go from the knee to the hip lock or key lock, from the knee to the Achilles figure-four foot lock, or from the knee to the heel hook or shin lock. These are what makes this a very versatile and usable lock. The first important factor that should be learned to make this lock effective is the application. The second thing is learning the variations in order to take the lock from every position. The third is your set-ups to your leg attacks or ways to get.

Technically, the fulcrum should be on the pubic bone or hip. The feet can be placed on the buttocks either with the legs bent for maximum bridging power, or the feet side-by-side or crossed. Another way is that the legs can be figure-foured with heavy emphasis on the knee squeeze. The foot can either go under the armpit closest to the opponent's body, or should be placed with the foot on the outside part of the face closest to the floor, holding the heel so you don't lose control of the knee.

My theory on leg attacks is that if the person is a good grappler they are going to consistently use their legs in their game because the guard is 360 degrees. So the legs are consistently coming into play. To catch the leg you have to attack something else in order to fool them into giving you the leg. For example, fake passing the guard so when they start defending with the legs—viola! Spin backwards over the leg into a knee bar. It is unorthodox in that you are giving them your back, but this also gives you an advantage in that they will not expect them to apply a finishing move from an "inferior" position. Next, when both fighters are evenly matched and both are at their peak of endurance at the beginning of a match, if you attack immediately and you miss the submission, you waste a lot of energy trying to take that leg, and you also end up in a bad position. So it is easier to attack the leg after you have "baked" your opponent.

Everyone now is learning the legs, especially in Brazil, and it is the latest craze all over the world. You need extensive knowledge on attacks and defense. The key is to get good at your attacks, learn how to hide your legs, and more so learn how to defend them. So many people spend 90 percent of their time learning how to attack the legs, but then ignore the counters and will get caught by a less-knowledgeable grappler. I learned how to defend leg attacks due to my extensive fighting in the Shooto organization, where all fighters attack the legs. The best person I could ever recommend to teach leg attacks is Yori Nakamura, the president and founder of Shooto in America. I learned many great leg attacks in Shooto but also Pancrase has many effective moves, as does Sombo. For selfdefense breaks, the Indonesian art of Pentjak Silat Mande Muda has many devastating moves. Two other great teachers of effective leg submission attacks in the United States are "Judo" Gene LeBell and Gokor Chivichyan.

Attention to the legs will enable you to diversify your arsenal, and will also make your arm attacks more effective as your opponents will have one more factor to confuse them. When they know you can attack their legs they will start to defend them, and then when that happens it will open up your upper body submissions and chokes.

For seminars, tapes and training products visit www.erikpaul-son.com or call (310) 785-5805.

Inside Guard Pass to Outside Knee Bar
Erik Paulson is trapped inside Marious' open guard. One of his opponent's hooks is inside his near leg, and his far leg is trapped by his opponent's opposite foot (1). Paulson posts to the outside of the hooked leg (2), puts his hips up and backspins over his opponent's far leg (3), and the secures the ankle and leans back in the knee-bar submission, while pulling on the leg to prevent the escape (4).

Best of Grappling, 2001

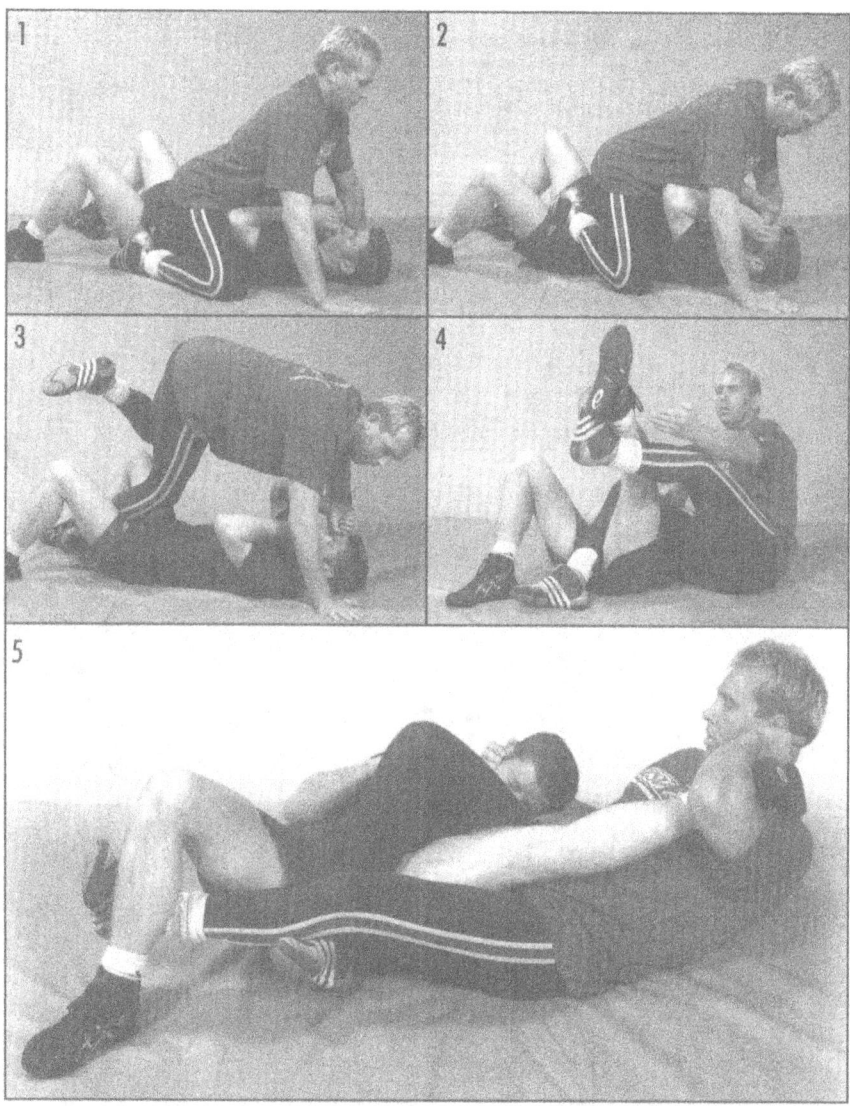

Top Mount to Reverse Jumping Knee Bar
Erik Paulson controls Marious from the top mount position (1). Paulson inserts a single hook inside Marious' near hip (2). Posting high, Paulson back-spins over his opponent's leg (3), sits down and traps his opponent's ankle with his foot (4), then grabs the foot, applies a figure-four knee squeeze, and applies the knee-bar submission while controlling the head (5).

Knee on Stomach to Reverse Knee Bar

Erik Paulson immobilizes Marious with a knee on the stomach (1). His opponent uses his bottom hand to shove Paulson's knee off to reduce the pressure (2). With the pressure reduced, Paulson's opponent scoots his hips away and makes Paulson's knee hit the floor (3). Using his knee as a focal point, Paulson back-spins over both his opponent's legs (4). To hold his position, Paulson grasps both of his opponent's legs (5), leans back while holding one leg and pinning the other (6), then puts his leg down his opponent's center, applies a figure-four on the far leg, controls the opposite elbow to eliminate the counter, and applies the submission (7).

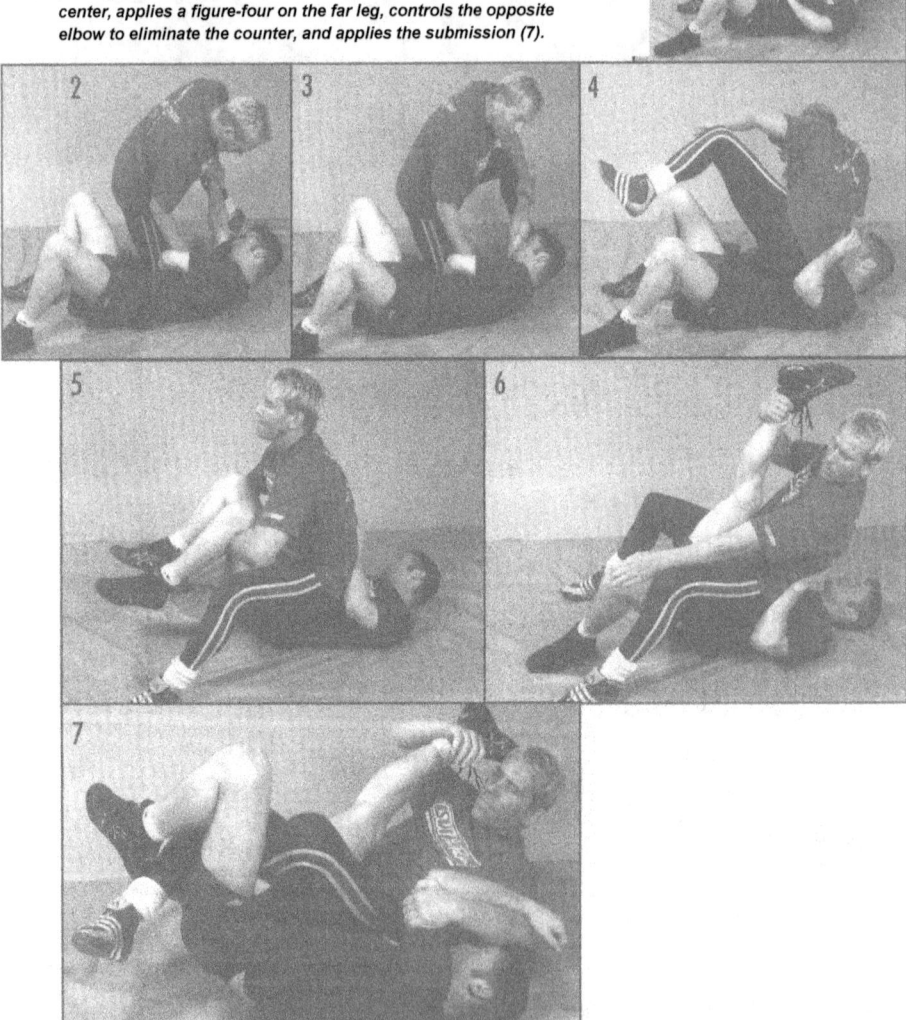

"So many people spend 90 percent of their time learning how to attack the legs, but then ignore the counters and will get caught by a less-knowledgeable grappler."

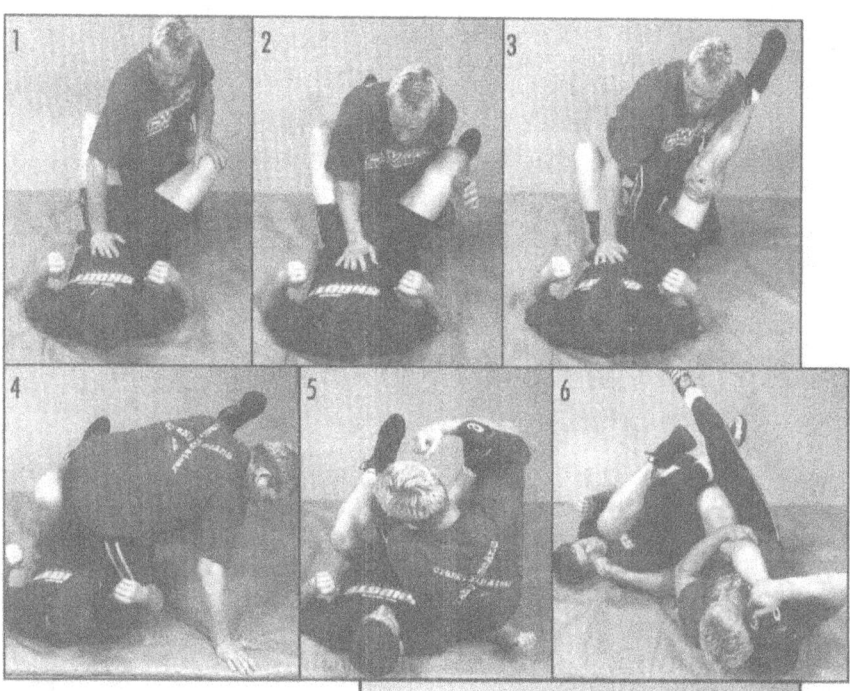

Inside-to-Outside Spinning-Guard Knee Attack

Erik Paulson is trapped inside Marious' open guard (1). Under-hooking Marious' leg, keeping his other elbow cinched tight to prevent the triangle choke (2), Paulson uses his forearm to open his opponent's legs and inserts his shin between the legs (3). Driving his shin through the hips, Paulson posts on his far arm (4), back-spins and kicks his leg through (5), controls the entire leg with a figure-four (6), then controls the heel and applies the finishing knee bar (7).

"Locking the knee is like locking a big arm. The same principles apply to the application of leg movements that you would use to apply an arm bar?

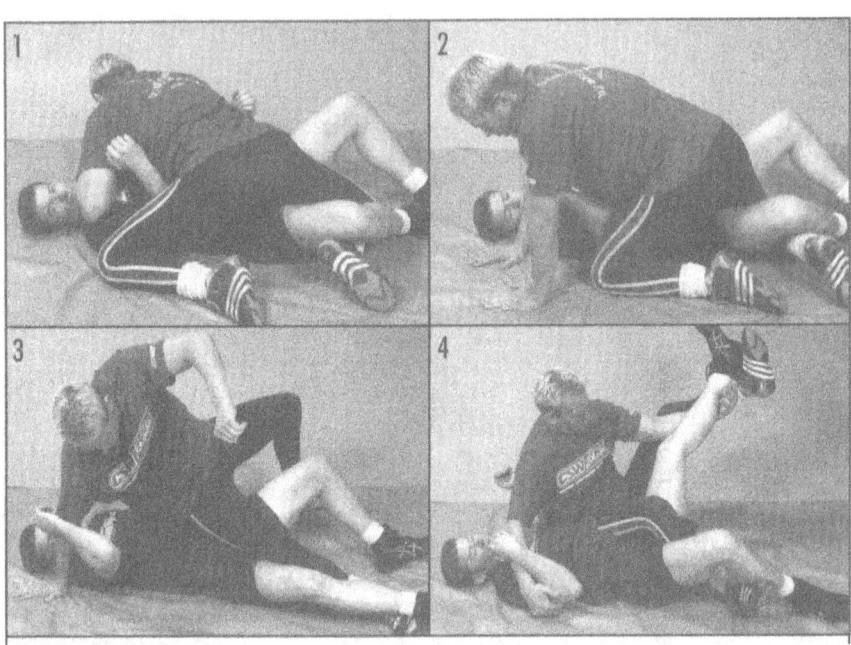

Half-Guard Back Spinning Knee-Bar

Erik Paulson fights for position from inside Marious' half-guard (1), and posts his hands on the opposite of the leg he will back-spin over (2). He quickly back-spins over Marious' near leg (3), using his own foot to flip Marious' far leg up, allowing him to grab the ankle with Ms hand (4). Putting a figure-four on the far leg, Paulson uses one arm to control Marious' foot, then stretches his hips to apply pressure for the finishing knee bar.